Giuseppe Boero, Henry James Coleridge

The Life of the Blessed Peter Favre of the Society of Jesus

Giuseppe Boero, Henry James Coleridge

The Life of the Blessed Peter Favre of the Society of Jesus

ISBN/EAN: 9783744660013

Printed in Europe, USA, Canada, Australia, Japan

Cover: Foto ©Lupo / pixelio.de

More available books at **www.hansebooks.com**

THE LIFE OF THE BLESSED PETER FAVRE

OF THE SOCIETY OF JESUS,

FIRST COMPANION OF ST. IGNATIUS LOYOLA.

From the Italian of

'FATHER GIUSEPPE BOERO,

OF THE SAME SOCIETY.

LONDON:
BURNS AND OATES, PORTMAN STREET
AND PATERNOSTER ROW.
1873.

PREFACE.

[BY THE AUTHOR.]

THE first, and I may say, the only complete Life of Blessed Peter Favre was the Latin Life by Father Nicolas Orlandini, which has been translated into several languages, and published at different times and in various places. It is from this work that other authors have taken whatever particulars are contained in their lives and panegyrics, except, indeed, Father Daniel Bartoli, who in the first book of his *History of Italy*, has written at greater length and added other details omitted by Orlandini.

As it has become my duty, since the sanction given by the Sacred Congregation of Rites to the veneration of this great servant of God, to relate his glorious actions and heroic virtues, I have thought well to take up the subject from the very beginning, and to compose an entirely new life—the first part comprising, in order of time, everything new which can be gathered from the three regular Processes, and from other authentic writings not known to early authors.

In the second part I shall give an Italian translation of the entire 'Memoriale' written by Blessed Peter Favre's own hand. For it ought to be known that in the year 1542 he was divinely inspired to note down in writing all his interior sentiments, all the mental illuminations and special graces which he received in prayer and meditation, that so, having them always before him, he might thereby be moved to gratitude to the Giver of all good. Thus, going through his life from his childhood and youth, he set down in succession everything which went on day by day in his soul, together with the resolutions which he made as to the exercise of Christian and religious virtues.

This memoir or diary of his life, discovered by God's special providence and arrangement after the death of its blessed writer, is the truest and most exact likeness of the man, and, above all, of the interior perfection of his soul, that can possibly be. Father Orlandini made good use of it in compiling his second book, which treats of Blessed Peter's virtues; but I think that devout persons will find still greater pleasure in reading it in full, and in the very words of the author.

And, indeed, every one who is in any degree able to appreciate spiritual perfection will take delight in seeing how liberally God communicated His lights to that soul, so free from all earthly taint, and how faithfully it corresponded with, and put in practice those divine inspirations. It will be seen, too, with astonishment, how a man always engaged in long journeys and Apostolical labours, was, notwithstanding, so continually united to God in heart and soul, that his thoughts and affections were immovably fixed upon Him. It seems, indeed, to me, that the peculiar and distinguishing characteristic of Blessed Peter Favre's perfection and sanctity is a close and unbroken union with God, combined with an unwearied and constant zeal for the eternal salvation of his neighbour.

But I will dwell no longer on this, but will leave the prudent reader to form his own judgment. It remains for me only to state that in translating the 'Memoriale,' I have thought it well here and there to express the spiritual ideas more concisely, especially when almost the same things are repeated in different words.

G. B.

NOTE.

[BY THE ENGLISH EDITOR.]

THE translation of the Life of Blessed Peter Favre, now presented to the English reader, is a faithful version of the Italian of Father Boero. I have, however, in order to make the book correspond to the other volumes of the series in which it appears, made his sections into chapters, and I have also substituted an analytical table of contents at the beginning for the short summaries prefixed to his sections. There is somewhat more discrepancy between the second part of the volume, which contains the 'Memoriale' of Blessed Peter, as it appears respectively in the Italian text and in the English version. I thought it better that the English translation should be made from the Latin lithograph, which has been for some years in limited circulation, than from the Italian translation, and a large part of the whole had been translated in this way when I discovered that the Italian version here and there differed from the common Latin copy, especially in being often a great deal shorter. I have not thought it necessary always to abbreviate the English version in order that it may correspond exactly with the Italian, but this has been done in many cases. There is often a good deal of difficulty in clearly expressing the meaning of the original—a difficulty only to be expected in the case of a diary jotted down from time to time, sometimes in Latin, sometimes in Spanish, and evidently meant for the writer's own use and for nothing else. I have often found that Father Boero's version makes a passage far more intelligible than it is in the Latin. At the same time the Latin (or Spanish) original seems now and then in a word or two to differ importantly from the

Italian version, and in this case I have followed the original. I have been able to use a very early transcript of the original, contained in an old manuscript volume which formerly belonged, I believe, to the College of Coimbra, and which was of great service to me in writing the *Life and Letters of St. Francis Xavier*. This volume contains a copy of Father Favre's 'Memoriale,' more complete than the common lithograph, inasmuch as it contains the additional matter mentioned by Father Boero in his note to page 389, but the copyist has omitted, apparently by mistake, a good many of the notes made in the early part of the year 1543. In one or two places, also, this transcript is fuller than the Latin lithograph, and, as far as I can judge from the Italian translation, than the copy from which Father Boero's version is made.

It is perhaps worth while to add a word as to the family name of the Blessed Peter, who is known to many of us as 'Peter Faber' or as 'Pierre Lefevre.' There has been some controversy among continental writers as to the proper name, and there can be no doubt at all that Blessed Peter always called himself Favre in his own language. His family, as Father Boero tells us (page 1, note), still exists, and is called by that name. If either of the two other forms, Faber or Lefevre (both of which are found in old English Catholic books), had acquired a prescriptive right in our language, I should not have hesitated to use that form, just as I should use the names Erasmus, Canisius, or Cornelius a Lapide. But I have been unable to find any satisfactory proof that this is so, and I have in consequence, though not without some hesitation, adopted the original form, at the risk of seeming to introduce a novelty. I trust that the reader, under whatever name he may please to invoke him, will ask the Blessed Peter's intercession for those who have undertaken the labour of making his life and virtues better known than before to English-speaking Catholics.

H. J. C.

London, Feast of the Holy Innocents, 1873.

CONTENTS.

PART THE FIRST.

The Life of Blessed Peter Favre.

CHAPTER I.

Birth and early years of Peter Favre. (1506—1513.)

	PAGE
Parentage of Peter Favre	1
His early piety	2
His zeal for souls	3
Traditions of his preaching as a child	4
Memory of him at Villaret	5

CHAPTER II.

First studies and early piety. (1514—1524.)

Peter sent to school	6
At the College of La Roche	7
Peter Veillard	7
Peter Favre's vow of purity	8
His advance in studies	8

CHAPTER III.

Meeting with St. Ignatius. (1525—1532.)

Peter at the College of St. Barbara	9
Arrival of Ignatius	10
Peter's scruples	10
Set at rest by Ignatius	11
Intimate friendship	11
Other companions	12

CHAPTER IV.

Priesthood and First Vows. (1534.)

	PAGE
Peter visits Villaret	13
The Exercises at Paris	13
First meeting of the companions	14
Agreement as to rule of life	15
The Assumption, 1534	16

CHAPTER V.

At Paris during the absence of St. Ignatius. (1535.)

Illness of Ignatius	17
He leaves for Biscay	17
Claude Le Jay	18
Paschase Brouet	19
John Codure	20
Influence of Favre at Paris	20
Occupation of the companions	21

CHAPTER VI.

Venice and Rome. (1536—1538.)

Journey to Venice	22
The companions go to Rome	23
Their ordinations	24
At Rome a second time	24
St. Lorenzo in Damaso	25

CHAPTER VII.

Peter Favre at Parma. (1539—1548.)

	PAGE
Favre sent to Parma	26
Reformation of religion	27
Favre and the Exercises	28
Jerome Domenech	29
Antonio Criminale	30

CHAPTER VIII.

In the Parmesian territory.

Strada at Brescia	31
Favre's visit	32
Letter from Parma	33
Congregation of the Holy Name	36
Favre's illness	36

CHAPTER IX.

Rules for the Congregation of the Name of Jesus.

Rules for the Congregation of the Name of Jesus	37—41

CHAPTER X.

The Diet of Worms.

Favre sent to Germany with Ortiz	42
The disputants at Worms	43
Timidity of Granvelle	43
Favre's letter to Rome	44
Uselessness of the conference	45
Bad state of things at Worms	46
Favre's work there	47

CHAPTER XI.

Spires and Ratisbon. (1541.)

Favre at Spires	48
Devotion to guardian angels	49
His way of travelling	50
Use of conversation	51
Adventure with robbers	52

CHAPTER XII.

Peter Favre at Ratisbon.

	PAGE
The Diet at Ratisbon	53
Desperate state of the Catholic cause	54
Letter from Spires as to the Exercises	55
John Cochleus	55
Distinguished men at Ratisbon	56
Favre's work among them	57
At Nuremberg	58

CHAPTER XIII.

Instructions how to deal with heretics.

Instructions how to deal with heretics	59—62

CHAPTER XIV.

Election of the General, and Solemn Vows.

Favre's letter on the confirmation of the Society	63
Election of Ignatius as General	64
Favre's profession	65
Favre sent to Spain with Ortiz	66

CHAPTER XV.

Peter Favre in Savoy.

Journey through Germany	67
Plots of the heretics	68
Peter Favre at Alex	69
At Villaret	70
At Thonon	71

CHAPTER XVI.

First Visit to Spain.

Imprisonment in France	72
Favre's devotion on arriving in Spain	73
Letter from Madrid	74
The Archbishop of Toledo	75
Favre ordered to return to Germany	77
John Aragonio and Alvaro Alfonso	78

CHAPTER XVII.

Peter Favre at Barcelona. (1542.)

Meeting with Araoz	79
The Viceroy Francis Borgia	80
Favre's sermon before Doña Leonora	80
Introduction to Francis Borgia	81
The Convent of St. Clare	82

CHAPTER XVIII.

Return to Spires.

Journey to Germany	82
Otho Truchses at Spires	83
False reports against Favre	84
Zeal of the Vicar General	85
Reformation of clergy and laity	86
Favre wins the people	86
Letter to Laynez	87
Great interior consolations	88

CHAPTER XIX.

Peter Favre at Mayence. (1543.)

Albert of Brandenburg	89
Favre preaches at Mayence	90
Great fruit among the people	91
The parish priest of St. Christopher's	91
Peter Canisius	92
He becomes a novice	93
Sent to Cologne	94

CHAPTER XX.

The Archbishop of Cologne.

Favre removed to Cologne	95
The Archbishop leaning to heresy	96
He promises amendment	97
Favre ordered to go to Portugal	97

CHAPTER XXI.

An illness at Louvain.

Students at Louvain	98
Cornelius Vishaven	98
Illness of Favre	99
Strada's sermons	99
Favre's apostolate while ill	100
Maria Vander Hove	101
Severe trials of Cornelius Vishaven	102
Recovery of Favre	102

CHAPTER XXII.

The Louvain Students.

Favre to remain at Cologne	103
Letter to Ignatius	104
Students to be sent to Portugal	105
Maximilian Cappella	106
List of the novices	107
Indignation in the city	108

CHAPTER XXIII.

Second stay at Cologne. (1544.)

Favre again at Cologne	109
His great exertions	109
Sermons and Spiritual Exercises	110
Melancthon and Bucer	111
St. Ursula's Chapel	112
Letter from Canisius	113

CHAPTER XXIV.

The Carthusians.

Gerard Hammond, Prior of the Chartreuse	114
His letter about Favre	115
Favre at the Chartreuse	116
Decree of the General Chapter	117
Friendship with the Society	118

CHAPTER XXV.

Peter Canisius and his family.

Peter Canisius and his property	119
Complaints of his stepmother	119
Letter of Favre to her	120

CHAPTER XXVI.
Peter Favre sent to Portugal. (1545.)

	PAGE
King John's request for Favre	122
Leaving Cologne	123
Arrival at Evora	124
The King determines to retain him	125

CHAPTER XXVII.
The College of Coimbra.

Favre at Coimbra	125
Fervour of the students	126
Letter to Ignatius	126
Admissions to the Society	127
John Nuñez Barreto	128
Favre's advice to him	129
He enters the Society	130

CHAPTER XXVIII.
Favre leaving Portugal.

Favre at the Court	131
Sent into Spain with Araoz	132
Letter to the College at Coimbra	133

CHAPTER XXIX.
At the Court of Prince Philip.

Salamanca and Valladolid	136
Prejudices against the Society	137
Removed by Favre and Araoz	137
Favre and the porter	138
Spanish and Portuguese nobles	139
Death of the Princess Maria	140
The Court moved to Madrid	141

CHAPTER XXX.
Valladolid and Cologne.

A conversion at the Court	141
Troubles at Cologne	143
Letter from Canisius	144
The students ordered to leave	145
Five of them remain	146
Letter from Favre	147
Letter to Hammond	148

CHAPTER XXXI.
Favre at Madrid.

	PAGE
Favre's work at the Court	149
The two Princesses	150
Foundation at Alcala	151
Story about the fathers	151
Don Alvaro de Cordova	152
Foundations in Spain	153
Influence of Favre	154

CHAPTER XXXII.
Favre summoned to Rome. (1546.)

Perfect obedience of Favre	155
The Council of Trent	155
Favre ordered to join it	156
Letter of Ignatius to Ortiz	156
The Patriarchate of Ethiopia	157
Favre's leavetakings in Spain	158
Sermon at Valentia	159

CHAPTER XXXIII.
Foundation of the College at Gandia.

Death of Francis Borgia's wife	160
The College and University at Gandia	161
Favre lays the first stone	161
Gives the Exercises to Borgia	161
The Pope's approval of the Exercises	162
Miracle at Gandia	162

CHAPTER XXXIV.
Favre's return to Rome, and death.

Favre's illness at Barcelona	163
Arrival at Rome	164
Joy of the fathers	165
Illness of Favre	165
He dies on the feast of St. Peter's Chains	166
Sorrow and consolation	167
Vision of Francis Borgia	168
He enters the Society	169
St. Ignatius assured of Favre's beatitude	170

Chapter XXXV.

Testimonies to Favre's sanctity.

Letter of Peter Canisius	171
Letter of Hermes Poen	173
Rejoicings at Gandia	174
Simon Rodriguez and Ribadeneira	175
St. Francis Xavier	176
He invokes Favre's intercession	177

Chapter XXXVI.

Veneration of Favre in Savoy.

Devotion to Favre at Villaret	178
Chapel where he was born	179
Restoration of the chapel	180
Honoré d'Urfey	181
He founds some Masses	182
Testimony of Peter Critan	183
Inscription	184
Continuance of veneration	185
Hospital at Annecy	186

Chapter XXXVIII.

St. Francis de Sales and Peter Favre.

Devotion of St. Francis to Favre	187
Visitation	188
Consecration of the altar	189
Letter of St. Francis to Father Polliens	190
Congregation of Priests	191
Successors of St. Francis	192
Toleration of *cultus*	193
Peter Camus	194

Chapter XXXVIII.

The last Process.

Testimony of the inhabitants of Villaret	195—198

Chapter XXXIX.

Graces and miracles.

Peter Critan	199
Honoré d'Urfey	200
Peter Vacheran	201
Pernette de la Motte	202
Auguste Larvaz	202
Josephine Dubourial	202
Rose Perillat Charlat	203
Frances Suize	203
Euphrosyne Blanchet	204
Michael Perissin	205

Chapter XL.

The Immemorial 'Cultus.'

Bartoli's account of the Process	206
Decision of the Bishop of Annecy	207
Visit of Father Maurel to Villaret	208
Petition of the clergy of Annecy	209

Chapter XLI.

Decree approving and confirming the Cultus.

Decree approving and confirming the Cultus	211—214

(*End of the First Part.*)

PART THE SECOND.

'Memorial' or Spiritual Diary of Blessed Peter Favre, of the Society of Jesus.

	PAGE
Introduction	217
Recollections of childhood (1506—1513)	218
,, of schooling (1516—1524)	219
,, of University of Paris (1525—1528)	220
,, of meeting with Ignatius (1529—1533)	220
,, of Orders and First Vows (1534—1535)	223
,, of Venice and Rome (1536—1538)	224
,, of Parma, Worms, and Ratisbon (1539—1541)	225
,, of first visit to Spain (1541)	230
Notes in Germany (1542)	234—311
,, ,, (1543)	311—376
,, in Germany and Portugal (1544)	376
,, in Portugal and Spain (1545)	377—396
,, in Spain (1546)	396

PART THE FIRST.

CHAPTER I.

Birth and early years of Peter Favre.

THE Blessed Peter Favre, who was, as St. Francis of Sales says, the first priest, the first preacher, and the first theologian of the Society of Jesus, as well as the first companion of St. Ignatius of Loyola, its founder, was born at Villaret, a little village situate in the valley of the Great Bornand, amidst the most rugged mountains of Savoy. It belonged at that time to the diocese of Geneva, which was not yet infected by the pestilent heresy of Calvin.[1] The day of his birth was the 13th or 14th of April, in the year 1506, for in his memoir he mentions that he was born during the festival time of Easter, which in that year fell on the 12th of the month. His parents were Louis Favre and Marie Perissin. Though the family of neither was rich in this world's goods, they were not badly off for poor people, in a village where all were poor. We gather from old documents that the mountain called Mairolle, in the Great Bornand, belonged to the Favre family, and that several of its members were employed in the service of

[1] We find Blessed Peter's surname differently written by different authors, especially among the French. Some make it Favre, others Fabre, Faure, Fébre, Lefèvre, and Lefébre. In his own autograph letters, written in French, Spanish, Italian, and Latin, it is his constant habit to subscribe himself Favre, Fabro, and Faber. There are several descendants of his family still living, and they are all known by the original name, Favre.

B

their native place, as mayors, counsellors, and notaries of the commune. But the parents of Blessed Peter possessed more important distinctions than these, being richly endowed with solid piety, steadfast religion, and Christian virtues. Not only they, but all their posterity, as we learn from the Processes, always enjoyed the reputation of good and fervent Catholics, who had never let themselves be contaminated by the errors of the heretics, whose doctrines had spread from the neighbouring cantons of Switzerland into the surrounding districts.[2]

As soon as he was more than an infant, Peter received from his mother his first impulses to piety. She instructed him in the rudiments of Christian doctrine, often to invoke the sacred names of Jesus and Mary, and to recite the prayers of the Church, especially our Lady's rosary. But his chief teacher was the Holy Spirit, Who took to Himself the charge of that beautiful soul, and began to fashion it after His own designs. As the child advanced in age he became more and more amiable and attractive from the composure of his demeanour and a certain gravity of bearing, which won affection as well as reverence from all. He took absolutely no pleasure in childish pastimes; all that he cared for was to dwell upon the lessons, and lovingly repeat the prayers, taught him by his mother.

At about seven years old, that is to say, as soon as he came to the use of reason, he felt rising in his soul such tender feelings of devotion, and such an attraction of his whole being to God, that thenceforth, as he himself says, our Lord seemed to desire to become the Bridegroom of his soul, and to take entire possession of it. At about this time his father gave him the charge of a small flock of sheep. The good child took occasion from the secluded country life which he had to lead in

[2] *Process. ord.* 1626, testis 1.

consequence, to unite himself more closely to God, and to detach himself from earthly things. Poor and scanty as was his daily fare, he began to fast strictly twice a week, denying himself even necessary things from the love of abstinence.[3] Besides the prayers which he recited many times in the day, he never failed to assist at the holy sacrifice of the Mass. There is near Vallaret a little spring of very clear fresh water, still called by the peasants the 'blessed fountain,' or 'Blessed Peter Favre's fountain.' It is said that the holy child, not being able to find the means of watering his flock conveniently, near at hand, caused it to flow miraculously from the rock; and certainly there is still something wonderful about this spring, for even in times of the greatest drought its waters have never been known to fail. The story goes, that no sooner did the little shepherd Peter hear the first stroke of the bell for Mass from his parish church of St. Jean de Sixt, than he gathered his sheep round the spring and ran off to the church, and that he never once found that they had strayed—there they all were, collected together just where he had left them.[4]

But the thing that struck every one as marvellous at that early age, was Peter's zeal for souls. When he was in the fields he would gather round him the boys and girls who kept sheep like himself, and very patiently teach them all that he knew of the Christian doctrine, ending by reciting with them various prayers and the holy rosary. He would also very gently admonish them and tell them of their faults, endeavouring at suitable times and places to move them to the love of virtue by his little sermons. On Sundays and festivals, when he used to stay longer in the village, he used even to preach

[3] *Process. ord.* 1596, testis 4.
[4] *Process. ord.* 1869, part 3.

publicly in the streets. A stone is still pointed out on which he used to mount and invite the people to listen to him. And not children only, but grown men and women hastened to the spot, wondering greatly at the wisdom and fervour displayed by so young a child, and weeping with emotion as they prophesied that he would one day be a zealous preacher and champion of the Gospel. When the sermon was ended, each vied with the rest in giving him apples, walnuts, filberts, and such fruits, as well as a few coins. He used to divide the fruit among the poorest of the little boys, and the money he took to his mother, begging her to give him more lessons which he might make the subject of his discourses.[5]

All these seeds of virtue, which were seen springing up in Peter's childhood, were so generally known and notorious that they passed into traditions among those simple peasants. His words and actions were minutely related by fathers to sons and grandsons, places and persons were pointed out, and every circumstance was particularly recorded. Hence many years after the Blessed Father's death the events of his childhood were talked of at Villaret as though they had but just occurred. We may give an instance. In the Process of 1596, Peter, his nephew, said 'that he had heard his father, Louis, say that when Peter was only six or seven years old, he was followed, whilst keeping the sheep of the family, by the little shepherd boys and girls, who delighted to hear him preach; and that seated on a stone, like a little preacher, he used to teach them to pray to God and to say the rosary and other devotions which he had learnt from his mother, with so much sweetness, that the grown up inhabitants of Villaret were drawn to hear him, especially on feast

[5] *Process. ord.* 1596 and 1626.

days. His manner of doing this was so attractive that his near relations were seen weeping for joy; and it was a marvel to behold how every one listened to him as attentively as though he had been a regular preacher. So that it became a common saying that the child would some day be a great and illustrious person.'[6] And George Favre, first cousin to the servant of God, makes declaration in the same Process—'That from his childhood he was thought to be a saint, and chosen by God to convert sinners. At the age of six or seven he used to preach about what he knew to both children and grown persons, who flocked to hear him on feast days; and the place was shown where he used to seat himself like a little teacher, while thirty persons or so, both men and women, took their places around him, listening as gravely as if he had been a preacher. More than this, when any of his audience made a noise, he would with an air of authority desire them to be silent; and when he had finished speaking, his hearers were so pleased with what he had said, that they gave him nuts and apples, which he divided among the shepherd children of his own age, by whom he was greatly loved and reverenced. The men also gave him money, but he took that to his mother, begging her to teach him more prayers, which he learnt with great ease, for the child was both very quick at learning and accurate in retaining what was taught him.'[7]

These are the words of George Favre. The same things are declared by the witnesses in the Process of 1626, nay, the very same particulars are related in our own day by the inhabitants of Villaret. And yet this Blessed Father lived but a very few years in his native place. He quitted it in 1534 for the last time, except that he spent a day or two there in 1541. It is plain

[6] *Process.* f. 8.   [7] *Process.* f. 10.

that the things which were remarked in his childhood must have been very extraordinary to be borne in mind and vividly remembered after so long a lapse of time.

CHAPTER II.

First studies, and early piety.

A MIND so well disposed by nature, talent, and inclination as that of Peter, a mind so occupied with the interests of God and of his neighbour, did not seem intended to waste its existence in so mean an employment as the keeping of a flock of sheep. And therefore God, Who designed him for far greater things in His service and that of His Church, kindled in him at this time an insatiable desire of knowledge and study. The good boy, unable to resist the interior impulse of his heart, began earnestly to beg his parents to send him to school. They desired it as much as he did, being well aware that he was in no way suited for advancement in temporal affairs, in which he took no interest whatever. They knew too, that if his mind were properly cultivated, he might in time bring great honour as well as great help to his family. Their poverty was their hindrance to their carrying their wishes into effect. The boy, however, pleaded his cause with so many arguments, entreaties, and tears, that he ended by prevailing on them to send him to begin his studies in the little town of Thonon, two long leagues from Villaret. There, under the guidance of a devout priest, he learnt to read and write, and he studied so diligently that in two years he completed his course of Latin.

His success delighted his parents and encouraged them to redouble their exertions, and it was decided that he should be removed to the College of La Roche, nine miles from Villaret, where he might pursue higher studies. No place could have been better chosen for the ability and wisdom of the master who presided over it. This was Dr. Peter Veillard, a very learned, and better still, a very holy man, who had been induced, not by the love of gain, but solely by the desire of guiding the young in piety and good manners, to undertake the troublesome office of teaching boys, with whom he lived a community life in his little college. Besides the other means employed by this holy man for inspiring devotion and the fear of God, he had a singular gift for introducing into whatever he was teaching or explaining, appropriate spiritual instructions and examples of virtue. He had the art of drawing useful comparisons with the history and moral teaching of the Gospel, even from tales and sentiments of profane authors, and by these means instilling into the minds of his scholars a perfect taste in the Greek and Latin languages, at the same time that he turned them betimes from whatever might soil the mind and heart.

Under such a master Peter made great progress both in learning and piety. As for piety, being already so well disposed naturally, he advanced in this so rapidly that he left all his companions behind, though there were among them several of rare excellence, and some who lived and died with the reputation of consummate perfection. Favre's whole mind was given exclusively to study and prayer, so that, when his school tasks were over, his whole time was spent in vocal prayer and reading pious books. He approached the holy Sacraments of Penance and the Eucharist as frequently as his director permitted. His manners were remarkably winning, his conversation frank and simple, and above all, his face expressed such innocence and purity of heart that he gained the homage and veneration of all. Of this purity he was most tenderly jealous; he omitted no possible means of keeping his mind and body pure, and of avoiding everything that might bring a stain of guilt upon his soul. And he gave solid proof of this, for when he was only twelve years old, and had gone home for the usual holidays, he one day withdrew to a wild and solitary place in the country, and there, lifting up his soul to God, he began to consider within himself what would be the most acceptable offering which he could make to Him, in return for the favours he had received. He heard as it were an inward voice, which answered, 'virginal purity.' Without a moment's delay, he knelt down and made a vow of perpetual chastity. Thenceforward he regarded and accounted himself as something consecrated, and he promised to serve God in some higher way of life, although he was unable to decide definitely on a particular state. A wonderful arrangement this of Divine Providence, Who was preparing him unconsciously to become the first companion of the holy founder of a religious order.

As to his studies, being very quick and intelligent, and gifted besides with an excellent memory, Peter very soon mastered the Greek and Latin languages; he then applied himself to rhetoric, and studied unaided some treatises in philosophy and scholastic theology, which he had copied from the writings of M. Veillard. He remained at the College of La Roche for nine years, and he would have stayed longer if Dr. Veillard had been able to direct his higher studies. But, as he was fully engaged with the younger pupils, he advised Favre to go to some celebrated University. This counsel was opposed by Peter's parents, both from a dislike to part with their son, and because their small income was not sufficient to bear the expense of his maintenance in a distant country. But Peter pressed the point, offering to live very sparingly if only he might study, so that they were prevailed upon, partly by his entreaties, and partly by the arguments adduced in his favour some years before by his near relation, Dr. George Favre, prior of the Carthusian Monastery of Reposoir,[1] to sanction his going to the University of Paris, where at that time, the study of all sciences, human and divine, flourished exceedingly.

CHAPTER III.

Meeting with St. Ignatius.

PETER FAVRE was nineteen years old when, in the September of 1525, he went to Paris, and entered the College of St. Barbara, there to commence the course of philosophy, which in those days was completed in three years and a half. His master was John Pegna, a distinguished doctor of the Sorbonne; and he had as college companion Francis Xavier, a young gentleman of Navarre, who for some time also shared his room. His bright intelligence, purity of manners, and sweetness of disposition gained the love of his fellow-students and the esteem of his master. He, on his part, ever watchful over himself, did not readily admit particular friendships and intimacies. Grave and reserved by nature, he applied himself to the cultivation of his mind, and studied philosophy with unwearied assiduity. Pegna honoured him

[1] The Rev. Father G. M. Favre, as we learn from the archives of the monastery, was prior from 1508 till 1522, the year of his death.

with a greater share of his confidence than the rest of his scholars, and often when he came to an obscure and difficult passage in the Greek text of Aristotle, he would consult Favre, who was extremely well versed in that language, as the best interpreter of the philosopher's meaning. On the 10th of January, 1529, he was made Bachelor, and after Easter in the same year, Licentiate; a year later he took his Doctor's degree, and was appointed to read philosophy publicly for a time, as was usual in that University.

It was in the October of 1529, when Favre was about to commence the theological couse, that Ignatius of Loyola came to reside in the College of St. Barbara. He had arrived at Paris from Salamanca the previous year, and was preparing to recommence his philosophy from the beginning, having studied it very superficially in Spain. He explained how matters stood to Pegna, who very willingly received him, and, the better to assist him in his studies, introduced him to Peter Favre, that he might go over privately with him the lessons given in the schools. These two understood and appreciated each other from the time of their first familiar intercourse. Ignatius, discerning Favre's excellent disposition, ability, and learning, formed the idea of getting him to join in the great work which he was meditating; and Favre, full of admiration for the prudence and sanctity of Ignatius, attached himself greatly to him, determining to take the opportunity of availing himself of him to the benefit of his own soul.

He was at this time tormented by frequent and violent carnal temptations, which were an intolerable distress and torment to a holy soul like his, all the more because of his vow of chastity. In addition, he was often assailed by temptations to gluttony and vainglory, and his mind burthened by a crowd of scruples which filled his soul with a thousand doubts, perplexities, and fears. His heart was dry, his mind agitated, and he was in a state of continual interior conflict. He prayed to God with many tears for help and succour, but finding no relief from his inward trials, he thought of retiring altogether from the world and shutting himself up in some solitary place where he might lead a life of austere penance in continual fasting and mortification of his body.

He was always brooding over these things in silence, without having courage to tell his troubles to any one: and this only made his condition doubly miserable. At last, one day, when more oppressed than ever by sadness and melancholy, it pleased God that he should break through his reserve and open his whole heart to Ignatius, who, having already suffered in the same way at the beginning of his conversion, was enabled by the teaching of experience to apply the proper remedies. He consoled Favre, advised him to make a very exact general confession, to purify his soul over and over again by frequent spiritual examination, and to fortify it by frequent communion.

By these and other means Favre speedily regained complete peace and tranquillity of soul. From that time forward, instead of being the master, he became the scholar of Ignatius in spiritual matters, holding frequent and delightful conversations with him concerning God and heavenly things. So great, indeed, was the pleasure he took in them, that it was necessary to put some check upon it. For when they met in the evenings to go over their lessons of philosophy, it would happen that one of them starting, even accidently perhaps, some pious subject, they would unconsciously prolong the conversation on the same topic late into night. This was a serious hurt to the studies of St. Ignatius, and they agreed not to make these digressions, nor to allow themselves to be diverted from the matter in hand during the hours appointed for their scholastic conferences.

It is quite true that, in undertaking the charge of Favre's soul, Ignatius looked not only to the present necessity, but aimed at higher things, namely, to lead him gradually to a loftier pitch of perfection. And thus for nearly 'two years he laboured by slow and sure degrees, till, having detached him from every earthly affection, and perceiving him to be capable of generous thoughts, he one day confided to him, in the familiarity of intercourse which subsisted between them, that it was his intention, as soon as he should have completed his theological studies, to go beyond the seas to the Holy Land, and there pass his life in labouring for the conversion of the infidels, or, in case this should be impossible, to offer himself to the Sovereign Pontiff, to be employed by him wherever he pleased, so that he might but promote the eternal salvation of souls. On hearing this Favre was greatly moved, and, as if he heard from Ignatius the express voice of God, he instantly gave himself to him, to be his follower and companion in that interprize. After him Francis Xavier joined Ignatius, and then four other youths of equal talent and merit —James Laynez, Alfonso Salmeron, Nicolas Bobadilla, and Simon Rodriguez.

CHAPTER IV.

Priesthood and First Vows.

FILLED with consolation by this generous and absolute offer of himself to God and St. Ignatius which he had made, Peter continued his theological studies with great ardour. In the year 1533, when the course was nearly completed, he left Paris for Villaret, to pay a last visit to his family, and to take leave of his father and receive his blessing. His mother had already passed to a better life. He spent seven months in his native place, where, with a heart filled with the love of God, he not only gave the example of a holy and perfect life, but succeeded by his admonitions in confirming his countrymen in the Catholic faith and in Christian virtue. Having thus accomplished his duty to his father, he returned to Paris without so much as a single coin, trusting to the charity of Ignatius, who undertook to maintain him and his other companions by means of the liberal alms which he received from the Spanish merchants.

On arriving at Paris, he withdrew himself into the solitude of a poor house, in order to go through the Spiritual Exercises, which, by the advice of St. Ignatius, he had deferred till now. It was an extremely severe winter, snow and ice everywhere; even the river Seine, which runs through the city, was frozen so hard as to bear the weight of carts. Nevertheless, Favre used to spend long hours, by night as well as day, praying and meditating in a courtyard open to the sky, in that bitter weather. He would have no fire in his room, and the only use he made of a great heap of fuel which had been placed there, was to lie down upon it to take a few hours of uneasy sleep. He also imposed on himself a strict fast, and passed the first six days without taking a morsel of bread or a drop of water. And he was disposed to go on still further, if St. Ignatius, coming to see him, and perceiving his state of exhaustion, had not prayed about it, and then commanded him to refresh himself immediately with food and a fire. Besides other advantages which were the result of this extraordinary fast, Favre derived this gain in particular—that henceforward he was never again troubled by the slightest return to those temptations to gluttony, which formerly had been so constant that he was unable ever to satisfy his hunger without annoying scruples. And it is a thing which frequently occurs to God's servants, that one heroic act of virtue entirely roots out of the soul all inclination to the contrary vice. After having gone through the forty days of the Exercises with great fervour, he prepared to receive Holy Orders, and on the 22nd of July, 1534, the feast of St. Mary Magdalene, his especial patroness and protectress, he for the first time offered the holy sacrifice.

Meanwhile, Ignatius, having, as has been said, gained five companions besides Favre, thought that the time was coming for inaugurating the great work which he had planned, and that the first step should be to unite all his associates for one common end, both as to their way of life and their work. As yet no one knew anything about the rest, and each one thought himself alone. He spoke to them one by one, exhorting them to consider seriously, and decide what kind of of life was most suited for the service of God and the conversion of souls. They were to prepare themselves by prayer and penance, and a day was fixed on which they were to bring their answer to his room, where they would find other companions who were meditating the same undertaking. This was done, and when they came back to Ignatius, nothing can express the joyful surprise with which that number of young men, so distinguished for talents and virtue, and who regarded each other with mutual affection and respect, found themselves for the first time united and bound together for a common end. They embraced with tears of tenderness. After they had given vent to their feelings, St. Ignatius was the first to speak. He said that it was his intention to conform his life to that of Christ, the most perfect example of all sanctity, and more than that, besides the care of his own salvation, to cooperate with Christ for that of the world. He thought that the first choice of place should be given to the holy places of Palestine, which he had already visited, and which he knew to be in pressing need of help, there to labour with the sweat of his brow, and there, if he should be found worthy, to shed his blood also, for the propagation of the faith. Meanwhile, until a favourable opportunity occurred for making this voyage, he had resolved to offer himself to God by a vow of perpetual chastity and voluntary poverty.

Hardly had he ended, when all the rest declared with one voice, that such, neither more nor less, were their own sentiments, such the resolutions which they had formed. Only some of them prudently suggested that they should consider what to do in case of being prevented by some impediment either from going to Palestine, or from remaining there. After a long discussion of this question, they agreed to wait in Venice for a year, at the end of which time, if they were not able to accomplish the voyage to the East, they would proceed to Rome, and offer themselves to the Supreme Pontiff to labour for the salvation of souls wherever it pleased him. In the meantime, those among them who had not yet completed their course of theology, were to continue it in Paris till January 25th, 1537, when they were all to go to Venice.

All this being decided by common consent, they resolved to confirm it briefly by vow, and for doing so fixed on the 15th of August, on which is commemorated the glorious Assumption of our Blessed Lady. On the 15th of August, then, 1534, they all met together in the Church of our Lady at Montmartre, half a league outside Paris. Peter Favre, the only priest among them, celebrated the holy Mass, and before communicating, they all, one after the other, pronounced the vow binding them to poverty and to perpetual chastity, to go to the Holy Land, and to present themselves, in case of the circumstances already mentioned, to the Sovereign Pontiff; and lastly, not to accept any stipend or alms for the administration of the sacraments. And in this manner were sown the first seeds of the Society of Jesus, which afterwards sprang up in Rome, and grew into a great and wide-spreading tree. After making their thanks to God, they refreshed themselves, in indescribable consolation and spiritual joy, with a frugal meal, which was prepared beside a fountain flowing at the foot of the hill. The rest of the day was spent in arranging the mode of life which they should thenceforth lead in Paris. As to this, they left themselves entirely to the direction of Ignatius, whom they began to regard as their master and father. He appointed a certain uniform number of prayers and penances, made it a rule to communicate on Sundays and festivals, and every year, on the same day, and in the same place, to renew the vows they had just made. Lastly, they were to meet together frequently for the purpose of keeping up and increasing their mutual charity, and of encouraging each other, by spiritual conversations, to the attainment of perfection.

CHAPTER V.
At Paris during the absence of Ignatius.

THE companions of Ignatius were still in the enjoyment of these sweet spiritual consolations, when an incident occurred which made it necessary for the holy father to go to a distance from them for a short time. The life of continual fasting and mortification which he had been leading had so injured his digestion that his strength seemed entirely gone, and all the remedies of art were in vain. The only thing which the doctors could suggest to save his life was that he should try the effect of his native air for a time. Ignatius was disinclined to this, but his companions urged it so strongly that at last he yielded—all the more readily, because some of them, Xavier, Laynez, and Salmeron, not wishing to return home themselves, begged him to undertake the settlement of their domestic affairs.

Ignatius left Paris for Biscay in the early part of the year 1535. Before starting, he commended his companions to the care and guidance of Peter Favre, his firstborn, whose singular prudence and virtue were respected and venerated by all. And well did Peter justify the confidence of his holy father. He not only maintained his companions in unity of spirit and charity, but increased their number by the addition of three more, who were already masters in theology. The first was Claude Le Jay, a Savoyard, a native of Aise, in the district of Faussigny. He had made his last studies in the

College of La Roche, under Peter Veillard, and it seems certain that while there he had contracted a friendly intimacy with Favre. There is ample proof of this in a valuable manuscript which, a few years ago, fell into the hands of the Jesuit fathers in Paris, at the beginning of which we find the following attestation—' This manuscript contains the commentary on the fourth Book of Sentences, dictated by Master Veillard, and copied with his own hand by our father, Peter Favre, of blessed memory, in the College of La Roche, about the year of our Lord 1519. I have compared it with the manuscript of Father Claude Le Jay. The matter and contents are the same, on the subject of the sacraments. From this we gather that these two men were at La Roche together, as Father Claude himself seems to hint at the close of the first part of his manuscript. They appear also to have gone together to Paris, as I was told a few years ago by an old man of the Le Jay family, the son of Father Claude's cousin. And in further confirmation of this fact, I and another father of the Society carefully compared these writings of Father Favre with those of Father Le Jay, and we found them to be the same, dictated by Master Veillard in the year above mentioned, and this, by order of Father Brossard, rector of the College, I certify under my own hand, this 1st day of August, on which is commemorated the happy death of Blessed Peter Favre. Chambéry, 1619. Nicholas Polliens, a native of the same diocese of Geneva in which those two fathers were born, and admitted into the same Society, and tolerated therein for thirty years, although the most unworthy of all who have been, are, or shall be in it.'[1]

---

[1] In the other page of the manuscript, Father Polliens again attests the authenticity of Father Favre's writing, comparing it with an original letter written to the prior of the Charterhouse of Reposoir. I, too, having seen and read the manuscript, am able to assert positively that it is written in Blessed Favre's own hand (*Author*).

These are the words of Father Polliens. But be it as it may, whether Father Claude came to Paris with Favre, or whether, as Bartoli, and Favre in his 'Memorial,' say, he did not arrive there till this very year, 1535, when he was already ordained priest, it is certain that having heard and seen the great things which were being done by the companions of Ignatius, and the still greater things which they were preparing themselves for, he was moved by God to join them.

Le Jay was a man of angelic disposition, and of rare ability, and he afterwards laboured greatly in the cause of the faith in Germany, where he was much loved by William, Duke of Bavaria, Ferdinand, King of the Romans, and by Cardinal Otho Truchses, Bishop of Augsburg, who appointed him to be his theologian and procurator in the Council of Trent. The second was Paschase Brouët, a Frenchman. He was born in the district of Bertraincour, five leagues distant from Amiens; and being sent to school at a very early age, made such rapid progress in learning and virtue, that as soon as he came to the proper age he was admitted to Holy Orders, and made a priest on the 12th of March, 1523. Desiring to improve himself in learning, especially in theology, he went to the University of Paris, where he made Favre's acquaintance. Under him, he went through the Spiritual Exercises, and came forth from them so detached from worldly things, that he instantly asked leave to be aggregated to the little Society. It was this Paschase Brouët whom St. Ignatius used to call 'the angel of the Society,' on account of his great purity and simplicity of manners, which were combined with so high a degree of Evangelical prudence, that Ignatius did not hesitate to propose him, after Favre, as Patriarch of Ethiopia. The last of the three was John Codure, another Frenchman, a man of most spotless life, born at Embrun, a city of

Dauphiné, on the festival of St. John the Baptist. On the anniversary of which day he was consecrated to the priesthood, and on the same festival also he died at Rome in 1541, being exactly the age of the holy Precursor. His was the first death in the Society, and his soul was seen by Ignatius ascending to heaven accompanied by a choir of angels. These three new associates made their vows on the same day on which the others renewed theirs, that is to say, on the feast of the Assumption, 1535, and they all renewed them together in the following year, 1536.

Not satisfied with this, Favre having now completed his studies, devoted himself entirely henceforth to the Apostolic ministry, and to the gaining of souls. One invaluable gift which he had received from heaven was a remarkable grace in conversing on spiritual subjects. He used to fall quite naturally and without any effort into discourses of this kind, and adroitly stealing into the minds of his hearers, he gained their hearts and gradually purified them from sinful and earthly affections, and drew them to the love of God and of heavenly things. He had besides so skilful a way of conducting the Spiritual Exercises, that St. Ignatius considered that there was not his equal in this respect. Partly in consequence of this gift, and partly by the example of his holy life, Favre worked great good in Paris during the two years that he spent there awaiting the time fixed for starting for Venice. He won over many young men of the University from the path of destruction to better ways, and was the means of inducing several priests and ecclesiastics of high dignity to reform their mode of life, and of inspiring them with great spiritual fervour. It is enough to mention that when the report got abroad that he was soon about to leave, an illustrious doctor of the Sorbonne raised the question whether he would not be incurring the guilt of mortal sin by leaving the certain good which he was doing in Paris, gaining so many souls to God, for that which perhaps he might do elsewhere, but which was uncertain. And in order to show that his opinion was not without foundation, he offered to get it confirmed and subscribed by all the theologians of the University.

Favre also kept up this active zeal for souls in the hearts of the companions committed to his charge. He frequently assembled them together in the College of St. Barbara, or in some other retired place; often he got them to meet at a frugal and simple meal, and with holy discourses encouraged them to make trial of their Apostolic vocation. They, on their part, did not fail so far as their studies permitted, to labour in the spiritual culture of their neighbours; such among them as were not priests, by means of private conversations and timely advice; and Claude Le Jay, Paschase Brouët, and Peter Favre, by their priestly ministrations, the preaching of God's Word, and hearing confessions. Thus, from that early time, they prepared themselves beforehand for the great things which, by the mercy of God, they afterwards wrought in different parts of the world, among Christians and infidels, Catholics and heretics, for the service of God and His Church.

CHAPTER VI.

Venice and Rome.

BEFORE Ignatius left Paris for Spain, it was agreed among the fathers that they should all meet in Venice by the 25th of January, 1537, as we have already mentioned. But as the Emperor Charles V. was making war against Francis I., King of France, and had already entered Provence with a powerful army, Peter Favre and his companions, after consulting together, resolved to hasten their departure, before all the passes from France into Italy were stopped. They already knew that their beloved father, St. Ignatius, had been nearly a year in Venice, and was anxiously expecting them; so without further delay, leaving a few of their number in Paris to see after their common property, and to distribute the little they had among the poor, the rest set out on the 15th of November, 1536, for Meaux, where they were all to meet and begin their journey together. In order to avoid the scouts of both armies, who were going about the country, they had to make a considerable detour by way of Lorraine and Germany, and this occasioned them many serious inconveniences and dangers. They all travelled on foot, poorly clad, and with their books and papers carried in bundles on their backs. The weather was rainy and cold, as it mostly is in that part of the country at the beginning of winter, and the roads they had to traverse were broken up by the heavy rains and blocked by snow so deep, that sometimes they had to wait three days till the passes were open. In the parts of the country which were inhabited by heretics, they had also to bear abuse and insults, and in some places their lives even were in danger. I do not here enter into particulars, which are related in full length in the Life of our holy father St. Ignatius.

At length, as it pleased God, after a trying journey of fifty-four days, they arrived safe and sound at Venice, on the 8th of January, 1537. Great was their joy at once more seeing and embracing Ignatius, and especially that of the three new companions, who had probably only known him hitherto by reputation. After a short time of rest, they divided their number between two hospitals, where they practised the spiritual and corporal works of mercy, to the great edification of the people ; and when the season of Lent approached, they all, with the exception of Ignatius, set out together for Rome, to beg for the Sovereign Pontiff's blessing, and to ask his leave to go to the Holy Land and there exercise their Apostolic ministry.[1] They were introduced to the Pope by Dr. Pedro Ortiz, the representative of the Emperor Charles V., and Paul III. not only received them with every expression of affection, but desired to hear them dispute on theological questions, in which he greatly admired their learning and ability. When he heard their request, he raised his hands and eyes to heaven, and tenderly blessed them. When they took leave of him, he ordered seventy crowns to be given to them as an alms, and gave permission to those among them who were not priests, including Ignatius, who was not present, to be ordained

[1] The original rescript of the Cardinal *Quatuor Sanctorum*, Grand Penitentiary, still exists, in which faculties are granted to Master Peter Favre and his companions, for going to Jerusalem and visiting the holy places, and remaining there as long as their zeal and devotion shall move them to do so ; also for receiving relics, either to keep them themselves or to give them away to others.

by any bishop, under the title of voluntary poverty and competent learning. They returned to Venice as they came, on foot, and begging their way; and renewed their vows before Jerome Veralli, the Papal Nuncio, on the festival of St. John the Baptist, in 1537. Ignatius, Xavier, Laynez, Salmeron, Rodriguez, Bobadilla, and Codure were ordained priests.

But the hopes of a passage to the East grew daily fainter. War had broken out between Soliman, the Turkish Sultan, and the Venetian Republic, and the seas were swept in every direction by the two hostile fleets, so that other vessels were not free to sail to Palestine. The fathers being thus released from their first vow, determined to retire to some solitary place, where they might have time for deliberation, and also for preparing to celebrate their first Masses with fervour. Ignatius, together with Peter Favre and James Laynez, went to Vicenza, and there spent forty days in intimate union with God, in the ruins of an ancient monastery, which they only quitted for the purpose of going into the city to beg the small supply of bread on which they lived. When their retreat was over, Ignatius summoned his other companions to him and proposed that, since the impossibility of their going to the East was plain, they should consider what to do in order to fulfil the other part of their vow. The opinion of each was fully discussed, and in the end it was agreed that Ignatius, Favre, and Laynez should go to Rome and offer themselves to the Pope, while the rest, dispersed in different cities of Italy, should give themselves up to labouring for the good of souls, and wait for the answer from Rome.

In the October of 1537, Favre arrived at the holy city for the second time. The Pope was delighted with the offer made to him, and at once appointed Favre Expositor of the Sacred Scriptures, and Laynez reader of scholastic theology in the University of the Sapienza. Ignatius applied himself to the work of gaining souls, and of sketching the first outlines of the Society of Jesus which he intended to form. As soon as he had thoroughly formed his plan, he summoned the rest of his companions to Rome, where they were distributed among different churches to preach the Word of God. It fell to the lot of Favre and Xavier to preach in the Church of St. Lorenzo in Damaso. During the time which was not occupied in spiritual offices or in the lectures of the schools, they met together for the purpose of discussing and considering the main points of the Institute which were proposed by Ignatius. There is an old book still preserved in our archives, in which these first resolutions, made by common consent, are registered, and they are written in Favre's own hand, so that he may fairly be considered as the first secretary to the Society.[2]

But he was not long engaged in these multifarious labours, for God had opened a wider field for the exercise of his burning zeal. Indeed, what we have hitherto written of his life and actions is nothing to what now lies before us, furnishing matter for a copious narrative. He lived only eight years after this time, and in that brief space he attained such a height of spiritual perfection, and accomplished so many enterprizes for the glory of God and the good of souls, as to make it very difficult for others to equal him in the space of a long life.

[2] It has been said that St. Francis Xavier was the first whom St. Ignatius employed as a kind of official secretary. But the fact is, that all these early writings are undoubtedly partly Favre's and partly Codure's, and that there are none at all in Xavier's hand.

CHAPTER VII.

Peter Favre at Parma.

IN the May of 1539, Ennio Filonardi, Cardinal of the title of St. Angelo, being sent from Rome to the duchy of Parma as Legate Apostolic of that State, which then belonged to the Church, requested permission before starting of Paul III., and by means of Ignatius succeeded in obtaining it, to take with him Father Peter Favre and Father James Laynez, that they might labour for the profit of the people by spiritual ministrations and exercises, so as to reform their manners and inspire them with fervour and Christian piety. On arriving at Parma the Cardinal wished them both to live with him in the palace. But they, according to directions given them by their holy father, refused, and chose the hospital for their lodging, living on what they begged day by day of the charity of the faithful. Soon after, Laynez was sent to work in Piacenza and its environs, leaving Favre alone in Parma, to bear the burthen of the labours which he had undertaken, and from which he allowed himself no rest. He began by preaching the Word of God in the Church of SS. Cosmas and Damian. At first people were drawn out of mere curiosity to hear a new preacher sent from Rome. But very soon they were attracted by the holiness of his life, the charm of his manner, and the force of his words, and every day greater numbers flocked to hear him, desiring to profit by his teaching. There were numerous conversions of sinners who were moved by divine grace to change their lives, and who had recourse to the holy father to set in order the affairs of their souls, and to obtain his counsel and direction.

At the same time he began to instruct the boys and girls in the Christian doctrine, which had been neglected for many years. He exhorted and moved the schoolmasters and some priests to do the same, and practise themselves in this most useful ministration. In some families there were girls who, because they were approaching womanhood or for other reasons, were ashamed to come and be taught in the church. Peter stirred up the zeal of some pious matrons who were highly esteemed for their virtue and gravity, to go from time to time into the houses of the citizens, and there teach the rudiments of the Christian faith.

One of the most efficacious means which he employed for effecting a reformation of manners, and for forming and strengthening good resolutions, was the frequentation of the sacraments. At that time very few persons confessed except at Easter. Thus when Favre succeeded in inducing a great many to approach the holy mysteries weekly, a great noise was raised in Parma in opposition to him: there was one person who even went so far as to blame his conduct in this respect publicly from the pulpit, as being more productive of disrespect to the sacraments than of an increase of devotion. Notwithstanding this, he remained firm, and continued to recommend his method, in which he was supported by the Legate and the ecclesiastical authorities. In the end, the example of the nobility, with Doña Ippolita Gonzaga, Countess of Mirandola, at their head, and that of the most respectable citizens, so encouraged the people to persevere in frequenting the sacraments, that Favre himself says that any one who did not cleanse his soul by sacramental confession at least once a month became a marked man. This pious practice was kept up throughout the duchy of Parma for a long time.

But Peter Favre's zeal was most wonderfully displayed in giving the Spiritual Exercises of St. Ignatius, in which, as we have already said, he had a remarkable skill and grace. No sooner did it become known what great fruit had resulted from this means in the case of certain persons who had put themselves under his direction, than great numbers, especially of the nobility and clergy, offered themselves to make the Exercises, and after experiencing their virtue in their own case, urged others to do the same, and instructed them in doing so. Among these was Doña Zerbina, a very devout lady, who passed for a saint in Parma. She had been for a long time confined to her bed by continual and severe illness, and at her desire her confessor, who had been instructed by Favre, gave her the Exercises. She found in them so much spiritual sweetness and consolation, that she could not keep it to herself, and spoke of it to those who were in the habit of visiting her. They all afterwards came to Favre, entreating him to impart to them this wonderful means of perfection. In this manner the desire of making the Exercises became general, and we have an account of more than a hundred persons of all conditions and ranks who went into retreat at the same time, to go through the course under Favre's guidance and direction. He says himself, writing on the subject to Rome to his dear friend St. Francis Xavier—'The multitude of persons who communicate every Sunday here in Parma and the neighbourhood is incredible. As to the Exercises, we cannot enter into minute particulars about them, but I may say that there so many who have made them and who are giving them to others that we cannot count them. Every one is anxious to go through them; and every priest as soon as he has made them comes out from them a master, and teaches them to others.' These are Favre's own words.

There would be matter for a long narrative in the successive particulars of the results which followed from Favre's method of preaching, by simple and familiar explanation of the Spiritual Exercises. Convents and other religious communities which had become somewhat relaxed and free in their way of life, were seen to return to the rules of regular observance. Curates, parish priests, ecclesiastics of every rank, reformed their lives, and became full of zeal not only for their own salvation, but for that of others. Men and women of every age and condition turned from a sinful to a blameless life, or passed from a virtuous life to a still better and more perfect. The habit and method of meditating well on the eternal truths, and on the examples of the Life, Passion, and Death of Christ, was introduced among a great number with all the profit which is the consequence of this practice. In short, the face of the whole city of Parma was altered, and could hardly have been recognized as the same place in rather less than a year and a half that Blessed Favre spent in labouring there.

The infant Society, too, gained greatly not only in the high place to which it rose in the esteem of persons of all ranks, but also by the accession of several men who afterwards added great lustre to it. The first of these was Jerome Domenech, canon of the Cathedral of Valence, who, passing through Parma on his way from Rome to Paris, made the Spiritual Exercises under Favre. This was enough to make him at once give himself up to him as a son and companion. Among the Italians who offered themselves were Paul Achilli, who was already a priest, Elfridio Ugoletti, John Baptist

Viola, John Baptist Pezzani, and Silvester Landini. The first martyr also of the Society, Father Criminale, came from among the scholars of Favre. Criminale was a native of Sissa, a large town ten miles from Parma. He had come to that city for the purpose of study, and was introduced by his countryman, Pezzani, who has just been mentioned, to Favre, under whom he made the Spiritual Exercises, and then consecrated himself to God, being ordained subdeacon. Burning with zeal for the salvation of others, he took Favre with him to sow the seed of God's Word in Sissa, his native place, and there observing more nearly the example of his life, his heart was touched by God, and he resolved to enter the Society. Accordingly, the following year, he went on foot as a pilgrim to Rome, and gave himself to St. Ignatius as a son. Being afterwards sent to the Indies, and appointed by St. Francis Xavier to the charge of the Christians of the Fishery Coast, he met, at the hands of the enemies of the faith, with the glorious death which he so greatly longed for.

CHAPTER VIII.

In the Parmesan territory.

THE zeal of the Blessed Father was, as we have seen, not confined to the city of Parma, but extended to the towns and villages of the immediate neighbourhood and elsewhere. We possess five original letters of his, written during his residence at Parma. The first three, dated December 4th, 1539, and March 25th and April 7th, 1540, are addressed to Father Peter Codacio and Father Francis Xavier; and the last two, of the 16th April and the 1st September, to his father, St. Ignatius. One of them is written from Brescia. The circumstances which led to his visiting that city were as follows.

Francis Strada, a very young man, not yet a priest, but exceedingly fervent, and possessing a natural eloquence, had arrived at Brescia from Siena, where he had been with Father Paschase Brouët, and where his preaching had gained him a great reputation. Immediately after his arrival he began to preach the Word of God in various churches with unusual fervour and spirit. Great numbers came to hear him, and many wonderful conversions followed; amongst others, there were more than a hundred young men who agreed together to change their lives and to serve God faithfully, either in the world or in religion. Several of them joined the Society; among them John Angelo Paradisi, who, soon afterwards falling dangerously ill, and desiring to confess to and be consoled by one of our priests, information of this was sent by letter to Favre, who immediately went to Brescia and remained there ten days, till the young man had recovered. He soon made himself known by his characteristic gentleness, and won the hearts of the citizens, who entreated him to prolong his stay among them; but he was not of himself able to make any promise, as he was at the disposal of the Cardinal Legate of Parma. They then begged that at least he would intercede for them that Strada might not be at once taken from them; and accordingly, on the 16th of April, as soon as he had returned to Parma, he wrote a letter to Ignatius, in which he says, among other things, 'As regards Master Francis Strada, I now repeat what I before wrote from Brescia, that every one is making efforts to keep him, so great is the delight of all the principal citizens in his learning, virtue, and holy life. They have written to Mgr. Datario, begging him to speak of this to your Reverence. The Vicar of Brescia also wishes for him very much, and would also like to have a priest of the Society to assist him in his spiritual ministrations. As I could not possibly remain, he has begged me to make intercession with your Reverence on the subject.'

Thus he writes[1]. And even before going to Brescia, and seeing with his own eyes the fruit which was the result of Francis Strada's sermons, he had written to St. Francis Xavier from Parma—'A good priest, a friend of ours, has told us that a person from Brescia has brought news of the immense crowds who go to hear Master Francis Strada preach, and that the whole city is in consequence stirred up to great fervour of devotion, insomuch that more than a hundred of the principal

---

[1] St. Ignatius received Favre's mediation favourably, and satisfied the wishes of the citizens by sending to Brescia Claude Le Jay, one of his earliest companions, who, together with Strada, continued to reap a rich harvest of souls.

citizens of Brescia have resolved to serve God with their whole heart.

He had often promised in his letters to give a minute report of all the good which, by God's goodness, had been effected at Parma. But he was so oppressed by incessant labours that he was only able to do so very superficially, just as he was on the point of setting out for Germany. We shall here quote his letter to the Society at Rome, translated from the original Spanish—

'*May the grace and love of Christ our Lord be with us always.*

'As I fear that I shall not have time for writing any more letters from this city of Parma, I will go a little into detail in this. And as to the plentiful harvest that has been reaped in this evangelical field, I will just say that it is a thing of frequent occurrence to see persons come every day to the Hospital where I am to confess and communicate. As a rule, a good number communicate every Sunday; and many of them are men and young students. I say nothing of the other parishes of the city in which this good custom has been introduced by several priests who went through the Spiritual Exercises during the first days of our residence in Parma, and who then became masters in them and have greatly propagated their use. Thus, even teachers in the schools have given them to such of their scholars as are most capable of making them. There are also some married ladies who make it their business to go from house to house to instruct the young girls who cannot freely come to the church. It would be impossible to say how much fruit has been obtained by these means in Parma and its neighbourhood. Neither can I express what good has been done in the city and neighbourhood outside it by means of frequent confessions. It is enough to say

D

that no one is now considered to be leading a good life unless he goes to confession at least once a month. In one little village more than three hundred persons went to communion on the feast of the Assumption. Canon Jerome Domenech will tell you by word of mouth better than I can write how many priests, and of what quality, have been moved by the Exercises to lead good lives, and how they have not only persevered in virtue, but have induced others to do as themselves. Much of this fruit is owing to the sermons, which are given not only by us two, but by three or four other priests, who, having made the Spiritual Exercises, have given themselves up to the work of spreading God's Word in the country about. Already ten or twelve of the most populous villages in the Parmegiano have returned to the way of salvation. I say nothing of the fruit which has been gained at Sissa, where there is a good priest named Orlando, who has devoted himself entirely to hearing confessions, catechizing children, and preaching on all festivals in three or four different places successively. The lady of the manor there, together with other noble ladies, has been to confession regularly every week from the Epiphany till now. And her husband also, hearing that I was about to leave, despatched a messenger begging me to go to Sissa, that I might hear his confession. The noble Pallavicini family, who live in a place at no great distance, made the same request to me. There is a lady named Giacoma,[2] who has an income of about five hundred scudi, besides her dowry, and she has offered voluntarily to spend all that she possesses in good works prescribed by me. This lady, having heard about a week ago of my approaching

---

[2] This lady appears to be Giacoma Pallavicini, to whom St. Ignatius wrote on the 17th February, 1554, praising her for the good and holy desires with which God had inspired her.

departure, went to the house of the lady Laura, who is the most distinguished matron in the city, and a relative of the Pope, begging her, with tears in her eyes, to write to the Lord Cardinal of Sta. Fiora to use his influence with his Holiness, that I might not be removed from Parma. I know that there is a great deal of stir in the city on the subject, and that the Pope has been written to. I do not take any part myself, you may be sure, in these matters. I beseech the Divine Goodness that the more we are separated in body the more we may be united in spirit; and so it will be if we pray to the Spirit of the Lord, Who fills the whole earth, to direct us all according to His most holy will.

'PETER FAVRE.

'Parma, the 1st of September, 1540.'

By way of rendering permanent the rich harvest which had been reaped at Parma, Peter established a congregation of excellent priests, his spiritual disciples, the object of which was to attend incessantly to the salvation of souls and to promote those exercises of devotion and piety which he had introduced. Besides this he formed another, consisting of laymen, to whom he gave very wise rules for their increase in number and in fervour. This congregation continued to flourish for many years, to the great profit of the city. In perpetual remembrance of its founder, there was placed on the façade of the church belonging to it a stone bearing the following inscription, which we translate from the Latin—'This oratory, dedicated to St. John the Baptist in honour of his decollation, belongs to the Congregation of the most Holy Name of Jesus, erected by Father Peter Favre, eldest son of St. Ignatius, founder of the Society of Jesus, for the greater glory of God and the salvation of souls.'

Peter's strength gave way under such great and incessant labours, and he fell sick. He was confined to his bed for three months; and while he was in that state, God, ever liberal of His graces to His faithful servants, visited him, pouring into his soul the most sublime sentiments and indescribable spiritual consolations. The citizens came to see him very often; and he, thinking nothing of his own state of suffering, was always ready to receive everybody, to hear their confessions, and to strengthen their good resolutions by his holy counsel. So that it may be truly said that even in his sickness he did not cease to work for the glory of God and the salvation of his neighbour. It seems that at this time his devoted followers would not allow him to remain in the hospital. They succeeded by their entreaties in having him removed to a private house, where he could be better nursed, and where also it was more convenient for his penitents to visit and converse with him. He mentions this himself in his 'Memorial,' thanking God, and saying, 'Remember also how greatly I am indebted to Master Laurence and Master Marino, in whose house I lay ill and had so many good opportunities granted me.'

CHAPTER IX.

Rules for the Congregation of the Name of Jesus.

As soon as his health was somewhat recovered, Peter Favre was about to resume his ministrations with redoubled energy, when he had orders from Rome to prepare to go to Germany with Dr. Pedro Ortiz, Ambassador of Charles V. As soon as the news spread in Parma, all the inhabitants were greatly troubled. Some of them, men of influence, wrote letters, as has been before mentioned, to Paul III., humbly entreating him not to call away from them so dear a father and so fervent a minister of the Gospel. But the Pope, looking rather to the general good of the Church than to that of one particular city, remained firm, and repeated the order for his departure. Then all pressed round Favre, particularly the numerous associates of the Confraternity of the Holy Name, which he had founded, entreating him to leave them some rules for their direction. The holy man consented, and wrote down full instructions for their manner of living and working, which we shall follow Orlandini in translating, as they may be useful, not only to societies of the same kind, but to all good Christians.

' I would not have you misled by the false notion, that in order to grow in godliness you require any sustenance other than that which has heretofore served to maintain you therein. Such was not the opinion or teaching of the philosopher, who, treating of bodily aliment, asserts that the substances suitable for the nourishment of our bodily frames, avail likewise for the increase of the same. Taught as you have been, by your own experience, that the holy exercises you are wont to perform are most efficacious in fostering the spirit of piety, you must needs be convinced that they will be of no less use in forwarding its increase. Among these you will ever chiefly prize the frequent partaking of that heavenly Bread, the soul's choicest food, whence the angels and spirits of the blessed continually draw their nourishment. This Bread is far more necessary for the life of the soul than that we daily break for our bodily sustenance. You will, in like manner, value your devout practices, such as calling oneself daily to account, getting rid of sin by confession, meditating on the things of God and the truths that concern salvation, and, lastly, assiduity in works of mercy. If by these several practices you have made any progress in self-knowledge, or in the love of God and your neighbour, be assured that, in order to advance in the ways of Christ, you must persevere in these works with ever increasing fervour and diligence.

'Your daily life may be ordered as follows—Every evening, before retiring to rest, kneel down, and think over the four last things: the day of death, the final Judgment, the pains of hell, and the glories of Paradise. And I should like you to give as much time to meditating on one or other of these things, as it would take to recite three times the *Pater noster* and the *Ave Maria*. After this, pass in review your spiritual condition, making your examination on all the actions of the day; and after rendering due thanks to the divine mercy for favours received, be truly penitent for the sins you have committed, and resolve to confess them at a given time, and to a particular confesssor. For this is a kind of spiritual confession, when a man finding out his sins, accuses himself of them before God with due sorrow, and with a firm resolution to confess them to the priest on an appointed day. Lastly, you must pray God to give to you and all the living a quiet and peaceful night, and to the dead who are in purgatory, pardon and relief, reciting three *Paters* and *Aves* for this intention.

'The same prayers in kind and number you must say on the following morning, that God may keep you and all living men from all stain of sin that day, and may give to the departed some relief from the fires of purgatory. If you have time, you may, before your crucifix, or during Mass, meditate on some point of the life of Jesus Christ, with the desire to conform your life and conduct to that great Model. After the priest has consecrated the Body of Christ, or when he elevates It in sight of the people, ask God to grant you the cure of your impurities and tribulations, and the graces you desire, such as fortitude of mind, the knowledge of yourselves, mutual fraternal charity; and, lastly, that hunger and thirst after justice, which is one of His most precious gifts. You must also ask Jesus Christ to visit your soul in spiritual communion; and this manner of communicating will increase within you a certain hunger after this sublime mystery, while your soul rejoices, both in the remembrance of having received it not long ago, and in the hope of soon doing so again. This spiritual communion will be an excellent preparation for the Sacrament of the Eucharist, just as the spiritual confession, of which I have spoken, is for the Sacrament of Penance. Nevertheless, I wish every one to keep looking forward to the day, even while it is still distant, on which he is to cleanse his soul by confession, and to nourish it with the food of heaven. Wake up and renew daily in your mind the thought of this sacrament, arranging your time in such a way that you may spend some of the days in thanksgiving for having received it, and the others in preparation for receiving it again. In this way, it will be clearly seen that you honour and reverence these holy and venerable mysteries; otherwise there will be danger either of your not preserving this heavenly food within you, as you ought, or of your not receiving it with becoming eagerness of desire. Do not be wanting to yourselves in this matter, and endeavour to receive these holy sacraments at least once a week.

'Now, with regard to other devotions, such as prayer, meditation, and the like, take care to direct them according to the following intentions, either to all, or to any one in particular. First to the glory of God and of the saints, then to the good of your own soul, and lastly to the profit of others; thus you will every day by means of these pious duties progress in virtue, such as humility, patience, prudence, and others like these, rendering yourselves by their means more fit to do good works. You will grow in the knowledge and love of God, your charity to men will be increased, and so advancing steadily, as by certain steps, in the spiritual paths, you will surely and safely proceed along the way of salvation.

'As regards the affairs of this world, and everything concerning the body, you must so regulate your thoughts and intentions that all your bodily occupations and exertions may be directed to the glory of God, your own spiritual good, or that of those for whom you are outwardly labouring. Strive therefore that, working or resting, God may be your first motive, then your own and your neighbour's salvation, and afterwards the welfare of your body and of that of others; and last of all, the care of your family and whatever may be judged needful for the life and sustenance of the body. Thus there will be no confusion or disorder in your life, so long as worldly goods are made subservient to the body, the body to the soul, the soul to God; if your gains are made with a view to the necessities of the body; if the health of the body is considered with reference to the salvation of the soul; and if the aims of your soul are always guided by the rule of the eternal law. This last then must be the first thing from which you start, and your duties must be arranged in this order: your first duty is to your soul, and then other things may come, always remembering that the good of the soul is to be the final object in everything. We must not be like those who think that they ought to begin from family cares and the interests of the body, and that when these things are set in order, they will find it easier to attend to their spiritual concerns. In the same way as regards your neighbour; you should, as far as possible, consider his soul before your body, so that, supposing it were in your power by the use of one and the same means to save yourselves from the death of the body, and him from that of the soul, you should far more readily think of the danger of the latter, than of the destruction of the former. If you observe this order in your actions, you will easily obtain that perseverance in leading a good life, which you desire.'

CHAPTER X.

The Diet of Worms.

WE must now relate the cause which obliged Blessed Peter Favre to leave Parma and go to Germany, there to begin a new kind of apostolate, fighting against the Lutheran heretics and leading back into the right way those Catholics who had strayed from it. It was now for many years that Dr. Peter Ortiz, in the name of the Emperor Charles V., had been in Rome, pleading the cause of Queen Katharine, who had been unjustly divorced by Henry VIII., King of England. On the failure of the efforts made by the Pope and others to arrange this affair, Ortiz was recalled to Spain, but with an order to go first to Worms, and there assist at a conference which had been already announced to take place between the Catholics and Protestants. Ortiz, a man of great piety and judgment, not wishing to undertake so very serious a charge unless he were accompanied by a good theologian and faithful counsellor, made request to Paul III., and through him obtained from St. Ignatius Father Favre to go with him. Favre, as soon as he received notice from Rome, broke off in mid career all his labours in Parma, and set out with Ortiz for Worms, where he arrived on the 24th of October, 1540. In the September of that year the Society of Jesus had been approved and confirmed as a religious order by Apostolic authority, and Father Favre was the first of its members who set foot in Germany. So God ordered it, that it might fall to the lot of a man eminent both for learning and sanctity to make the Institute known, and thus to inspire princes and prelates with a desire to receive the Society into their states and dioceses. So that the five provinces which it afterwards possessed, and the numerous houses and colleges which were founded in that vast country, were in great measure due to the virtue and merits of this truly apostolic man.

Eleven heretics and eleven Catholics were already met at Worms to dispute on religious questions. Out of the latter, three were evidently inclined to the Lutherans, and the other eight were either weak or suspected. Thus the enemies of the faith, divided in opinion as they were among themselves, but thoroughly united in the matter of hostility to the Church, were already triumphantly shouting victory. In the private houses all about and even in the pulpits of the churches they were disseminating fearlessly their errors, openly, with public challenges, defying the Catholic party to combat; and, because their opponents, either from disunion or fear of defeat, did not answer the challenge, boasting with intolerable arrogance, to the disgrace of all religion. The leader and chief support of the heretics was Philip Melancthon, then a young and fiery-spirited man, who, puffed up with conceit, had passed from the school of humanities, which he taught, to the professor's chair, as a teacher of false theology. Favre's arrival put the good Catholics into fresh heart, for they hoped, that once confronted with the heretic, as he desired and requested to be, even if it were only in a private conference, he would soon quell his audacity. But Antony Perrenot de Granvelle, who presided over the conference in the Emperor's name, could never be induced to consent to this. He was one of those men whose only idea of prudence is to give and take time; and who, while waiting for what they call a favourable opportunity, let the mischief have free course without taking the least trouble to check it effectually. He fancied that the opposite party might be gained by patient toleration and soothing attention, and was afraid of making them still worse by irritating them. With this object he had strictly ordered the eleven Catholic disputants to exercise the greatest moderation, and to discuss the points of controversy only in writing, and in a tone and letters full of respect. As for Favre, though he pledged and bound himself to keep within proper limits, he not only refused his consent to a dispute between him and Melancthon, but would not even allow him to teach the elements of the Catholic faith to the children, for fear that the Lutherans might thence take excuse for greater violence.

But it will be better to hear what Favre himself says in a letter to the fathers in Rome, dated the 27th of December.

'As to the conference,' he says, 'I cannot say that, so far, any good whatever has been done. Not a single Lutheran, either belonging to Worms or who has come thither from other places, has abandoned his errors through the efforts of those who are assembled here for their conversion. Meanwhile it is evident that they are gaining ground, and the right cause losing it; for three out of the eleven Catholics opposed in the conference to eleven Lutherans have agreed with the heretics in several articles, and some of the remaining eight are wavering before the fight begins. . . . Many of these doctors were anxious that I should have a meeting with Melancthon, saying that it was better for me to see him than the others, who show that they have certain reserves on the controverted points. To tell the truth, I am conscious of good desires which have been awakened in my heart as to the matter; but I do not like to do anything against the judgment and opinion of the presidents, and they will not allow any *vivâ voce* dispute with the heretics, for fear that it might hinder the good progress of affairs. For this reason Dr. Ortiz also has desired me to refrain, although his private inclination is the other way, knowing that, with the help of God, I should not be likely to argue with them out of a spirit of contradiction, nor by exasperating any one to hinder the good which is hoped for. The presidents think it best for the eleven Catholics to reply in writing to the articles of the Protestants, and to discuss the points which they can or cannot yield, with courtesy. Up to this time, however, no answer has been given, on account of their want of union among themselves, and this furnishes the Protestants with a good argument for becoming more confirmed in their opinions. For, however much they may differ in certain ways of thinking, they are all agreed in receiving the Confession of Augsburg and the Apology of Melancthon, and consequently in attacking the Catholic faith.'[1]

In another letter, dated January 1st, 1541, he adds—

'The Catholic doctors have at last sent in to the presidents their answers in writing to the Protestant articles, but there has not been any meeting with them. This does not satisfy our adversaries; they would like to dispute man against man, with the eleven Catholics, and only with them; for they are in hopes of gaining them all over to their side, as they have gained the first three, and in a measure unsettled the rest. Besides, they want to protract the whole thing, and meanwhile

[1] Autograph letter.

to get together the German princes and detach them from the Roman Church and from the spiritual authority of the bishops. . . . I have no confidence in the success of this plan for bringing back Germany to the unity of the faith. . . . These Protestants pretend that all that they desire is the reformation of the Church; and there are too many people ignorant and stupid enough to believe them, even when they are seen to profane the sacred images and to destroy the altars in the churches; besides forbidding private Masses and denying the worship of the saints. It is really a melancholy thing to see the blindness which has fallen upon this nation.'[2]

As there was no possibility for the holy man to deal directly with the heretics, he turned his attention to the task of doing good to the Catholic laity and clergy, more particularly the latter. And indeed the need of it in both cases was so pressing, that it is sad to hear the account given of it by Favre himself. 'I can only wonder,' he says, 'that the number of the heretics is not ten times greater than it is, since a bad life naturally leads to a false belief. The apostasy of so many countries, the rebellion of so many cities and provinces, is to be attributed, not to the garbled Scriptures, not to the plots, open or secret, of the Lutherans, but to the scandalous lives of the clergy. Would to God that there were in this city of Worms but two or three priests not living in concubinage, or guilty of other public and notorious crimes! I feel convinced that if even those two or three possessed a little fire of zeal for the salvation of souls, they could do what they liked with this simple people. I speak of cities which have not as yet revoked the laws, abandoned the customs, and shaken

[2] Autograph letter.

off the authority of the Apostolic See, but where those who are bound by their sacred calling to inspire the heretics with the desire of being Christians, are the very persons whose bad lives occasion the Catholics to turn Lutherans.'

Notwithstanding all difficulties, he devoted himself with fervent zeal during the time (little more than two months) that he spent in Worms to confirm the faith of the Catholic laity by his sermons, and by private exhortations to heal the wounds of the clergy. He was powerfully seconded in his efforts by the dean, who was at the same time Inquisitor and Vicar General of Worms. Left, as he had been, almost alone to defend the cause of God and religion, he had done his utmost to stem the torrent of impiety and corruption, but finding himself deserted by every one, and deprived of advice and succour, he was on the point of going away and leaving his wretched flock a prey to wolves. Favre encouraged him to remain, and persuaded several persons whom he had previously brought to a better mind, to cooperate with the Vicar for the common good.

He had, besides, a great deal to do for the spiritual advantage of the courtiers and attendants of the princes assembled at Worms: and he himself mentions in his letters the gentlemen attached to the service of the Minister, de Granvelle, of his son, the Bishop of Arras, of the Papal Nuncio, John Morone, and others who followed his counsel and direction in spiritual things. And the fruits of these labours of his were all the more abundant for their not being showy and conspicuous; and he says distinctly that he had in his heart a strong feeling of affection for the German nation, and a great confidence that in time the Society would do a great work there, adding these words—'I have no doubt whatever that these interior feelings of mine proceed from some great good which our Lord has in store for this country and people.' Subsequent events proved the truth of this prediction.

CHAPTER XI.

Spires and Ratisbon.

ON the 16th of January, 1541, Father Favre left Worms with Ortiz, and went to Spires, whither the conference was transferred, the eleven being reduced to one on each side—Melancthon for the Lutherans, and John Eckius for the Catholics. There he witnessed the second utterly unprofitable dispute on original sin, which had to be broken off after three days (during which time nothing was settled), and everything was put off until the General Imperial Diet, which was to be held at Ratisbon in April.

In these journeys, the holy man, as he has left us in writing in his 'Memorial,' began to use a method of his own for keeping himself constantly united to God by means of prayer, partly mental, partly vocal, which he afterwards continued and added to during the rest of his life. And before going further, we may here explain this method for the instruction of others, together with other particulars connected with his Apostolic journeyings. No sooner, then, did he catch sight in the distance of the walls or tower of any hamlet, village, or city, than he raised his heart and mind to God, affectionately invoking first the archangels to whom were committed the protection and guardianship of the place, and then all the angels who had charge of its inhabitants, and lastly, Jesus Christ, the Redeemer of them all. He gave them most humble thanks for the benefits bestowed upon the bodies and souls of those persons, and besought them to enlighten their minds with holy inspirations, and to inflame their hearts with divine love; to confirm the strong, to support the weak, and to raise up the fallen. He especially commended to them the sick and the afflicted, the persecuted, the poor, the dying and the dead, asking for them health, comfort, succour, patience, and refreshment. He found out what saints were venerated as patrons of the different places as he passed on, or whose bodies lay in the churches dedicated to their names, and he invoked them from a distance, lovingly commending the welfare of the citizens to their care. So, on seeing the mountains, hills, farms, and lands which he passed on the road, he gave God thanks for their lords and owners, begging pardon for those who were guilty of ingratitude to God by abusing the gifts which He had mercifully given them. On arriving at inhabited places, he visited the Blessed Sacrament, then the churches of their holy patrons, and renewed his prayers for the souls of others, adding a petition for strength, energy, and zeal in advancing the honour and glory of God.

He himself bears witness to many very special graces and benefits which he obtained from God for himself and others by means of this method of prayer, especially by devotion to the guardian angels of places; saying that he had thus escaped many serious and mortal perils, many plots and snares of heretics who sought his life, and obtained the signal conversion of apostates, unbelievers, and hardened sinners. Hence it became his custom to recommend this devotion to the ministers of the Gospel, and to all with whom he had intercourse; as St. Francis of Sales affirms, who practised it himself, and thus speaks of it in the sixteenth chapter of his

Introduction to a devout life—'The great Peter Favre, passing through this diocese of Geneva, in which he was born, on his return from Germany, where he had achieved great things for God's service, related, that in travelling through several heretical districts, he had received numberless consolations by means of his custom of saluting the guardian angels of whatever parish he came to. Of this he had had sensible proof, both in their delivering him from the plots of the heretics, and in making a great number of souls pliant and well inclined to receive from him the truths of salvation. And by relating this experience of his own he so greatly recommended the practice to others, that a lady who was then young told me, four years ago, with great feeling, that she had heard it spoken of by Favre himself, when she was young, sixty years since.' And in the Process which was made at Thonon, in 1596, the same thing is attested by a noble lady, Doña Wilhelmina of Arenthon, of whom we shall have to speak in due course.

As to his way of travelling, he went mostly on foot, carrying the bundle of his writings round his neck. He had made a vow never to take any payment or compensation for his spiritual ministrations; and this was afterwards made a rule in the Constitutions by St. Ignatius. All his provision for sustenance, therefore, was his trust in God, and the charity of the faithful. At night he used to retire to take a brief repose in the hospitals; and in places where there were none, he went to some house or small inn, always choosing one of the poorest and meanest. When it chanced that he had to stop for a short time at any village or hamlet, he took the first opportunity of speaking publicly and privately on sacred subjects. The religious communities to whom he was already known by reputation vied with each other in eagerness to hear him, and sometimes begged him to turn a little out of the way to console them. In one place he preached two or three times to different congregations; and we are told of some famous abbey in Germany where the lord abbot and all his monks, after hearing Favre deliver an extempore discourse on religious perfection, were so impressed, that after vainly trying to induce him to stay a little longer, they insisted on accompanying him for a good distance, with many marks of reverence and affection, till he was again on the main road.

But, apart from incidents like this, the holy man was so filled with the Spirit of God, and with a burning zeal for souls, that he might be described as sowing the seed of the Divine Word during the whole of his journey. Whomever he fell in with by land or by sea, in inns or private houses, everywhere and at all times, he was always on the watch, always at work to gain souls for God. From everything he saw, from everything that happened, from everything that turned up in conversation, he took at once occasion to speak of spiritual things; and he did this not in a forced or studied manner, but so naturally and appropriately, that nothing could seem more fitting and timely. He used to say in his humility, and we record it to his honour, that he was the broom of God's house, always employed in sweeping the floor—that is, in cleansing sinners from the stains of sin. He used to add, that all the sons of the Society ought to be the same, because their vocation obliges them to occupy themselves in every possible way with the salvation of their neighbour. And as he was gifted both by nature and grace with an incomparable power of sweetly and powerfully winning all hearts to himself, these accidental meetings were invariably followed by great conversions. Once as he was travelling from Parma to Rome to join Dr. Pedro Ortiz, he was overtaken by the night between

Florence and Siena, and not being able to find any place of shelter, he turned a little out of the way, and going up to a poor labourer's cottage, begged the peasant who lived there to take him in. A few hours later, a party of sixteen highwaymen came unexpectedly to the same place, and ordering supper to be got ready for them, ate and drank voraciously, diverting themselves, as low people of that brutal sort will do, with very indecent talk. Favre was sitting silent in the chimney corner, with his heart and mind fixed on God, thinking over what he should say in case these wretched men spoke to him. By and bye, one of them, irritated at his silence, said—'Now, you stupid priest; what are you about? Why don't you share in our merriment? What are you thinking about, sitting there sad and silent?' Then the holy man, turning full round on them, answered, with his face full of compassion and also of love—'I am thinking how sorrowful a thing is the merriment of sinners, who are the enemies of God; and this fire, by which I am sitting, brings vividly before me the hell to which those wretched men are already condemned for their wickedness. I am thinking how they, who have no certainty of living another moment, and are in danger every instant of falling into that abyss without any hope of coming out again, can nevertheless go on laughing and rejoicing and boldly offending God, without restraint, as if it were all nothing. Reflect, dear brothers, that the divine justice may strike you with its chastisements when least you expect it; and that if once you lose your souls, they are lost for ever.' And then he went on, pointing out the danger they were in of everlasting damnation, and the way of escaping it, by leaving the bad ways in which they were living, and turning to God with true penitence. And he said it all with such fervent zeal and such affectionate tenderness, that those poor wretches were filled with compunction, and all sixteen repented, and resolved to lead a new life, beseeching Favre to hear their confessions at once, and reconcile them to God on the spot. And all that night was spent by the blessed father in a holy joy of spirit over the treasure he had gained in those lost souls. Other occurrences like this happened in the course of his travels, which we shall relate from time to time in due order. It is now time to resume the thread of our narrative.

CHAPTER XII.

Peter Favre at Ratisbon.

THERE were already assembled at Ratisbon, to be present or to vote at the Diet, great numbers of the German princes and prelates, the delegates of the free cities, the ambassadors of kings, together with the flower of the Spanish and Italian nobility, whom the Emperor Charles V. had brought with him. The two nuncios, John Morone and John Pozzi, were there to represent the Pope, with Cardinal Gaspar Contarini as legate extraordinary. Those chosen to take part in the conference on religious questions were, on the Catholic side, John Eckius, Julius Pflug, and John Gropper, Archdeacon of Cologne; and their three Lutheran opponents were Philip Melancthon, Martin Bucer, and John Pistorius. The propositions and the answers were put in writing, and copies of them were distributed everywhere, to the great scandal of the faithful, who saw there the most essential articles of the Catholic faith impugned and denied.

Peter Favre was more grieved at this than any one. Writing on the subject to St. Ignatius, he says—

'It pierces my very heart to see so great and noble a country of Europe as Germany, where the lustre of religion and the incomparable dignity of the churches and clergy were formerly the glory of Christendom, threatened now with total ruin, and to find that so great and wise an Emperor, with all his Ministers, and so dignified a body as this Diet, are utterly powerless to check this wreck of the faith, or even to re-establish the poor remains of this Church.'

Nevertheless, desiring greatly to oppose some barrier to the mischief which was threatening to burst, he was divinely inspired to adopt a course which reason and experience showed him to be, perhaps, the only way likely to be successful. This was to induce the more influential Catholics to amend their lives, so that, having inflamed them with a zeal for God's glory, he might encourage them to cooperate for the help and defence of religion. With regard to the heretics, seeing that the only result of disputes and conferences was to make them more obstinate in their error, he resolved to attack and conquer them by gaining over their perverted will, convinced that if this were conquered the intellect would follow, being darkened more by vice than false doctrine.

As to the Catholics, he had already begun to work upon many of them, both at Worms and Spires. The Dean of St. Martin's, at Worms, had only been able to finish the first week of the Spiritual Exercises, as Favre was on the point of departure, yet even this had so impressed him that he could not sufficiently praise the holiness and excellence of this means of grace, and wrote letters to the Bishop of Spires in hearty commendation of it. Favre, writing from Spires to the fathers in Rome, on the 23rd of January, says—

'I think no one was more grieved and troubled at my departure from Worms than the good Dean of St. Martin's, who had begun the Spiritual Exercises, and had scarcely finished the first week. He has, by God's grace, so profited by this that he is burning with zeal to soften the hearts of others, which are as hard as stones. There are many such in this city of Spires, to whom he has written about our concerns, and who, in consequence, have a great wish to make the Exercises. He has also written to the bishop here, who is one of the princes of Germany, and very well disposed. I have spoken to him several times, describing our manner of life, with which he is much edified. Last Thursday, he invited me to dine with him, when there were present the Duke of Bavaria and the Archbishop of Trêves, and he afterwards sent to me his vicar general, whom, judging from our conversations on spiritual subjects, I consider very desirous of making the Exercises. I cannot, however, begin them, or undertake anything solid, as our departure for Ratisbon has just been fixed. However, as his lordship the bishop is to be there with the other German princes, it will be possible to take up the affair again, and to cultivate these good dispositions.'

Dr. John Cochleus also, an exceedingly learned man, and theologian to the King of the Romans, having heard Favre discourse on the difference that there is between the knowledge and the relish of divine things, was quite beside himself with delight. 'I am full of pleasure and joy,' he said, 'that there are such people as masters of affective theology.' He afterwards made the Spiritual Exercises under Favre, and came out such an altered man, that instead of a scholar he became a master in the art, and gave them to the Bishop of Meissen and to others of equal dignity. These men and several others, first by letters, and then by word of mouth after their arrival, raised the reputation of Favre's sanctity to the greatest height in the Diet of Ratisbon. Hence the majority of those princes and noblemen applied to him for counsel and direction in matters concerning their souls. In this manner, he opened a regular spiritual school in Ratisbon, and one or other of these great persons was so continually coming to him, that he had no time for saying the divine office except by cheating himself of his night's rest. To mention a few of those who were most constant in visiting him. There were D. Jerome della Cerda, son of the Duke of Medina Cœli, D. Juan Manriquez, brother of the Duke of Najara, D. Sancho of Castille, D. Francis of Toledo, D. Juan of Granada, and the regent Figueroa, all of whom were Spaniards; and of the Italians, the two Apostolic Nuncios, Morone and Pozzi, the Bishop of Girgenti, the Marquis of Terranuova and his two sons, the Count of Mirandola and his son, and Prince Camillo Colonna. Ortiz also introduced to him Charles III. of Savoy, called "the Good," who inquired whether he were one of those priests who went about the world after the manner of the Apostles, for the purpose of doing good to their neighbours. Favre gave him a brief account of the Institute, and the Duke was much delighted with it, and was lavish of courteous and kind words and acts. Afterwards he chose Favre for his confessor and spiritual father, never letting a day pass without hearing him discourse for an hour on the things of eternity. The same thing was done by the Ambassador of D. Juan, King of Portugal, and D. Sancho of Castille, whom Favre calls his eldest son in that Court.

But it was in the German prelates and ecclesiastics, who were there in great numbers, that the holy man strove most to kindle a more fervent spirit of Apostolic zeal. He placed before their eyes the melancholy condition into which religion had fallen, and the obligation laid upon them to use every means for defending, supporting, and advancing it. And as his manner of doing this was both most sweet and most forcible, he induced them to promise this with all their hearts, and, after returning to their churches, to keep their promise, of which they gave signal proof in instructing and reforming the clergy and laity. These good desires and magnanimous resolutions were, in a great measure, the fruit of the Spiritual Exercises, which, being handled by Favre with his usual incomparable ability and address, always produced wonderful results. He began by giving them to a few persons privately, then to several together, and at length the numbers of clergy and laity of all ranks so increased, that not being sufficient for the work by himself, he asked to have ten of the Society to help him. 'I can say with truth,' he writes to St. Ignatius, 'that if ten others of the Society were here we should have quite work enough to do in accordance with our Institute. Dr. Ortiz would like a hundred of us, as he says there would be plenty of employment for them all in this Court. You may imagine, therefore, how incessantly I am occupied here, principally from having to converse with numerous princes, each of whom would require a much better workman than poor Favre.'[1] But whatever he may say out of humility to himself, the fact is that every one in the Court was speaking of the sudden and thorough changes from evil to good, and from good to better still, which were seen to result in those who had gone through the Exercises. Many persons, indeed, not being able to guess at the cause, openly accused Favre of magic and witchcraft. When he heard this, he was very glad, hoping to be accused of these arts by the heretics before the Diet, for he did not doubt that if he should

---

[1] Autograph letter, May 23, 1541.

have to give an account of himself before that great assembly, and to explain what kind of magic it was that was practised in the Exercises, he should be able to bring over the most stubborn and obstinate, and therefore the most in need of help, to make proof in themselves of what they could not understand in others, and in this way he hoped to gain over many even of the heretics.

But without this opportunity he really did gain several, partly by private conversations, and partly by the Exercises. He made it his aim to win their affection, and then taking their souls, as it were, by surprise, to discover and heal the sores which sin had made there. And it frequently happened that, after breaking off evil habits and emptying their hearts of sinful affections, they found their minds at once cleared of doubts and errors. On one occasion, when he was sent for to Nuremberg to attend an Italian who was dying, he not only helped the poor man to make a good death, but induced another of the family and two rich merchants who had apostatized to renounce their heresy and be reconciled to the Church, besides, in addition, baptizing two Mahometans. We have no record of any other particular cases, but we possess a full account in his own words of the plain and successful method which is to be observed for the conversion of heretics. He wrote a letter full of wisdom on this subject to Father James Laynez, who had asked for it, and in it he may be said to describe himself. And I have thought well to translate it faithfully, for the good of other labourers in the Gospel.

CHAPTER XIII.

Instructions how to deal with heretics.

'You have more than once written to ask me to trace out some sort of rules for the guidance of those who may desire to labour among heretics for the salvation of others without prejudice to their own. I have not hitherto answered, for many sufficient reasons. In the first place I have never yet been able to find time for maturing the subject sufficiently, as the concerns I am occupied in leave me no leisure; next, my late illness has so weakened me that it is with difficulty that I can guide my pen; and lastly, nothing that satisfied me came to my mind. However, I will now write down what comes to my pen.

'First of all, it is essential that whoever desires to be useful to heretics in our day should both nourish in himself a great affection for them and show it in action, removing from his own mind those unfavourable imaginations which make us think less well of them. The next thing is, to win their goodwill and inclinations to such an extent that they may reciprocate our kind feelings and think well of us. This may easily be done by speaking to them affectionately, and dwelling in familiar conversations on those points only on which they agree with us, avoiding everything like a dispute, in which one side always assumes an air of superiority, and shows contempt of the other. Those subjects should be first chosen in which there is a sympathy and union of wills, rather than those which tend to disunite them by opposition of opinion. These Lutherans are, as the Apostle says, children led away to their destruction. The first thing that they lose is their piety and power of doing good works; after this comes the loss of the true faith. Hence the work of their redemption should begin by replanting in the will good principles leading to right actions, and then go on to those which lead to a right belief. This order of proceeding is the reverse of that which was followed in the early times of the infant Church, when Gentiles were being converted by the faith. Then, the first thing was to convince unbelievers of their errors, and afterwards, with great prudence, lead them on to the ways of living and acting according to the rules of the faith.

'Therefore, if it falls to our lot to have the care of the soul of a person whose intellect is darkened by errors, and at the same time whose heart is full of vices, we must first employ every effort and art to heal him of his vices, and then to convince him of his errors. A priest once came to me, begging and entreating that I would, if possible, prove to him by sound arguments the falsehood of the opinion which he held, that priests ought to be allowed to marry. When I had heard this I got him, by courtesy and kindness, to open his heart to me, and discovered that his soul had been for many years in a bad state from his being ensnared by love for wicked women. I put the question of his doubts altogether aside for the time, and tried to lead him adroitly to detest his evil ways, and the result was that no sooner had he, by the help of God, abandoned his sin, and dismissed a woman of bad life whom he maintained, than his mind was set free from all doubts, and I heard no more of those errors contrary to the Church's teaching which had arisen and increased in consequence of his dissolute life.

'Since one of the commonest errors of the Lutherans is the ascribing merit to faith alone, denying it altogether to good works, the right way to proceed in the matter of their conversion is to begin by exciting them to the performance of good works, and to come to the question of faith afterwards. Thus, when a heretic denies the Church's power to make the hearing Mass or reciting the divine office an obligation under pain of grievous sin, we should strive to bring him to practise these and other pious exercises, because he abandoned them before forsaking the faith. Besides this, we should remember what is the principal prop on which these leaders and teachers of heresy rely in maintaining their errors, in opposition to the precepts of the Church and the rules of the holy Fathers. They say that they have not sufficient strength to obey God, and that the Church's laws and precepts are intolerable to human nature. They ought, therefore, to be encouraged to trust in God with all the energy of their minds, and so to make themselves capable, by His help and grace, not only of keeping the precepts, but of advancing to greater and more perfect things.

'My own belief is, that if it were possible, by force of learning and ardent zeal, to persuade Luther himself to root out his vicious inclinations and observe the pious practices of the Church, and so to resolve readily on obeying the precepts, he would by these means alone, without any religious controversy, cease to be a heretic. It is nevertheless true that it demands great force of virtue, and much grace from God, to acquire this interior submission of mind and readiness of will; and, as it is difficult to conceive the existence of such sentiments in these men, steeped as they are in the mire of vice, and wholly estranged from God, there can be little or no hope of bringing them back to a better way. However this may be, it is my opinion that there is more good to be done to the souls of heretics by conversing with them familiarly on the amendment of life, the beauty of virtue, the diligent practice of prayer, the final judgment, eternal punishment, and every subject relating and tending to a reformation of morals, than by confounding them with many arguments and authorities. To sum up the whole briefly, what I say is, that these persons need to be properly incited and encouraged to correct their vicious habits, and to open their hearts to the fear and love of God and the desire of doing good works. By these remedies they will be healed of their spiritual diseases, especially of that disgust for divine things which is found in them, and of their continual mental distraction; for these are not the least of their spiritual maladies, seeing that they have the effect, not only of blunting the edge of their intellects, but of weakening their whole mental and bodily vigour. May Jesus Christ, the Redeemer of men, Who well knows that it is not in the power of His written Word thoroughly to soften their hearts, deign to touch and move the souls of the heretics by His divine grace!'

CHAPTER XIV.

Election of the General, and Solemn Vows.

WHILE Blessed Peter Favre was making the Society of Jesus known in Germany by his successful labours, and gaining for it great respect by the holiness of his life, St. Ignatius and his other companions were in Rome, engaged in regulating it and establishing it on a proper footing. As far back as the 27th of September in the preceding year, 1540, Pope Paul III. had issued an Apostolic Bull confirming it and declaring it an Order.

Favre had heard this on his way from Italy to Germany; and on his arrival at Worms he received letters from Rome containing fuller information. In his answer, dated the 27th of December, 1540, he says— 'I have already written this week, to let you know that I received your letters and the copies of those written by our brothers on the 17th of this month. I am not able, at present, to write or explain the pleasure they gave me; principally because they show how every day our designs are more and more blessed by God. I rejoice exceedingly at the spiritual privileges granted to the Society by his Holiness, and at his approbation of it, and I have great confidence in God that all this is but the pledge of more and greater graces which Christ, Whose Vicar his Holiness is, will give us if we do not make ourselves unworthy of them. If I had nothing else to do, I could certainly find matter in these things to occupy myself for many days in praising and thanking the Divine Goodness, from Whom come all these mercies to us.'

The Society, being thus established by Apostolic authority, it was decided by election, in the spring of 1541, who should govern it as General. Before starting for Portugal, Father Francis Xavier and Father Simon Rodriguez had left their votes in a sealed letter, and Father Peter Favre, who was then in Ratisbon, sent three copies of his by different routes, to avoid all danger of miscarriage and delay. When the letters were opened, it was found that Ignatius was elected General by the unanimous votes of the three who were absent and the five who were present. And indeed there could be no doubt that the voices of all would be given for him whom all already acknowledged as their common father and master. Nevertheless some, particularly those who were absent, who desired to name more than one by way of guarding against any possible accident, agreed in voting, after Ignatius, for Favre only. This was done by Francis Xavier and Simon Rodriguez, and also among those who were present by John Codure, who gave a reason for it which reflects the highest praise on Favre. After naming Ignatius, he adds these words—'After him, I think the venerable Father Dr. Peter Favre ought to be preferred as being a man of equal virtue.' And it is certain that if they had all named more than one, they would all, in like manner, have voted for Favre, after Ignatius. He himself named Xavier after Ignatius, as Xavier had named him, and this shows the mutual esteem of these two great and saintly men.

As soon as Peter Favre had news of the election of St. Ignatius he prepared to make his solemn profession, which the others had made already in the Church of

St. Paul fuori le mura. He made his preparations very devoutly, and on the octave of our Lady's Visitation, the 9th of July, 1541, in the Church of our Lady in Ratisbon, called the Old Chapel, he offered himself to God by the vows of religion, with the deepest feelings of humility and submission, and placed himself entirely at the disposal of the Vicar of Jesus Christ and of the General of the Society. In his 'Memorial' he has himself preserved for us the form which he used, there not being at that time any common form in existence. This is, however, a little different from that written by his own hand, which he sent to Rome, and which we still possess. It runs thus—

'I, Peter Favre, promise to Almighty God, in the presence of His Virgin Mother and all the company of heaven, and to my Reverend Father Ignatius of Loyola, who is in the place of God in the Society of the Name of Jesus, perpetual chastity, poverty, and obedience, according to the rule of life enjoined in the Bull and in the Constitutions of the Society of our Lord Jesus, already promulgated or hereafter to be promulgated. In like manner, I promise special obedience to the Sovereign Pontiff regarding the missions mentioned in the Bull. And lastly, I promise obedience with regard to the instruction of children in the rudiments of the faith according to the same Bull, and to the Constitutions. At Ratisbon, in the Church of our Lady, called the Old Chapel, before the high altar, July 9th, being the octave of the Visitation of our Lady, Mother of God, 1541. Which profession and vow I confirm and repeat to Almighty God, to His Virgin Mother, and to all the saints, and to you, Reverend Father, who hold the place of God, as though I were present before all the Society, praying your Paternity and all the

Society to be pleased to accept and receive this my profession, incorporating me, though unworthy, in your holy Society. And all this I write with my own hand, signing it with my name. This 10th day of the same month and year. PETER FAVRE.'

Words cannot express the floods of consolation which deluged his soul in thinking over and attentively considering the wonderful ways by which God had guided Ignatius and the companions he had gained in Paris up to this last step by which they were all united in one and the same purpose, and joined together by one and the same bond of religion. The life which he had led up to this time had been one of great hardship, long journeys, continual dangers, incessant labours, and privations of every kind; but he had ample compensation in seeing the work begun by him and the others, under the direction of St. Ignatius, in our Lady's Church at Montmartre in Paris, thus firmly and durably established. For this he gave infinite thanks to God, and felt his heart inspired with new strength and vigour to undertake greater labours, and to endure greater sufferings for the good of souls. At the same time he received new lights from God on different methods of prayer, and on detaching his heart from created things, and entirely subjecting his will to the orders and injunctions of holy obedience.

As to this last point, he gave proof of it a few days later. Dr. Ortiz had pressed, as soon as the Diet was concluded, for permission to take Father Favre with him to Spain. The holy man no sooner received notice of this from Rome than he immediately broke off all his successful labours and prepared to start. There were many who opposed this resolution of his, on account of the spiritual good he was effecting in Germany. But they did not prevail with him; for it was his invariable habit to abandon himself completely into God's hands, and to execute His orders, as manifested to him through his Superiors, without delay; leaving without a moment's hesitation all the works he had begun, or nearly completed, to betake himself to the new country whither he was sent, to begin everything over again. Indeed, he protested, as he told St. Ignatius in a letter, that he desired never to do anything except by obedience, and that he was ready, if his Superiors so pleased, to do nothing but travel for the rest of his life.

CHAPTER XV.

Peter Favre in Savoy.

On the 27th of July, 1541, Peter Favre left Ratisbon with Dr. Ortiz. In passing through Germany, he was exposed to the secret attacks of the heretics, who hated him mortally, who plotted and lay in wait for him, and posted assassins ready to kill him in different parts. But God, and the guardian angels of places, whom, according to his custom, he invoked as he travelled, protected and saved him from every danger. He was well acquainted with the intentions and designs of those treacherous sectaries, yet so far from fearing them, he may rather be said courageously to have confronted their fury; frequently stopping on the way to sow the seed of the Word of God, and to defend the cause of religion, in cities and towns which were in great measure infested by heresy. As he approached Switzerland, the danger to his life increased in consequence of his having discovered a secret and horrible conspiracy while he was in Ratisbon. He came to know that the heretical cantons had combined with Geneva and some German cities, in a plot for making a sudden descent upon Savoy, occupying the fortresses, reducing the country to their detestable rule, and rooting out the Catholic religion. He gave information of this to the Duke, his sovereign, who promptly dispatched soldiers and arms to the frontiers, so that the wicked designs of the traitors came to nothing, and the only harm done was the burning of a few little villages, which were found unprovided with means of defence.

In spite of this, the plague of heresy had crept into several places in Savoy, and this was, as I think, the motive which induced Favre, as he had entered the diocese of Geneva, to go a little out of his way to visit his native place, to purify it from, or fortify it, according to the necessity of the case, against the infection of false doctrine. He only remained nine or ten days among those rugged mountains of Upper Savoy; yet in that short time the hearts of all the mountaineers were so filled with love and veneration for him, on account of the holiness of his life and wonderful works, and he left behind him such recollections of himself, that in the year 1596, Dr. Peter Critan, the parish priest at Thonon, drew up a little process in which he collected the testimony on oath of five persons, almost all of them eighty years old, concerning the childhood of Favre, and this visit of his to his native country. And it is from the acts of this process, which was approved and confirmed in 1607 by the saintly bishop, Francis of Sales, that I shall extract the notices of those particulars which are about to be related.

He travelled then through Savoy, in company with a priest, who, the witnesses say, belonged to the Society, and a noble layman. I find no mention in our annals of his having taken one of our fathers with him on this journey: so that the priest must have been Dr. Ortiz, and the gentleman one of his suite. They all travelled on foot; and when they reached Alex, a small village not far from Geneva, they fell in with the noble D. Mark of Arenthon, the lord of the place, who recognized Favre, and courteously invited him to take up his abode in his house, and rest there for awhile. He stayed there three days, to the infinite consolation of all the family, who were never weary of gathering round him to hear him speak of heavenly things, and of his hopes for the conversion of the German heretics. He never went out during that time, and passed many hours in prayer, either in the solitude of his chamber, or in the chapel of the castle, where he said Mass daily. Wilhelmina d'Arenthon, Mark's daughter, at that time a girl of eighteen, was determined, with some companions of hers, to watch and find out what the father did when he was alone, and not once only, but many times, she saw him with his face all on fire, quite out of himself, and rapt in an ecstasy. Struck with astonishment, she ran to tell what she had seen to the household, and she always retained so lively a recollection of it, that fifty-five years afterwards she was able to declare it on oath in the Process, always speaking of Favre as 'Blessed' or 'the Saint.' Another miraculous thing happened which increased the veneration in which he was held. There was a servant of the house named Claude Morac, who had lain sick of almost incessant fever for a year and a half. When Peter Favre heard of his state, he paid him a visit, and after hearing his confession and giving him Holy Communion, he recited a few prayers over him, and without more the disease left him and he was perfectly cured. All these things made so deep an impression, that after the three days, when the holy man was about to take leave, all that noble family came and knelt before him weeping, and begging his blessing : and Mark, not satisfied with this, insisted on accompanying him on foot for more than a league on his way.

From Alex he went to his native place, Villaret, and finding that the inhabitants kept very firm in the old faith and in solid piety, he set himself vigorously to increase their zeal for good works. He preached several times in the Church of St. Jean de Sixt, fervently enjoining on all a great devotion to the Blessed Virgin Mary, and teaching them how to recite with profit the holy rosary. He introduced the custom of wearing our Lady's beads round the neck, which continued for many years after. He visited one by one all the sick in the village, heard their confessions, and tried to soothe their sufferings by the sweetest spiritual discourses. In the neighbouring parish of the Great Bornand, he preached four times, besides instructing the children in the Christian doctrine. There he was told that an old aunt of his, named Jane Favre, had lain for eight months grievously and hopelessly sick in a poor cottage at the top of one of the mountains. He determined to visit her, and finding her surrounded by a numerous family, he was filled with compassion. He celebrated the holy Mass; and then, making her drink some holy water, and commending her to God in a few short prayers, he restored her whole and in health to her poor children. In short, during the one week that he spent in those parts, he did great things for the service of God, preaching to the people, administering the sacraments, sowing the good seed everywhere, as the witnesses say, and doing infinite good in saving and consoling so many souls. The good people of that country left all their occupations, and hastened to see the saint, to hear him, and to have his help in settling their consciences. It is no wonder, therefore, that when he was going away, all the inhabitants of Villaret, and many others from the neighbourhood, including his two younger brothers, John and Louis, went with him as far as Thonon, where they knelt for his last blessing, and then returned home rejoicing that they had seen him, and grieving that they had so soon lost him. At Thonon, he was requested to preach, and produced such an impression that the small body of clergy there did all they could to keep him with them for a few days; but he was not able to give them that satisfaction, being compelled to resume the journey with Ortiz which had been interrupted; and so, having given them all his blessing, which they earnestly entreated, he finally quitted Savoy, and turned his steps towards France.

This was the visit which he paid to his native place, a truly Apostolic visit. He left behind him so great a name and reputation, that on hearing of his death five years later, all the people of the place immediately began calling him 'Saint' and 'Blessed,' invoking him as their advocate and patron in all their troubles, and going in procession to the devout little chapel which they dedicated to his honour. And this popular devotion was not a passing one, but it went on increasing up to our own days, as we shall show in the proper place.

CHAPTER XVI.

First visit to Spain.

WAR had broken out afresh between the King of France and the Emperor Charles V., and as they were passing by a fortress, Ortiz and his suite, being surprised and recognized as Spaniards by the scouts who were scouring the country, were taken prisoners and led off. Favre, who had the art of making an opportunity of labouring for the good of souls out of everything that happened, won over the soldiers of the garrison by his sweet and loving manner of conversing with them about God, and especially the governor of the fortress, who, having heard him several times, invited him to a private and confidential interview, in which he was so moved by the grace of the Holy Spirit, that he made a general confession to him, and received from him rules for the new way of life which he resolved in future to lead. After a week, during which time he treated his prisoners, for the sake of Favre, with the greatest courtesy, he set them at liberty without demanding a penny of ransom. Such is the power of virtue in a holy man to make friends and benefactors even of the most determined enemies.

Having passed through France and set foot for the first time on Spanish ground, Favre saw what a vast field was opening to him for promoting the glory of God. Distrusting his own strength for the work, he turned, as he always did, to ask help from heaven. With a wonderful warmth of fervour, he entreated the angels guardian of that kingdom to be favourable to him; then he prayed our Blessed Lady, enumerating in his mind all the places where she is specially honoured; and lastly, the most celebrated saints of Spain, St. James, St. Narcissus, St. Isidore, St. Ildephonsus, St. Eulalia, and the rest, begging them to give efficacy to his words and fruit to his labours. He was the first, after Father Antonio Araoz (who had been there for a very short time the year before), who went to that country to prepare the way for the Society, and to incline the minds of the inhabitants to receive it. And truly he attained his end, although this first visit was more like a rapid course through the country than a regular stay. His very presence removed many hindrances out of the way, destroyed many adverse prejudices and false charges which clouded men's minds, and he left behind him an inheritance of fair fame and reputation for his successors.

In company with Dr. Ortiz he visited the principal cities, leaving everywhere traces of his Apostolic zeal. The long intercourse he had had in Paris and Rome with St. Ignatius had made him master of the Spanish language, which he both spoke and wrote fluently. Hence all his letters to Ignatius are in Spanish. He was thus able without any difficulty to preach God's Word, to hear confessions, and to converse familiarly on the things of God and the salvation of souls. Here, as elsewhere, he had only to be seen and heard to win all hearts, such was the power of his spirit and the sweetness of his manner. He found matter for valuable instructions to high and low in everything that came before him. Neither did he disdain, great as was his credit, to gather around him the roughest of the populace and the most neglected of the children, and to teach them the Christian doctrine. There is a letter of his, in which he says that he had received special heavenly illuminations and great spiritual consolation in doing this.

On arriving at Madrid, he gave a particular account of his journey in Spain.

'We left Ratisbon,' he writes to the fathers at Rome, 'three months ago, and it has taken us all that time to reach Madrid. In my last letter, from our Lady of Montserrat, I related all that had happened up to that time, repeating some things which I had already written from Lyons and Narbonne. I will now tell the story of our journey from Montserrat to Madrid. We were very kindly received at Saragossa by the leading persons of the city. I in particular found great favour shown to myself and the Society in the House of the Hieronymites, and by the canons of our Lady of the Pillar, and those of the Cathedral. A doctor of theology, Michael of Santangelo, who was with us in Paris, offered very willingly to make the Spiritual Exercises, if I had stayed there for any time. At Medina Celi I found the Bachelor Guttierez, a native of Almazan, a famous advocate, and a very devoted disciple of Father Master Laynez. He promised me to go to Galapagar, to make the Exercises for a whole month. I also spoke to the Duke, the father of D. Hernando della Cerda, who, after some conversation, took me apart and opened his whole soul to me with intense feeling, as if he had been on the point of death. There was with the Duke a brother of the Count of Monteacuto, the Lord of Almazan, who is well acquainted with our affairs. I wrote a long letter to the father of Master Laynez, not having been able to get permission from Dr. Ortiz to go to that place, which is six leagues off, though I wished to do so more than if it had been my own native spot. From Medina Celi we went to Torrigo, where a sister of D. Hernando della Cerda, a daughter of the Duke's, named Catarina, lives. I preached there, and held long spiritual conversations with her and her husband. The Bachelor Guttierez insisted on accompanying us as far as Siguenza, where again we found many persons of distinction acquainted with our affairs, especially some who were in Rome at the time of our persecutions. From Torrigo we went to Guadalaxara, and as several relations and connections of Dr. Ortiz were living there, we stayed there four days, not without spiritual profit. Leaving Guadalaxara we came to Alcalà, and there remained more than ten days. In this place I became very intimate with the vicar general, who opened to me his whole conscience, as though I had been his confessor, and manifested a keen desire to make the Exercises. To begin at the beginning, you must know that, as I wished the morning after our arrival to say Mass at St. Giusto's Church, the sacristan called a young man, who took me to the vicar to obtain permission to celebrate, as I was a foreigner and not known to him. He asked me a few questions, to which I replied, then taking me, first to the reception-room and then to his own apartments, we talked on various subjects till we fell to speaking of our concerns, and of our Father Ignatius and his companions, of whom he had heard something. He was so pleased and edified that I cannot describe it. After spending an hour or two in this way, he took me himself to the church and gave orders that I should be supplied with everything, begging me afterwards to dine with him. I did so, and after dinner we spent two more hours in various discourses. After leaving Alcalà, it was God's will that we should meet the Cardinal Archbishop of Toledo at about two leagues from the town. I went up to kiss his hand, and the Doctor spoke of me and our affairs. Then the Cardinal asked us to return with him to Alcalà, so that I was able to inform him fully and at leisure of everything concerning the Society. He was much pleased, and gave me in writing ample faculties for exercising my ministry throughout his archdiocese, as you will see by the copy which I send. The Cardinal was accompanied by Dr. Bernard, one of his most trusted counsellors, and who has long been much attached to the Society. With him I had a familiar conversation on spiritual matters, and also with two others, doctors of arts, Master Miranda and Master Campos, whom I had known in Paris, one of whom promised to come to Galapagar to make a month of Exercises. On my taking leave, the vicar said to me with great feeling, that if I were able to remain with him a few days he should be ready and willing to follow me to prison and to death. We arrived here at Madrid last Thursday, and I find many opportunities and various ways of labouring with profit, for, independently of my being known and approved by the Cardinal, Don Pedro of Castille, who was my spiritual son in Ratisbon, is here. Two days before our arrival, Don Francis Manriquez, who made the Exercises with me in Ratisbon, came here from the Imperial Court. But nothing will come of all these good opportunities, because, having several other places to visit, we are unable to remain here. I was anxious to write full particulars of all these things, that you may see that I have not been burnt in effigy in Spain, and that our work here is regarded with greater favour than I can describe. And if I am to say what I think, it is my belief that this fair weather which we are enjoying was merited by the storms of persecution endured here by our Father Ignatius, God so ordering things, that where he went through so many sufferings we should find so much favour. I pray Christ our Lord, of His divine clemency, to grant us grace not to grow weary of labouring in His vineyard, for which He gave His blood and His life."¹

From Madrid Peter went to Galapagar, which is a large town, from which Dr. Ortiz received a great part of his ecclesiastical revenues. On his way, Father Favre preached a kind of mission in three places, and heard the confessions of several persons, who were moved by his sermons to turn to God. In Galapagar, where he remained longer than anywhere else, he took on himself the instruction of boys and girls in the Christian doctrine daily in church, and not only those belonging to the spot, but many from neighbouring places, who were sent by their parents to hear him. The people, too, flocked in crowds, and the holy man, seeing them so desirous of the Word of God, undertook the additional labour of preaching on every festival to the adults, and giving them more solid instruction on the precepts of the law of God. And the fruit which was the result was so abundant, that when the Doctor had to go to Occagna to visit the Infantas of Spain, he had not the heart to deprive his people of the presence of Favre, but left him behind to continue his Apostolic labours.²

He was in the midst of these labours when, quite unexpectedly, he received letters from Rome containing express orders from the Sovereign Pontiff to return immediately to Germany, as things there were taking a bad turn, and required his presence and assistance. He, perfect in obedience, without delay prepared to go back all that long and dangerous journey by himself, but God provided him most opportunely with two companions, the more welcome for being unexpected. In passing through Occagna, he was obliged to yield to a pressing

[1] Autograph letter, October 27, 1541.
[2] Autograph letter.

request made to him, that he would give two daughters of the Emperor Charles V. the consolation of a visit from him. They were Mary, afterwards married to the Emperor Maximilian, and Jane, afterwards wife of Don Juan, Prince of Portugal. He stayed a very short time in that Court, yet he did much good there, and gained the veneration of the Princesses, who, when he was about to leave, desired two priests attached to them as chaplains to bear him company as far as Toledo. Their names were John Aragonio and Alvaro Alfonso. On the way they entered into familiar discourses with Favre, and were so struck with his exalted virtue that the heart of each was at the same time touched by God, and they obtained leave from the Princesses to follow him to Germany, not only as companions for the journey, but as brothers in religion.

The holy man received them as novices, and he so trained them during the journey, and afterwards in Germany, by the brightness of his example and the power of his words, to a high degree of virtue and perfection, that they both, as we shall see, became very zealous labourers in the Lord's vineyard. In 1544. Aragonio went to Portugal; after finishing his studies at Coimbra, he was appointed, with two others, to found the College of St. Antony at Lisbon. Father Balthasar Tellez, in his Chronicle of Portugal, writes of him thus—

'This Father was a great servant of God, much given to prayer, and very zealous for the salvation of souls, which he strove to compass by every means, chiefly by the Sacrament of Penance. And as he was singularly attractive and affectionate, he gained the hearts of all with whom he had to do. By his holy words and efforts he not only persuaded every one whom he came across to be reconciled to God, and to begin a new life, but as soon as he had gained any one he made him an instrument for gaining also his family, relations, and friends.'

Father Alvaro Alfonso remained at Cologne to study, from which place he too was sent to Portugal and to Spain. He was a most zealous labourer for the divine glory and for the salvation of his neighbours; indeed his fervour had to be somewhat restrained by Father Favre, who, on leaving Germany, left for him some written spiritual counsels, full of wisdom.

CHAPTER XVII.

Peter Favre at Barcelona.

FAVRE, joyful at having gained these two companions, began his journey with them at the beginning of January, 1542. On arriving at Barcelona he unexpectedly found there Father Antonio Araoz and Father Diego d'Eguia, who had been sent to Spain by St. Ignatius, for the purpose of publishing in that country the Bull approving and confirming the Society. They had arrived the night before, having walked all the way from Rome to Barcelona without any means of support, except the alms which they begged from pious persons on the journey. The fathers' mutual joy and consolation in seeing and embracing each other was all the greater for being so unexpected. And as Favre was obliged to wait for a time for better weather for his journey to France, he at once took counsel with Araoz; and the two Apostolic men resolved to begin their sacred ministrations the next day, preaching the Word of God to the citizens of the place, whose remembrance of and veneration for St. Ignatius were still fresh. A few years before, he had made himself a great name in the city, for his holy life and wonderful works. Father Araoz preached in the parish Church of St. Maria del Pino, and Father Favre in the Church of St. Clare, belonging to the Benedictine nuns.

There was at this time in Barcelona, in quality of viceroy, lieutenant, and captain-general of the principality of Catalonia, Don Francis Borgia. Ever since his great change for the better, after seeing the disfigured countenance of the deceased Empress Isabella at Granada, he had given himself entirely to the concerns of his soul, and was leading a very holy life in frequent fastings, long prayers, and works of great piety, as well as of mercy and zeal towards others. He was admired and praised as the mirror and model of true Christian princes, and his Court was more like a religious community than an assemblage of knights and grandees of the State. He did not then know the Society of Jesus—perhaps not even by name; and I will now relate the way in which he learnt first to know and love it, then to advance it, and lastly to resolve on dedicating himself to it.

His wife, Doña Leonora di Castro, who resembled him perfectly in piety, was that morning at the Church of St. Clare with some of her ladies, to hear the sermon of Father Favre. She was so greatly struck and moved to compunction by his powerful words and zeal, that when the sermon was over, she went to him to speak on spiritual subjects, and having thus tasted the sweetness and unction of his spirit, she earnestly begged him to be so kind as to preach another sermon the following day. On returning to the palace she told everything to her husband, Don Francis, and was profuse in praise of the virtue and sanctity of Father Favre. Soon after, Father Araoz called upon her, and set forth briefly the purpose for which he had come to Spain, giving her an account of the institute of the Society of Jesus, founded in Rome by Ignatius, and approved as a religious order by Pope Paul III. All this was related to Don Francis, and kindled in him the desire to make closer acquaintance with the two fathers, and to learn from them the true object of their vocation.

Accordingly, next day, he was present with his whole Court at Father Favre's sermon. That first time of hearing him was sufficient to bind his heart to that great man, and give him the highest esteem for him. Francis made him dine with him; and all dinner time was spent in hearing him speak of God, and give a full account of the object of the Society, and of the great good to souls which it was already doing in Italy, Germany, and Portugal. Francis conceived so high an opinion of the perfection and wisdom of St. Ignatius, that from that time he began, and continued, as long as he remained in the world, to write to him for advice and direction as to the rules he should observe in frequenting the sacraments and in the practice of virtue. And as he could not keep Favre, he earnestly requested and obtained leave to have Father Araoz for some time in Barcelona. When, after the death of his father Don John, he went to rule and govern his duchy of Gandia, his first thought was to establish there first a college, and then a university for the Society. And at length, as we shall see in due course, he resolved to leave the world, and to give himself to St. Ignatius as his son in place of Father Favre, whom he saw after his death ascending gloriously into heaven.

For the rest, during the few days that Favre remained at Barcelona, he won the goodwill and affection of every one, as he always did even in the shortest visit, by his winning manners and exemplary life. The Benedictine nuns of the Convent of St. Clare, where he often preached, desired to hear him discourse privately on the perfection

G

suited to their state. He complied, exhorting them to a complete union with God by means of prayer, detachment from the world, and continual mortification. Many of them were very spiritual persons; and remarkable among these, were Doña Geronima Oluia, and Doña Teresa Regadella, both of very noble birth, and, which is a far higher distinction, favoured by God with singular gifts and graces. The holy conversation of Favre inspired them with so strong an affection for the institute of the Society, that they wrote to Rome for permission from the Apostolic See to place themselves under the obedience and direction of our fathers. But St. Ignatius, who, for very valid reasons, was exceedingly averse from undertaking the direction of nuns, or women living in community, constantly refused to accept the charge, and exhorted them to persevere cheerfully in the path of perfection, according to their rule, as may be seen in his letters to Doña Teresa Regadella.

CHAPTER XVIII.

Return to Spires.

THE weather being now somewhat improved, Father Favre took leave of the holy viceroy, Don Francis, of his two companions, and of his friends in Barcelona, and resumed his journey with his two novices. Before leaving Spain he was in danger of meeting with the assassins who infested the roads; in France he was on the point of again falling into the hands of the soldiers, and in Switzerland of being seized by the heretics. The journey was long, and full of disasters, in the depth of winter, sometimes in floods of rain, sometimes through ice and snow. The plague was raging in some cities, some were in all the confusion of war, others were the prey of intestine discord and strife. Nevertheless, full of trust in God, he generously overcame every difficulty, though often delayed by failure of strength and by illness. He was ready and willing to lay down life itself if only he might obediently accomplish the will of the Vicar of Jesus Christ. Thus, visited by continual spiritual consolations and bodily sufferings, he only reached Soleure, on the borders of Switzerland, on Holy Thursday, after preaching at a place in Savoy which was in great spiritual need. On Easter Day he came to a place where there was no priest, and there, acting as parish priest, he sang solemn Mass, to the great delight of the good inhabitants; and not there only, but elsewhere in Germany, he found, as we see from his letters, many quite populous places where there was but one priest, and some where there was not one, all of them having either died of the plague or been perverted to the Lutheran heresy.

On the 14th of April he arrived at Spires, where he was very courteously received by Otho Truchses, who gave him a letter which Father Nicolas Bobadilla had left for him a few days before, informing him that Morone, the Bishop of Modena, and the Pope's Nuncio, left it to his choice either to join Mgr. Jerome Veralli at the Court of the King of the Romans, or to remain at Spires till further orders from his Holiness. After imploring to be enlightened from heaven as to his course, he yielded at last to the pressing entreaties of Truchses, and remained, with his two companions, at Spires. He was already well known there by his labours in God's service during the preceding year. Now that he returned he was greatly surprised to find the minds of the inhabitants, particularly of the clergy, prejudiced against him. The reason of this feeling was that, shortly before his arrival, a report had been set on foot, which spread among the people, that he was sent by the Pope and his Nuncio, with the most ample faculties, in the character of a reformer of the clergy; and as the very name of a reformer is always hateful, every one was filled with horror and indignation, and, in consequence, stood upon his guard and held himself in readiness as if to repel the attacks of a declared enemy. Neither were these guilty feelings merely cherished in secret, they showed themselves openly, and men avoided speaking to Favre, and even seeing him. He perceived the state of things, but appeared not to know it. After asking the help of God with fervent prayers and many tears, he set himself to gain by meekness and patience the goodwill and affection of some few of the clergy, showing them that the only commission he held was supplied to him by his own zeal, which was, to promote, with all discretion, the eternal welfare both of the clergy and laity. Having won over these persons, it was not a difficult matter to him gradually to draw over others by their means; and indeed there was much need that they should reform their lives, which were, for the most part, very irregular and scandalous. He had to endure many labours and sufferings in bringing them back to purity, but at length, by private exhortations, and still more by the Spiritual Exercises, he succeeded in persuading them to abandon their vices altogether, and to lead lives worthy of their state. In order to make their conversion permanent, and any relapse difficult, he stirred up the zeal of the bishop, Philip Fleschein, whom he had known before, both at Spires itself and at the Diet of Ratisbon. He spent four whole days in conversing with him on the great obligations of the pastoral office, at the same time devising exceedingly wise laws and regulations for the extirpation of scandals and abuses, and for driving away the devouring wolves from the flock. The zeal and energy of the bishop's vicar general were of no slight assistance to him in this work. He was able to spend only eleven days in retreat, making the Spiritual Exercises; but in that time he found himself changed so entirely into another man, that, filled with a profound disgust for worldly greatness and rank, he determined on giving himself up to Favre for life as a disciple of his wisdom and his companion in religion. But good and zealous prelates were too scarce in Germany in those days to allow of the few that there were leaving the cities in which they were. Favre was obliged to persuade, or rather to command, him to remain at his post, and to do all he could, animated by the true spirit of charity, for the salvation of his neighbours. And so, indeed, he did; beginning by declaring war on the practice of concubinage, especially among priests, insisting that such women should either lead a virtuous life or be altogether banished from Spires.

And now that Favre had restored the clergy to primitive simplicity and austerity of life, and thus removed that great excitement to evil, he turned his attention to the instruction and amendment of the laity; and, with the help of his two novices, Aragonio and Alfonso, he effected so much, that when the parish priests and their curates took the account of the confessions and communions the following Easter they were found to be more numerous than those of all the twenty preceding years put together. Besides this, he brought back several religious communities of both sexes to the observance of their rule, and purified them from the taint of some Lutheranism which secretly lurked among them. He saved from impending ruin a learned and gifted man, who had fallen into the hands of a treacherous master, from whom he had already imbibed the poison of heresy, and so was on the point of doing serious injury to the Church. He made him enter into himself, and convinced him of his errors; and then turned him into so ardent a champion of the Catholic faith that thenceforward the teacher who had perverted him had no more terrible opponent, nor one whom he feared more. In like manner he earned the goodwill of a religious preacher, who was in the habit of boldly propagating false doctrines from the pulpit, and whom Favre induced to retract publicly. Moreover, lest he should be tempted by poverty, which is often the worst of counsellors, to do wrong again, he obtained ample help and alms for him and his.

So marvellous were the effects produced in the city of Spires by the gentle spirit of Father Favre that, having begun by being shunned and hated by every one in it, there was at last not one, even of the heretics, who did not greatly love and respect him. He speaks of this himself, in his letters to Rome, as something wonderful, giving the glory to God.

' I laboured in this city,' he says, ' with my two Spanish companions, till the 10th of October, making the people friendly to my person and to our habit, which is that commonly worn by priests in Spain. My previous letters have made your charity acquainted with all that happened in the earlier part of the time. Blessed be God, Who has made the end and issue so much better than the beginning. At the present time there is no one in Spires, priest or layman, who is not very well and kindly disposed towards us; even those who most differed from us on points of faith, have become friendly to us from observing our way of living and working. We quitted Spires with regret, and it may truly be said that we have left our hearts there.'

At the same time he did not neglect the spiritual cultivation of his two novices, John Aragonio and Alvaro Alfonso. Having by this time thoroughly initiated them in the things of God, he sent first one and then the other as pilgrims to Cologne, begging their bread on the journey. They had to endure many inconveniences, and no slight danger, on the way; but they returned full of joy at the great benefit which had resulted to their souls. The good father received them again with expressions of the tenderest affection; and, on hearing the account of their adventures, he was transported with spiritual joy, and dwelt a long time in contemplation on the effects of the divine goodness and providence, giving infinite thanks to Him and to the saints of heaven. And it was very common with him to lift up his soul in this manner to God, and to be favoured by Him with frequent lights and supernatural inspirations, which he was often unable to explain in words when he wished to do so. As an instance, we give a passage from a letter which he wrote from Spires, on the 30th of August of this very year, 1542, to Father James Laynez, his intimate confidant.

'Would that it might please the Blessed Mother of our Lord and God to enable me to relate to you the many and great spiritual goods which, since I left you at Placenza till this day, have come into my mind and remained there, both as to knowing and as to feeling aright the things which concern our Lord and His most Blessed Mother, the saints and angels, and the souls in purgatory. And what can I say of my own interior? Of the elevation and depression of my soul, of the way in which I have entered into and gone forth again from myself? How can I speak of the manner in which I have learned to purify my body, soul, and spirit, to cleanse my heart, and by removing every hindrance to prepare it for receiving, retaining, and preserving the floods of divine favour; asking for all these various graces, and striving and praying with importunity to gain them? And as to what regards my neighbour also, I could tell you many things of the methods and ways which my God has shown me; how He has revealed His truths, and laid bare to me the lives of men that I might know them; so as to rejoice in their welfare, and for Christ's sake to compassionate their misfortunes: showing love to some, bearing with and pitying others; teaching me again to return thanks for one, and beg mercy and pardon for another, seeking and finding excuses for, and speaking well of, this and that man in the presence of God and His saints. In short, I declare to you, my brother, Master Laynez, that I should never be able to come up to in word or deed, nor even to conceive in thought, the favours which our Lord God has shown, and is still showing, and is most willing to continue to show me—dressing and binding up all my wounds, healing all my infirmities, and showing Himself so wonderfully good in blotting out all my sins. To Him be all the glory given! Amen. Blessed be His Name everywhere, and by all creatures! Amen. May He be for ever honoured in Himself, His Mother, His angels, and all His saints! Amen. May He be magnified and exalted above all things by all His creatures! Amen. I say this Amen for myself, and I entreat you to praise Him for me, your brother, as I do for all the Society.'

CHAPTER XIX.

Peter Favre at Mayence.

FROM Spires, Father Favre went, by permission of the Nuncio, John Morone, on whose commands he was dependent, to Mayence, whither he was invited by the Cardinal Archbishop and Elector, Albert of Brandenburg. They entered into familiar discourse on the grievous injury that heresy was doing to religion in Germany, and Favre, taught by his experience elsewhere, proposed and suggested to the Cardinal various measures and plans to be adopted for saving his States from the infection. The Cardinal, a very single-minded and zealous man, took up these proposals without delay, and issued very wise and timely regulations. This stirred up the blood and bad humours of some who sought to escape from the hand of the physician who wished to cure them; so that here in Mayence, as formerly in Spires, Favre met with aversion and dislike. But he, employing the same means as before, very soon succeeded so completely, by the modesty of his deportment, the affability of his manners, and the gentleness and forbearance of his speech, in gaining the regard, not only of his opponents, but of all classes of persons, that there was not, perhaps, a city in Germany where he was more loved and respected. He availed himself of these favourable dispositions to cultivate the souls of both clergy and laity by means of the Exercises, which produced, as was infallibly the case, abundant fruit.

Meanwhile, the Ecumenical Council was announced as to meet at Trent, and the Archbishop had intended to send Favre there in his place as his proctor and theologian. But the opening of the Council was deferred to a more fitting time, in consequence of the war which was still raging among the Christian princes, and so he kept him with him at Mayence. After Christmas he took him with him to Aschaffenburg, and intrusted him with some very private controversial writings and treatises, leaving to his learning and discretion the task of separating the good from the bad, which had been artfully mixed up therein. On returning to Mayence, Favre undertook to explain the Psalms of David in the University, and to preach in Latin in the church on Sundays. A numerous and distinguished circle of men of letters crowded to hear him, as well as ecclesiastics of every rank. All were astonished at the depth of his learning and the fervour of his zeal. In his sermons he touched very lightly on controverted points of religion, dwelling more at length on the eternal truths of faith, the necessity of good works, and the reformation of manners. At the same time he continued to give the Spiritual Exercises, sometimes to a few, sometimes to a large number. He gave them also to two bishops, the Suffragan of Mayence, and the Bishop-Elect of Naumburg. Each came forth from them with a firm resolution to do everything in his power to promote the salvation of the souls of his neighbour. By the same means he effected the conversion of several priests who had for some time led a scandalous life, and were in consequence, as so often happens, wavering in their faith also. As for the laity, as they did not all know Latin, and were therefore not able to enjoy the privilege they so much desired, a good interpreter was found to translate Favre's instructions and meditations into their own language for them.

People were continually going to him for spiritual advice and his direction as to their souls, and those thought themselves very fortunate who were able to make even a single confession to him. In short, his labours were rewarded by such abundant fruit, that it was that which chiefly made him begin to hope for a possibility of curing the many evils of Germany, if the supply of zealous Gospel labourers could be increased. And writing on the subject to St. Ignatius, he had no hesitation in saying that as the fruit gained in Parma had prevented his regretting leaving Rome, so, trusting in the merit of obedience, he had received great consolation from God in leaving Parma for Germany, Germany for Spain, and then again, Spain for Spires, and Spires for Mayence. It is true, moreover, that at the same time he did not forget or neglect the places which he had visited, nor the persons whom he had instructed; for besides continually bearing them in mind and commending them to God in prayer, he often wrote them letters full of power and breathing the fire of charity, encouraging some and consoling others; supporting and animating the weak, and restraining the bolder spirits within the bounds of discretion.

At first the Cardinal wished him to lodge in his palace with him, so as to converse more at ease with him on public and private matters; but as soon as Favre had satisfied this wish for a time, he asked and obtained permission to live elsewhere in a poor manner. The public hospital would, as usual, have been his choice; but as he had to receive frequent visits from great persons, and to converse with many people on their spiritual concerns, he hired some humble little rooms, where he stayed for a time, and then went to live with a certain Conrad, the parish priest of St. Christopher's, whom he had brought, by means of the Exercises, to that bright spiritual perfection of which he afterwards made profession as a Carthusian monk. In the beginning of the May of 1543, he received immense consolation by gaining for himself, for the Society, for Germany, and for the Church, a new and most valiant soldier.

There was at that time studying at Cologne a young man from Nimeguen, named Peter Canisius. He was already famous, though but twenty-two years old, for his keenness of intellect, virtuous life, and religious zeal. Having heard what great things were spoken of the virtues and learning of Peter Favre, he greatly desired to make his acquaintance and consult him on questions of conscience, especially as to his choice of a state of life, about which he was in doubt and uncertainty. Accordingly, late in April or early in May, he went from Cologne to Mayence, and called on the priest of St. Christopher's, by whom he was most kindly received. As Favre was not at home at the time, the priest told him so many wonderful things about that saintly man, that the ardent youth longed impatiently for his return, that he might have an interview with him and open his heart to him. Favre came in; and after Canisius had heard him speak a few times on divine subjects, and had learnt from him the institute and object of the Society of Jesus, he felt no doubt at all that this was that new community of priests which, according to a prediction made to him many years before at Arnheim, he was to join. Nevertheless, in order to make himself more sure as to the will of God, he made the Spiritual Exercises under Favre's direction; and hardly had he gone through the first meditations than, utterly unable to resist the vivid light which God communicated to his soul, he bound himself on the 8th of May, by a vow signed with his hand, to dedicate himself wholly to the Society.

Canisius becomes a novice.

No words can describe the consolation, joy, and fervour which took possession of him when, at the close of the Exercises, Favre received him as a novice. He went about in an almost ecstatic state with wonder and interior emotion. And after he had, in calmer moments, had a more thorough taste of Favre's spirit, he spoke of him as an incomparable man, and could never satisfy himself with hearing him and learning from his life ever new lessons of perfection. Indeed, unable to keep to himself the high opinion and veneration with which Favre inspired him, he communicated his sentiments to an intimate friend of his at Cologne, to whom he wrote from Mayence in the following terms—

'Here I am, thank God, safe and sound at Mayence; and I have been very fortunate in finding the man here of whom I came in search; if, indeed, he is a man, and not rather an angel of the Lord. I have never seen nor heard a more learned or profound theologian, nor any person equal to him in sanctity. His only desire is to labour for the salvation of souls, in union with Christ. Whether he is working, or speaking, or conversing familiarly, even when sitting at table, whatever he says or does is full of God; and although he is exceedingly fluent, it is never possible to be weary of hearing him, however long he speaks. So great is his credit and reputation, that many doctors, religious, and bishops have made him their master and guide in spiritual things. Among the number is Cochleus himself, who declares that he shall never be able to repay the vast debt that he feels that he owes him for his direction in the spiritual life. Several priests and ecclesiastics of every rank have dismissed and separated entirely from the women with whom they had formerly been living, or have, by his persuasion, abandoned other grievous sins and begun to lead a better life, so much as even to have retired altogether from the world. And if I must speak of my own case, I can hardly find words to tell you how these Spiritual Exercises have made my soul better, changed my heart, enlightened my mind with the brightness and beams of heavenly light, and inspired me with extraordinary strength and courage, so that this abundance of choice favours overflows even into my body, and I feel altogether invigorated and changed into another man.'

A few days later, having received instructions from Favre how to go through the usual probations of the novitiate, he was sent with Father John Aragonio and Father Alvaro Alfonso to Cologne, to continue the course of theology which he had begun there. This is that Peter Canisius who, on account of his shining virtues and Apostolic labours in aid and defence of religion, was afterwards called the Apostle of Germany, and in the end raised to the altars of the Church.

CHAPTER XX.

The Archbishop of Cologne.

BLESSED PETER FAVRE had been labouring unweariedly in Mayence for nearly a year, when a messenger arrived unexpectedly from Cologne with very pressing letters from the inhabitants of that city, and from the Nuncio, John Pozzi, requesting him to go thither immediately to minister to the spiritual needs of the Church there, which was in great peril. The Archbishop Albert was not then in Mayence, and Favre would not leave without his consent. He therefore detained the messenger, who was a priest and theologian, and in this interval took him through the Spiritual Exercises as he desired, and this alone was sufficient to make him dedicate himself for ever to the Society. When the Archbishop of Mayence returned and heard of the envoy's mission, he was very much grieved at the prospect of losing such a man, whom he so greatly loved and respected. But as so important a service to religion was in question, he did not dare to oppose his going. As a mark of his gratitude and affection, he sent him a great many valuable presents, among others some silver plate of great value. But Favre sent back everything with much courtesy of manner, saying that he was not a man to use silver plate, but so poor that wherever he went or stayed, he carried all his property with him. The next day, however, when Favre came to take leave of the Archbishop and to ask his blessing, the latter held him by the arm, and by force put a hundred gold florins in the bag which hung from his girdle to carry his breviary in; and courtesy forbidding him to refuse, the holy man accepted them with thanks. He would not, however, keep any of the money himself, but sent part to the members of the Society at Louvain, who were living in great poverty, and distributed the rest among the most necessitous of the poor.

He arrived at Cologne, probably, before the middle of September, and found religion in a very bad state there. The Archbishop, Hermann von Weiden, had not only been for same time wavering in his faith, but leant, though so far secretly, to the Lutherans. The clergy and laity, being convinced by many signs of the existence of hidden plots, were much scandalized, and trembled for the fate of that flourishing Church. No one, however, ventured to face the Archbishop, nor to give him the slightest hint of the sinister reports which were current about him. Favre being informed of all this, in the first place commended the matter to God, then, putting aside all human respect, he presented himself before the Archbishop, and with the utmost freedom and boldness, explained to him how much his flock feared that they had in him, no longer a loving shepherd, but a hireling keeper ready to leave them in the mouths of devouring wolves. He bade him think on the terrible account he would have to render to God, should this ever happen by his fault, and besought him, for the love of Jesus Christ, not to fall a prey to the wicked devices of the heretics, but to cleave firmly to the old faith, and to maintain it undefiled among his people, who were so well disposed to resist the recent innovations of the reformers. Hermann listened in motionless silence, and the words pierced his soul. No sooner had Favre ceased speaking than he broke out into violent weeping, professing, whether deceitfully or at the time sincerely, who can say? that he was convinced, and repented of his error, and promising to have nothing more to do with the heretics. Full of joy, Favre wrote to the Nuncio Pozzi, who was at Bonn, saying that as his business was accomplished he thought of returning according to his promise to Mayence. But Pozzi had no confidence in the steadfastness of the Archbishop of Cologne, and considered Favre's presence there necessary, so he replied by commanding him to remain where he was, saying that he would take it upon himself to obtain the consent of the Archbishop of Mayence.

Things were in this state when a letter arrived from Ignatius, with positive instructions to Favre to leave Cologne and proceed to Portugal with John Aragonio. The reason was, that King John III., having betrothed his daughter Mary to Don Philip, Prince of Spain, was going to send her to that country, and had most earnestly begged Ignatius to let him have two fathers to accompany her, expressly mentioning Favre as one of them. He knew him only by reputation, but had the greatest desire to see and converse with him. Ignatius could not refuse so pious a prince, who had moreover deserved so well of the Society. He therefore laid the matter before the Pope, and on his signifying his approval ordered Favre to start. News of this reaching the Nuncio Pozzi, he represented to the Pope that Cologne would run great risk by Favre's absence. Favre himself wrote, informing Ignatius of everything, and then set out for Louvain without delay.

CHAPTER XXI.

An illness at Louvain.

THERE were at Louvain several young men of the Society, principally Spaniards, who had come from Paris, where they had been prevented from remaining by the war which was still going on between Francis, King of France, and the Emperor Charles V. They all lodged in the house of a good priest named Cornelius Vishaven, a man of very holy life, exceedingly strict and austere towards himself, liberal and charitable to the poor, most zealous for the honour of God and the salvation of souls, and regarded by all as a saint on account of his great works, some of which seemed even to surpass nature. This man longed exceedingly to see and make the acquaintance of Father Peter Favre, of whom he had heard many wonderful things from those of the Society who were living with him, and, quite recently, from his intimate friend, Peter Canisius, who had written to him about Favre. On seeing Favre, therefore, come quite unexpectedly to seek a lodging with him, he was extremely consoled, and made great rejoicings over it. But no sooner had Favre embraced him than he said—'I know who you are, Cornelius, and know what you desire; but at the end of two days we shall be separated by obedience.' Immediately Cornelius answered—'I shall not oppose or contradict obedience; but I shall have recourse to God, Who is able and knows how to detain even obedient people if He pleases, and I shall ask Him to detain you for the good of the people here.' Favre smiled; and the day after went to Antwerp, and to the port of Vera, where, finding that the ships for Portugal were on the point of sailing, he went back to fetch his companions, who were to accompany him to Lisbon.

But hardly had he reached Louvain, than he was attacked by a violent fever, which compelled him to take to his bed; it turned out to be of the kind called tertian, and lasted two months. This long and tedious illness did not prevent Favre from labouring zealously for the salvation of souls, and the fruit which followed very plainly showed that it was God's special providence which detained him in that city. Among the students of the Society who have been mentioned was Francis Strada, then a young man of four-and-twenty, whom Father Ignatius had received in Rome, and trained for some time in his spiritual school. He had a great force and vigour in speaking, more from nature than art, and wherever he had been God wrought numerous conversions by his means, as has been said in speaking of what happened at Brescia. He attended the course of philosophy in the college known as the College of the Falcon, where his courteous manners and pious discourse, and still more his holy life, had gained the esteem and goodwill not only of the masters but of the students, whom he strove to advance in virtue and piety. Favre, knowing how much might be done by such a genius if it were properly disciplined, undertook to instruct and train him in sacred eloquence, and by way of practice ordered him to compose and recite some Latin sermons in the University. And the result was that his audience daily increased, till it was necessary for him to move two or three times to a larger and more convenient place, and at last he was requested to explain the Word of God every Sunday at the Church of St. Michael, one of the principal churches in Louvain. Favre consented to this, and in order that his study of philosophy might not suffer by it, undertook the task, while confined to his bed, of giving him the subject of his discourse, dividing and arranging the matter and arguments, and showing him, step by step, the method and the limits to be observed in enlarging on his theme, and giving full course to his eloquence. With these instructions, Strada gained the reputation of an excellent preacher, and, what is a far greater distinction, he was the means of rousing men's souls and producing very fervent conversions; religious of different orders, and the flower of the men of letters, professors and students of the University, all flocked to hear him. Not being yet a priest, he sent on to Favre all those who consulted him about their souls. As to Vishaven, he was beside himself with delight, speaking in terms of the highest praise of Favre's perfection and sanctity; and as he was a man very much thought of, he inspired every one with a great desire to see and know him, and to profit by his counsel. Thus great numbers of persons of every sort and grade began to visit Favre's bedroom: some to set their souls in order, others for his advice in choosing a state, or amending their life. The holy man denied himself to no one; he was always ready to receive, instruct, confess. and direct all who came; the fervour of his spirit strengthening the weakness of his body, and the abundant fruit which blessed his labours filling him with consolation. There were several who even desired to make the Spiritual Exercises under him, among these were Ruardo Tapper, chancellor of the University, and dean of St. Peter's at Louvain, and Theodore Hesius, who had been secretary and confessor to Pope Adrian VI. Although far advanced in years, he wished to leave the world and spend the remainder of his life in the Society. But Favre did not think that he ought to leave Liége, where he was Vice-dean of the Cathedral and Inquisitor of the Faith. He advised him rather to use his influence and official position for the honour of God, the glory of the Church, and the good of souls. So well did the good old man follow this advice, that Favre was able by his means to reform several convents of nuns in Louvain, to whom he gave very useful regulations for the observance of their religious rule.

A miraculous occurrence which took place, greatly increased the reputation of Favre. There was at Louvain a girl of nineteen, named Maria Vander Hove, who afterwards dedicated her virginity to God as a Carmelite nun. She suffered many different kinds of mortal maladies, besides being frequently tormented by devils. She was taken to Favre, who exhorted her to put her confidence in God, and for nine days recited over her the Gospel in the Ritual, and other prayers; on the last day she was, as the father had predicted, entirely delivered from all her troubles. In the year 1600, on the 20th of April, fifty-seven years afterwards, she affirmed every particular on oath, in the presence of five witnesses, who signed her deposition.

But there was no one who made better progress in Favre's school than Cornelius Vishaven. He had, very early in his acquaintance with the father, begged to be admitted into the Society, but before giving him any assurance on this point, Favre saw fit to put him to a severe trial in order to eradicate from his mind certain methods of conduct in spiritual matters to which he was addicted, which savoured too much of ostentation and eccentricity, and were in consequence liable to fallacy and illusion. He put this before Cornelius as a condition, and the good priest accepted it, giving himself absolutely into the hands of Favre, to be treated just as he pleased. The latter began his work by mortifying him in his will, which he crossed in everything and in every possible way. If he showed an inclination for anything, even though in itself praiseworthy, it was abruptly refused. Everything he did was badly done, and he was blamed and reproached for it, and ordered to do it over again three or four times. Very often he was sharply reprimanded before the inmates of his house for very slight things in which there was no blame. In spiritual matters he was placed under obedience to Strada, whom he had to attend as companion while he was preaching, having to sit in sight of the people on the pulpit-steps, with the hour-glass in his hand to mark the time. As to obedience, Favre told him every evening what he was to do the next day, purposely mixing up and confusing things in his instructions; afterwards he called him to give an account of himself, and when, according to his own judgment, he had no fault to find, he received a reproof and a penance. For two months, Vishaven's virtue was tried in these and other ways, and he not only stood the test with imperturbable peace and serenity of mind, but showed himself ready to persevere in this till death. Then Favre, laying aside the false semblance of severity and rigour which he had assumed, embraced him with marks of the tenderest affection, and received him into the Society, nominating him Superior at Louvain.

All this time the fever continued, and the physicians seeing all the remedies which they had successfully employed in similar cases to be in vain, were obliged to say that this sickness did not follow any natural law, but that perhaps God had sent it because of the great good which his presence in Louvain produced. And these words of theirs recalled to Favre's mind the last words spoken to him by Vishaven on the day of his arrival; and, therefore, calling him to him, he said, ' This fever came to me through you, and it is now time that it should leave me through you. You prayed, and I fell ill. Let your prayers now cure me.' Vishaven did not deny the fact, he promised to pray, and as soon as he had done so, Favre rose from his bed cured of the fever, and very quickly regained his former strength.

CHAPTER XXII.

The Louvain Students.

WHILST these things were passing at Louvain, letters came from Rome ordering Favre to send our students to Coimbra, in Portugal, where the King, Don John, was establishing and founding a college of arts and sciences for the Society, and to return immediately himself to Cologne, where Pope Paul III., having received the information sent to him by the Nuncio Pozzi, considered his presence absolutely necessary to prevent the imminent ruin which evidently threatened the Church there, in consequence of the apostasy of Archbishop Hermann. Pozzi had before this written to Favre, telling him that the Pope's intention was that he should return to Cologne; but, not having received an explicit order to that effect, such as the order commanding him to go to Portugal had been, the holy man was in some perplexity, not knowing which course to take to perform his obedience exactly. On the 6th of December, accordingly, he wrote to St. Ignatius from Louvain, in these words—

'I wrote a letter with my own hand, from Antwerp, on the 13th of October, informing your Reverence that a week after receiving orders to go to Portugal I left Cologne, and went direct to Antwerp, fearing that I might be too late to find an opportunity of sailing. I showed your Reverence's letter to the agent, who offered to find what was requisite for the sea voyage, and told me to wait at Louvain, where he would let me know when the time came for starting. I accordingly returned to this city, and was attacked by fever immediately on my arrival. May the will of Jesus Christ be done, Who knows, that if it had been possible, we would have acted in simple obedience. Meanwhile an incident occurred, which only God knows whether or not it is for His greater service. Mgr. Pozzi having been informed of the order I had for Portugal, began, before I left Cologne, to try every means to stop me, thinking that it was more useful for me to remain in Germany than anywhere else. He wrote to me on the 12th of last month, saying that he hoped very soon to get the Pope's permission for me to remain, and that Mgr. di Santa Croce had written to him after the feast of St. Andrew, giving him a promise to this effect. He afterwards sent me word by one of his secretaries that some despatch or letter had arrived from his Holiness, giving him full license to keep me in these parts. Up to this time I have neither seen this letter, nor been informed of its contents. Nevertheless, I am in great perplexity; seeing, on the one hand, your Reverence's order, and on the other, his Holiness' will to the contrary. It surprises me extremely that your Reverence should know nothing of this letter from his Holiness, more especially considering the mediation of Mgr. di Santa Croce in the affair; for in his reply to a letter of mine of the 18th October, he did not appear to know anything of my being sent to Portugal. I say all this, not that I am in the least more inclined one way than the other, but merely to let your Reverence know everything. If, in the letter which Mgr. Pozzi has, I should see the Pope's will clearly expressed, I shall still not be able to set my mind at ease until I receive a reply from your Reverence. I entreat you, therefore, for the love of Jesus Christ, to do all you can to give me a speedy answer.'[1]

In this letter he shows, as always, an entire indifference in his obedience, ever ready to undertake or to abandon anything at the sign of the will of his Superiors. And his father, St. Ignatius, was so struck and touched by his conduct, that he could not refrain from marking these beautiful words of Favre with his own hand, and writing twice on the margin of the letter, as an expression of his admiration, these words—' See what obedience ! See what obedience !'

Soon after this, having received fresh letters from Rome, in which the will of his Superiors was clearly notified, he at once prepared to send several of his companions to Portugal, and to return himself to Cologne. But as soon as it was rumoured through the city that the members of the Society were about to leave, there was a very great and general lamentation; but there were several young men belonging to the University who, on the contrary, were full of joy on hearing it. God had already deeply touched their hearts by means of Francis Strada's sermons, and they were

[1] Autograph letter.

firmly resolved to dedicate themselves to His service in the Society; they no sooner heard that the fathers were on the point of leaving, than they courageously determined to follow them. Eighteen came at the same time to Favre, who, after examining them very closely, was satisfied of their vocation, and received them all. Since the shortness of the time did not allow of a longer instruction, he assembled them all in a room, and gave them lessons, full of wisdom, for their guidance in the new life which they had embraced. They were all of one mind, full of spiritual consolation, and ready to beg their way on foot wherever they should be commanded by obedience to go.

The general gladness was increased by the accession of another companion, the more welcome for being unexpected. Maximilian Cappella, a youth of eighteen, of an excellent disposition and great talents, had for several months had an inspiration to join the Society; but, fearing that this mental attraction might arise from some lightness, and not from the voice of God, he had paid no attention to it. On hearing of the departure of our fathers, he was conscious in his heart of the revival of the same desire; yet even then he resisted the interior movement, arguing with himself, and purposely seeking reasons for rejecting and setting aside the idea. He was strengthened in this course by a certain preacher, who spoke publicly against our fathers and particularly Francis Strada, pitying people who were so blinded as to crowd to hear a beardless boy. Nevertheless, as Cappella had several times been to confession to Favre, he thought it only courteous to pay him a farewell visit; and going to Vishaven's house for that purpose, he met Favre on the threshold just in the act of leaving. As soon as he saw Cappella, he said, 'You, too, Maximilian, do you wish to join us?' At these words, as he afterwards said himself, Maximilian felt his mind instantaneously cleared of all doubts, his heart glowing with fervour, and irresistibly impelled to answer with resolution, 'Yes, father, I, too; I desire to be with you.' 'Very well,' rejoined Favre; 'go upstairs, and you will find some more companions.' He obeyed, and when he saw that band of youths, all of whom he knew, five of them masters in philosophy, and the rest either bachelors of theology or some of the first students in civil and canon law, he burst into tears of emotion, embraced them one by one; and, that he might never leave them again, he gave the keys of his rooms to a friend, begging him to take charge of his effects, and to send them to his parents at Lille.

The numbers of the Society having so greatly increased, Favre did not think it well to remove them all from Louvain, especially as some of the more influential citizens were meditating an appeal to Charles V. for the establishment of a college. He therefore made choice of twelve to be sent to Portugal, three who had been some time admitted, Francis Strada, Andrew Ovieda, and John Aragonio, with nine novices, Peter Favre de Hallis,[2] Leonard Kessel, Hermes Poen, James Lost, John Covillon, Daniel Dondermund, Cornelius Vishaven, the younger, Thomas Pogh, and Maximilian Cappella; leaving the rest in Louvain under the direction of Father Cornelius Vishaven, the elder, with the exception of Emiliano di Loyola, nephew to St. Ignatius, and Lambert Castrio, from Liége, bachelor of theology, whom he took with him to Cologne. But immediately after Favre's departure a perilous tempest unexpectedly arose, which all but ruined everything. The professors of the University, who had at first been

---

[2] He added the name of Favre to his own name, Peter, on account of his great affection for the holy father, and he kept it all his life.

so kindly disposed, now, irritated by the loss of so many promising students, became suddenly hostile ; and, not satisfied with complaining, they worked upon the natural affection of the parents and relations of the young men, till the whole city was in a tumult against the fathers. The good Father Cornelius Vishaven was marked out for universal indignation. Instead of being regarded, as before, in the light of a saint, and being respected and venerated by every one, he was looked upon as a person who went about deceiving the young, and who deserved to be shunned as a domestic enemy. Things reached such a pitch that the members of the Society were obliged to keep in the house by themselves for several days, not venturing to show themselves in public. Yet none of the novices wavered or yielded to either the threats or entreaties of their families. They all bravely defended their own cause, repelled every attack, and conquered every trial. And so far from the students of the University being deterred from the desire of a religious life, five more, influenced by the example of such constancy in their fellow-students, joined them. These were Adrian Adriaen, Anthony Vinck, Peter Gillon, Nicholas Gauden, and Oliver Manara, all of whom were afterwards of great use to their country and to religion.

CHAPTER XXIII.

Second stay at Cologne.

WE must now return to Father Favre. He quitted Louvain at the end of December, 1543. He stayed a few days at Liége, Maestricht, and Aix-la-Chapelle, to sow the Word of God in those cities; leaving in them all such a desire of his presence, that soon afterwards several of the inhabitants followed him to Cologne, in order to confer with him more at leisure, and to make the Spiritual Exercises under him. On reaching Cologne, he found reason for the bitterest sorrow, religious matters having fallen into a much worse condition since he left it. The Archbishop Elector, Hermann, faithless to the promises he had made at the Diet to the Emperor, and a few months before to Favre at Cologne, had begun to take the part of the heretics openly. Nor was this all, he had summoned Martin Bucer from Strasbourg, and Melancthon, Pistorius, and Sarcerus, all leaders and teachers of their sect, from Saxony, giving them the fullest power to propagate their false doctrines with impunity.

Favre was filled with a burning zeal at the sight of these terrible evils, and he generously resolved to employ every exertion, every means to remedy them, not hesitating, in case of necessity, to lose his own life. And, finding the clergy, nobility, and people well disposed to resist the assaults of the heretics, and to refuse to admit their new doctrines, he mounted the pulpit, and continued to preach for many months, encouraging his hearers to remain firm and faithful to the old faith of their fathers. He set forth the true sense of the Scriptures with great solidity and clearness, drawing thence arguments and proofs in confutation of the new heretics. Combining the characters of theologian and preacher, he mingled instruction with the defence of true doctrine in his discourses; thus, at one and the same time, enlightening the intellects of his hearers that they might know the truth, and moving their wills to the amendment of their lives. From the very beginning the first persons in the city crowded to hear him: consuls and senators, doctors and members of the University, canons, and all orders of the clergy, the Bishop of Liége, and other distinguished strangers; and, as the fame of the servant of God spread abroad in the city, the numbers of his audience continued to increase. The fruit of these labours of his was, that some members of the University, who had partially joined the Lutherans in opinion and way of living, returned to the right path. Many more, whose faith was wavering and in imminent danger of altogether giving way, were confirmed in the truth.

The man of God did a still greater work by his familiar conversations in society, and by giving the Spiritual Exercises privately. No heart, however hardened and obstinate, could long resist him, or refuse to be softened by his gentle persuasions, and by the attractions of his most loveable spirit. Those who had had personal experience of his power inspired others with a desire to know him, and undertook to introduce and present them to Favre. He was now constantly besieged by penitents, who wished to make their confessions to him; and, not being able to hear them all, he was compelled to avail himself of the assistance of Father Alvaro Alfonso, although he was new to the work. Before this time, very few indeed approached the sacraments, except at Easter; but now great numbers, many of them, too, persons of consideration, did so very frequently, to the great edification of the people. The rites and ceremonies of the Church, and the pious practices of religion, began once more to be reverenced, and several convents and religious communities were brought back to ancient discipline and to the strict observance of their rule.

Having thus, as far as possible, repaired the losses of religion among the Catholics, he next set himself to quell the pride and blunt the weapons of the heretics. He wrote very pressing letters to John Gropper and Antonio Perrenot de Granvelle, entreating them to interpose with the Emperor, at whose Court they were, to prevail upon him to provide for the Church of Cologne, by driving out the heretics by public proclamation, seeing that they made his name a pretext for the purpose of dissemination of errors with impunity, under the name of reform. And that they might not venture in the meantime to pervert the people with their sophistries, he challenged the two leaders of their party, Philip Melancthon and Martin Bucer, to a public disputation. Puffed up with pride, and trusting to their own boldness, they both, one after the other, accepted his challenge and met Favre, who, pressing them with incontrovertible arguments and proofs, and entangling them in their own answers, reduced them to silence, their intellects convinced, but their wills remaining more obstinate than before. The consequence was just that which Favre aimed at. They were ashamed again to risk their reputation after being thus publicly disgraced, and therefore left Cologne, to diffuse the poison of their heresy secretly in the country round. Even the Archbishop, seeing these champions thus defeated, contrary to his expectation, was somewhat checked in his mad course, and the senate by public edict banished the heretical preachers beyond the bounds of the city. Thus was Cologne then saved, mainly by the instrumentality of Favre.

It is true that he used another, and a most efficacious, means besides these labours for accomplishing his object, namely, prayer. He very often retired to St. Ursula's Church, and there, in the chapel called the 'golden chamber,' where rests her relics and those of the holy virgins her companions, spent long hours in prayer to God, commending to Him the cause of religion and the salvation of the citizens. Every day he said Mass there, shedding an abundance of tears, and crying to God for mercy. He returned infinite thanks to the angels guardian and the holy patrons of the city for the firm allegiance of its inhabitants to the true faith and for their perseverance in Christian virtue, of which he had fresh evidence every day. And we know that he became so strongly attached to the people of Cologne, that even when he was far away from them he kept them in remembrance. The following year he wrote thus to our students whom he had left at Cologne—

'I always knew perfectly well that in other universities you might make greater advance in study than in Cologne; but, notwithstanding this, I thought the good of so many souls was a more important consideration. The very tender affection that I bear to this city has made me prefer exposing you to the danger, or rather I preferred that you should be less learned in Cologne than exceedingly learned elsewhere. God grant that this zeal may be in conformity with His will, Who gave His only-begotten Son for the salvation of sinners. Don Alvaro is well acquainted with these sentiments of mine, which may have seemed to be to his own detriment; but, as I have already said, my mind was made up on the point, and I may add that I would rather hear that any one of you, including Master Peter Canisius and Don Alvaro, had died and was buried at Cologne, like Master Lambert, than that he was living and in good health elsewhere.'

Not to speak of the others, Canisius entered thoroughly into these feelings, and in his reply to the holy father on the subject, he says—' Since I have been admitted to the baccalaureate, my friends insisted on me giving the lectures on the Scriptures; and I do this three times a week in the school of theology. I am engaged upon that golden epistle of St. Paul to Timothy. My audience is very numerous, and it increases daily, for my lectures are public. I continue also to preach to the clergy, and I do the same on all feasts, at the Gymnasium, where I explain St. Matthew's Gospel. Moreover, I very often have to dispute before the professors of the University. You may easily imagine how all these things tax my poor wits; but I am very happy in thus labouring for the service of my neighbour, more particularly as it is done to please my venerable father, Peter Favre, who loves me so truly in Jesus Christ. I am sure that if he were here he would give me energy and strength. I feel nothing too much for me, nothing a trouble, if only, by fulfilling your wishes, I can be of some use to the citizens of Cologne; for I well know how greatly your Reverence desires to do them good by your prayers and labours, and by those of your sons. And I tell you frankly that, unless obedience should summon me elsewhere, I am ready and willing to devote this soul and body of mine, with all my time and study—my whole self, in short—to live and to die, to teach and to labour, for the good of the citizens of Cologne.'[1]

The affection borne by Favre to the people of Cologne was equally returned by them, and they proved it in the July of this year, 1544, when they had the first news of his intended departure. They were full of grief about it, and knowing that the holy man would not consent to accept any other mark of their gratitude, they offered him the heads of six of the holy virgins, St. Ursula's companions, which he valued more than any amount of treasure, and took with him to Portugal. But before speaking of his departure, I must relate two circumstances which are connected with the affairs of Cologne.

CHAPTER XXIV.

The Carthusians.

THE first of the two things alluded to in the last chapter, was that Father Favre gained for the Society, not only the affection of the sacred and venerable Carthusian Order, but its formal brotherhood, and a participation in all its good works. When Peter Canisius returned to Cologne full of holy fervour, and, as it were, out of himself with rapture at the wonderful things he had seen in Favre, and at the Exercises which he had made under him at Mayence, he poured forth all that was in his heart to Father Gerard Hammond, the prior of the Carthusians, telling him so much of the holy life of the man of God, and of the wonderful effect of the Exercises when handled

[1] Autograph letter.

by him, that he was full of eagerness to know Favre and to have personal experience of the Exercises. He moreover desired to inform the Prior of Trèves of the particulars related by Canisius, and wrote to him, accordingly on the last day of May, 1543, as follows—
'Amidst the storms with which all Christendom is shaken in these deplorable times of ours, it has pleased God, blessed be His Name! not to forsake His Church, but to raise up to help her some Apostolic men, fitted with His Spirit, and adorned with virtue from on high, who labour with fervent charity in leading back wanderers and sinners into the path of salvation. This they do, and great is the fruit which blesses their work; for the Master of these men works invisibly in their souls, and their words, like sparks from red-hot iron, set on fire the hearts on which they fall. There is one of their number with the Cardinal of Mayence, Master Peter Favre by name, a theologian of the University of Paris, and a man of great sanctity. He puts the souls under his direction through certain Spiritual Exercises, which are so powerful and efficacious, that in a very short time they produce in those who follow them a true knowledge of themselves and of their sins, with the gift of tears, and of a real and hearty conversion to God, their last end; together with growth in virtue, and the enjoyment of an intimate familiarity and loving union with Him. Would to heaven that it might be given to me to find out some necessity for travelling to Mayence! Certainly, it would be worth while to go as far as the Indies to find such a treasure. However, I trust before I die to be permitted to see this servant and dear friend of God, and to be guided by him to the reformation of my interior spirit and to union with God.'

Favre was unable to satisfy his wishes on the occasion of his first visit to Cologne, as he only stayed there a fortnight or a very little more. But in this second stay, which lasted six months, he had leisure for long conversations with Hammond; indeed he lodged in his monastery, and was able to give the Spiritual Exercises to that devout community. So marked was the fruit and consolation which those holy men experienced from this, that they were never tired of sufficiently praising to the skies that divine teaching of the spiritual life. In order to have it always within reach, and to profit by its instructions, they requested to have a copy of the Exercises, which they preserved ever after among the most precious manuscripts of the monastery. It is unnecessary to say that they cherished an undying remembrance of the virtues and sanctity of Favre. After his death, two years later, he was never named amongst them except by the title of 'Blessed;' and he is so styled by Theodore Petreius, in his *Carthusian Library*, where, speaking of the bright example he gave in the Charterhouse of Cologne, he says—'So great was Blessed Peter Favre's gravity of manners and holiness of life when he was a guest in the Carthusian monastery at Cologne, before the name and labours of the Society were so well known in the world as they afterwards became, that he carried every one away with admiration of him,'[2] and it was mainly for his sake, that from that time the Carthusian fathers began, and afterwards continued, to consider and cherish as brothers all who belonged to the Society. It is certain that so close a bond of mutual charity was formed between them and us in Cologne, that each regarded the others as one with themselves; and on the death of Lambert Castrio, who had accompanied Favre from Louvain, the Carthusians buried him among their own dead, and admitted him to a share of their suffrages.

[2] Vol. i. pp. 35, 36.

In the following year, 1544, when the General Chapter was being held at the Grande Chartreuse, the fathers assembled not only approved of the union subsisting between our Society and their House at Cologne, but resolved unanimously to give the former a share in all their spiritual goods, and the decree, drawn up in proper form, signed, and sealed, was sent to St. Ignatius at Rome. The following is a translation of it.

'Brother Peter, the unworthy prior of the Grande Chartreuse, and all the other definitors of the General Chapter of the Carthusian Order, to the Reverend Father in Christ, Ignatius, General of the new Society of the Name of Jesus, and to his devout brethren, in every part of the world, that salvation which God has prepared for those who love Him.

'Ever since we have known, dearest brethren in the Lord, of the sweet odour of your holy life, salutary doctrine, voluntary poverty, and all the other virtues by which we understand that you, as lights shining in the darkness of this miserable world, labour to turn into the narrow path of salvation those who are in the broad way leading to destruction, to confirm the wavering, to urge on the tepid and spur them to progress in virtue, and so to be of great use to the Catholic Church, we have been filled with joy in the Lord, and give Him thanks that even in this so great desolation of His Church, and in the midst of the heavy calamities which have befallen us, He has been mindful of His mercies, and has raised you up and sent you forth as new labourers in His vineyard. In which holy undertaking we also, greatly desiring to aid you, so far as is possible to our weakness, earnestly beseech you, brethren, by the love of that dear Lord Who vouchsafed to die for us, *ne in vacuum gratiam Dei recipiatis;* but continuing to persevere in your holy resolution, *exhibeatis vos sicut Dei ministros in multa patientia*, not relaxing in your labours, nor being cowed by danger, or the persecutions which are always in store for such as will live a holy life, *tempore enim suo metetis non deficientes*. And for ourselves, brethren, if our divine sacrifices, our prayers, fastings, and pious exercises, in all of which we give a share to you and to your successors, living and dead, are of any avail before the Lord, we gladly unite in all your holy intentions and labours, entreating you likewise to admit us in return to a share of your prayers and spiritual goods.

'Given at the Chartreuse, under our seal, in the year of our Lord 1544, on the Thursday after *Cantate* Sunday, May 15th, during our General Chapter.'

This decree, together with other favours, was again confirmed in another General Chapter, held in 1583. And as time went on this mutual brotherhood and participation of spiritual privileges, far from diminishing, continued to increase in the two orders. But, to return to early days, it is certain that the Society owed its existence at Cologne to the Carthusian fathers. It was the Prior Hammond who, in 1553, provided a house for our fathers to live in, and who, the following year, promised what was necessary for their support. He it was, too, who, with John Gropper and Everard Villichius, induced the consuls and magistrates of Cologne to give to the Society the College and University there, known as those of the 'Three Crowns;' and all this was due, in the first instance, to the merits of Peter Favre; for it was he who won for the Society the love and protection of those venerable fathers. And the holy patriarch Ignatius did not fail to correspond, to the utmost of his power, with the great affection of the Carthusians, especially those of Cologne, writing many times to thank them for their kindness to his Society. There is one of these letters, dated the 11th of June 1547, in which he expressly speaks of having admitted them to a share in the works, prayers, and merits of the Society.

CHAPTER XXV.

Peter Canisius and his family.

ANOTHER event happened while Favre was at Cologne which deserves mention, although it was of a private nature. Peter Canisius had been suddenly summoned to Nimeguen, his native place, to attend his father, James, in his last moments. As soon as he had passed to a better life, the pious youth, following the Evangelical counsel, distributed among the poor his portion of the inheritance, reserving only a sum of money sufficient for the maintenance of himself and his companions, who were living at Cologne very hardly, on alms. His step-mother, Wendelina Vanden Berg, was very angry at this, and, not satisfied with raising a great commotion on the subject in the family, she spread a false report, that Father Peter Favre, whom she described as a vagabond foreigner, had used certain arts to bewitch her step-son, and attach him to himself for his own ends, which were to appropriate the largest and most valuable portion of the property, and to ruin the family. She wrote the most insulting letters on the subject to Cologne, spreading her complaints and lamentations all through that distant city.

Favre, who knew by experience how prejudicial such damaging reports and false accusations are to the Apostolic ministry, thought it necessary to put a stop to them. He took up his pen and wrote to the lady in question a letter full of boldness and prudence in defence of himself and her son.

'Very dear and honoured lady in Christ,—

'You complain that Master Peter Canisius, hitherto your much loved son, has degenerated from that respect which he has of old paid to you, and you say that the blame of this rests with me. I, on the other hand, who behold this excellent and most virtuous young man united with me in the closest bonds of spiritual affection, so that we are one in heart and mind, cannot but desire and wish every kind of good for him and for his relations and friends. And in saying this, I do not mean those only who are united to him by Christian charity and Evangelical perfection, but those also who are his friends and relations according to the flesh. For this reason, I often pray to our Lord God for the soul of his late father, and for your consolation and for your children and relations. But perhaps you will say, Why, in that case, have you taken from us Master Peter, who was, by his presence and counsel, our joy and consolation? I answer, What would you do, pious and excellent lady, if you saw on the one side Jesus Christ wishing that he should serve Him, and delighting in his spiritual profit, and on the other his natural relations and friends, wishing, at any cost, to enjoy his society in the midst of the deceitful and transitory pleasures of this world? If you think my judgment right in the matter, you certainly must agree with me, that I have done wisely in helping and confirming him in this resolution of his, all the more because in doing so I have not regarded my own interests, nor derived any advantage from the smallest portion of his property. The whole question, as it seems to me, is made one of worldly interest; and it seems to cost no one a thought that Master Canisius' soul should go to perdition. People find it too hard to bear that the property which falls to him by right of succession should be alienated. It is thought a great matter that our lands should be diminished by a few inches—a miserable hand's breadth of soil; and it is a thing of no moment that a soul should be separated from God, Who is our supreme felicity! For the rest, I declare that not the very smallest portion of these worldly goods is applied to my advantage. God is faithful, Who has for His own glory kept me free in this respect, and it would be impossible for me even to think of putting my trust in any earthly thing. Why then, you may say, do you not forbid his doing what you are aware must be displeasing to us? I am ignorant what, or how much property he has disposed of; but if I am to express my opinion freely, I can only say that I do not disapprove of what he has done. I know that the disposal he has made is for pious objects; and that therefore, to speak correctly, so far from having alienated his property, he has restored it to the one real, rightful, and supreme Master, that is, to God. What can there be wrong in this? Besides, the possessions which he brought with him are his own to dispose of as far as he pleases. Our Society aims at objects, at desires, and at gains very different from these poor and perishable things. As to the reports spread about me, they are, I think, too trivial and contemptible to be believed, at all events by persons like yourself, who fear God, and are not given to think evil of their neighbours. They say that I am an unknown person and a stranger; and I do not deny it. Yes, I am a pilgrim, and so are all my companions, and not only in this part of the country, but all the world over, and so I shall be, thank God, till my death. For all my cares and all my efforts are directed to one only end—that I may one day be an inmate of the house of God and a fellow-citizen of the saints.'

After receiving this letter, Wendelina withdrew her opposition; indeed, a few years later, she gave her son, Theodoric Canisius, to the Society.

CHAPTER XXVI.

Peter Favre sent to Portugal.

MEANWHILE, Don John, King of Portugal, had not at all abandoned his resolution already mentioned. He besieged his Ambassador at Rome with letters in which he continually urged him to press for Father Favre's departure. It was not possible to resist the reiterated request of so great a prince. Accordingly St. Ignatius, with the Pope's consent, ordered Favre to leave Cologne and begin his journey to Portugal immediately. As soon as this news was told to Father Claude Le Jay, also one of the first ten companions, who was in Germany at the time, he represented in vivid colours the irreparable loss to religion which would be the consequence. 'For,' he writes to St. Ignatius, 'there is here so high an opinion of Father Favre's sanctity and wisdom, that the very sound of his name is a support and an encouragement to the Catholics. And it is by means of his presence and labours that their princes and nobles hope to repair the losses sustained by the faith in this country.' But Favre, although a vast harvest lay before him, promising abundant fruit, showed all willingness to take a final leave of Cologne, being firm in that principle of his, that every change of place made under obedience would lead to greater glory for God than remaining where he was. And so indeed it turned out in those two last years of his life which he spent in Portugal and Spain. And so, taking leave of the clergy, nobility, and people, he quitted Cologne on the 12th of July, 1544, leaving there eight of the Society, under the government of Father Leonard Kessel, who had returned from Portugal. Among them was Peter Canisius, the heir of his spirit and zeal. He continued the work of supporting the Catholic cause in that city, and after two missions, to George of Austria, the Bishop of Liége, and to the Emperor Charles V., succeeded in obtaining the removal of the wicked pastor, Hermann, against whom Pope Paul III. had issued sentence of excommunication. In his stead was appointed Adolphus of Schaumburg, a prelate of irreproachable life and faith.

At Louvain, Favre was greatly consoled by the society of his dear children, and when he was about leaving, Father Cornelius Vishaven insisted on bearing him company as far as the port of Vera, where the Portuguese ships lay at anchor. To reach that port from Antwerp, it is necessary to cross a wide arm of the sea, and while doing so, it happened that a dead calm came over, and obliged the sailors to take to their oars to hold on their way. While they were doing this, Favre and Vishaven were talking together on spiritual subjects, and one of the crew said, half angrily, as he passed them—'What is the good of your chattering there? Why do you not get us a breath of favourable wind from God by your prayers? We shall never be in port to-night without it.' Favre, not knowing Flemish, asked his companion what the sailor had said; and when he was told, he added pleasantly—'The good fellow is quite right; let us begin to pray.' They both knelt down, and immediately a fair wind blew, and took them into the port in two hours, to the wonder and delight of the passengers. There, with a last embrace, the two holy men parted; and Vishaven returned to Louvain, whilst Favre sailed for Lisbon, where he arrived safely on the feast of St. Bartholomew.

We are told by Father Balthazar Tellez, in his *Chronicles of Portugal*, that after visiting our brethren in the House of St. Antony, Favre went straight to Evora, the residence of King John, his Queen, Doña Catarina, and the Princess Doña Maria, who was betrothed to Philip II. He was introduced to the King by Father Antonio Araoz, and he thanked his Highness humbly and gratefully for the many and signal favours which he had granted with so free and lavish a hand to the Society, and for the fatherly care which he took of it in supporting and extending it, not only in his own dominions, but in other countries also by his good offices and recommendation.

King John, who had been led by the great things spoken of Favre by Father Simon Rodriguez and Father Antonio Araoz to form a very high opinion of him, now that he had seen him, and still more when he had conversed with him familiarly, thought that the reality far surpassed the idea that he had conceived. He was a very practised observer and judge of character. He seemed to see in Favre the exact and living likeness, as it were, of the spirit of Ignatius, and thought that, as regarded personal holiness, and the gift of governing others, the Society did not possess his equal in Portugal. He therefore, after consulting with the Queen, who was as much delighted with Favre as himself, abandoned the idea of attaching him to the service of his daughter, for whose sake he had begged for him, and determined to keep him in Portugal, and not to suffer him to leave his Court.

The holy man, not guessing at the King's intentions, and supposing that he should soon be going to Spain with the Princess Maria, took a journey to Coimbra, for the purpose of embracing the fathers and brothers there, who were very desirous of seeing him ; and after spending a few days at the College, returned in haste to Evora. But his health suffered from the journey in the rainy autumn season, and he fell sick. This strengthened the King in his determination, now that he saw it to be in accordance with the will of God ; and without more delay he sent some of his own suite to accompany the Princess to Spain, and then turned his attention to the diligent use of every means for restoring the health of Favre.

CHAPTER XXVII.

The College of Coimbra.

AT the beginning of the new year, 1545, when Peter Favre had recovered from his illness, he returned to Coimbra, to inspect more at his ease the beginnings of the College, and to enjoy a longer time of intercourse with the numerous students. Words cannot tell the joy and reverence with which he was received, not as a stranger or a guest, but, to use his own words, as if he had been the common father, lord, and master of all, ardently desired and loved by all. There were there upwards of sixty young men of different nations—Portuguese, Spaniards, Italians, and Flemings—but all united most closely in heart and mind. They pursued their scientific studies with the greatest ardour, without neglecting their own perfection, and the whole city was greatly edified by their generous acts of humility, mortification, and self-contempt. All of them, from the oldest there down to the novices, rendered him a most exact account of their consciences, and he, who possessed a remarkable gift and grace of discernment of spirit and of direction of souls, gave to each the particular guidance and counsel which was most suited to his disposition. The result was such an unusual revival of fervour, and such a wonderful progress in the practice of the most difficult virtues, that the Superiors were obliged to restrain the excessive zeal of some who were inclined to outrun the bounds of discretion. Favre was filled with consolation at this, and wrote letters to St. Ignatius, speaking highly in praise of the students. In one of these letters he says—

'It is a month since I came from Evora to visit our brethren here at Coimbra, where, by the grace of our Lord, I was received, not as a guest, but as the father, lord, and master of all. I must put in the first place, Father Santa Croce, the Rector of the College. I assure your Reverence that if no fruit had come of my visit here except the indescribable joy it caused to all the brothers, and to other persons who desired it, the fault must be entirely my own, either because I take too much advantage of their perfect humility and obedience, or because I have not been able to direct each one to his own real profit. I do not believe there is a single person, out of more than sixty who are in this house, who has not been making great exertions to increase daily in perfection, and to persevere unto death in the fervour with which they have begun. Great peace and harmony reign among them. There is brotherly charity, there is obedience, humility, and entire submission of every one. Order is observed in everything—in bodily, literary, spiritual exercises ; and in saying this, I do not make my own way of thinking and acting a standard, knowing that there is always a great want of order in it, but I mean that everything is done exactly as your Reverence would desire. Thanks be to Him Who is the author of all good.'[1]

At the close of this letter he defends some of the fathers who had been suspected by Ignatius, not without apparent reason, of following certain rules in the government and direction of others which did not seem in harmony with the spirit of the Society. Nevertheless, he observes, with his usual prudence, that this unwonted and impetuous fervour requires regulation to prevent its becoming excessive, and shaking off the restraint of obedience from too much freedom being allowed to individual judgment. This very thing happened a few years later, and to correct it St. Ignatius was obliged to use firm and vigorous measures. Outside the house, men's minds were no less stirred up by the Blessed Father. He preached several times from the pulpit of the principal church, and drew to himself the admiration and affection of many who came to him for the purpose of private conversation and to make the Spiritual Exercises under him. It will be enough to say that about thirty of the choicest students of the University came to him, requesting admission into the Society. He only received some few of them, all men worth many others from their noble birth, talents, learning, and

[1] Autograph letter, January 8, 1545.

virtue, such as Manuel Sa, Antonio Gomez, a doctor of the Sorbonne, Michael de Sousa, John Azpilqueta, a relation of the famous Martin Navarro and of St. Francis Xavier, and Louis Gonzalez de Camera, son of the Count della Calleta. The last mentioned had known both Favre and his companion at the University of Paris. At Coimbra he now observed the example of his holy life more closely, and became inflamed with a desire to imitate it; so, generously abandoning the wealth and honours of his paternal home, he entered the Society, thereby closing the door to any dignity, ecclesiastical or secular.

But no vocation was so wonderful and worthy of record as that of John Nuñez Barreto. He was already a priest and commendatory abbot of a noble church, and was leading in the world a truly saintly life. He had felt drawn by an interior attraction from God to make the last sacrifice which remained for him to make, that of his own will, by placing himself under obedience in the Society, of which his brother Melchior was already a member. He could not make up his mind to this, fearing that that new kind of active life, devoted to the welfare of others, might check the flow of that stream of sweetness and consolation which he drew from the contemplation of heavenly things, in which he passed a great part of both day and night. He was in this state of uncertainty, when he dreamed that he saw a foreign priest celebrating High Mass, and that he himself was assisting as deacon. He was offering him the pax to kiss in the usual way, with the right hand, when the priest made him a sign to use the left. There followed a dispute between them, each persisting in maintaining his own opinion. On awaking, and thinking over the vision, he heard an interior voice telling him not to seek the peace of his soul only in the contemplative life, represented by the right hand, but in the active life also. Nevertheless, in order to know God's will more clearly, he promised to say several Masses for this intention, and meanwhile he constantly prayed for light from heaven, begging for the intercession of our Blessed Lady, to whom he was greatly devoted. The Mother of God appeared to him visibly, having by her side the priest whom he had seen in his dream, and ordered him to go to Coimbra, where a faithful servant of hers would tell him what it was God's will that he should do. He obeyed instantly; and no sooner did he reach Coimbra and present himself to Father Favre, than he recognized him as the priest whom he had already seen twice. Throwing himself at his feet, full of joy, he opened his whole heart to him, giving him a full account of himself, and asking his advice and direction.

When Favre had heard everything, he warned him, that in embracing a mixed life he would have to be ready to give up sensible consolation and spiritual sweetness. 'For,' he said, 'so long as you thought you could not do better than lead a solitary life, God gave you undisturbed peace and tranquillity of soul in large measure. But when your obedience places you in the midst of the labours, dangers, and persecutions which always attend an Apostolic life, and you no longer feel in your soul those interior delights of spiritual consolation, will you have strength to go forward, to conquer yourself, and to labour effectually for the promotion of God's glory and the salvation of souls?' John replied that he certainly should. 'Well, then,' rejoined Favre, 'rise to-night, according to your habit, to pray; defy the devil to make all those attacks on you which he would make

J

if you were in religion, then, in the morning, after saying Mass and again asking God to enlighten you, decide on your state of life.' He obeyed, and after meeting and conquering the enemy, who assailed him with every kind of temptation, he offered himself to God, in the act of celebration, as a perpetual holocaust, and resolved to live and die in the Society, entirely subject to obedience. And perfectly did he accomplish this, so that Favre himself, having observed his conduct, was obliged to say, in great astonishment, that he had never seen any one who suffered himself to be ruled and guided by the will of others in the smallest things, as Nuñez did.

This was the John Nuñez Barreto who, after enduring many fatigues and dangers in Africa for the redemption of Christian slaves, took the place of Favre, as we shall see later, in the dignity, or rather the Apostolic burthen, of Patriarch of Ethiopia, and who, being prevented from making the passage to his Church, lived and died in a saintly manner at Goa, in India.

CHAPTER XXVIII.

Favre leaving Portugal.

PETER FAVRE was not able to remain at Coimbra longer than a month, as the King was very pressing for him to return, that he might converse confidentially with him both on his own spiritual concerns and on the affairs of the Society. Accordingly he returned to Evora; and when there, he went regularly on appointed days to the Court, which he never left without having given a bright example of virtue and sanctity. His gracious and winning manners gained the respect and attention of all the noblemen, who crowded about him to hear him speak of divine things. Not that he needed pressing to do this; he had a graceful way of voluntarily entering into discourses of this kind, and the enthusiasm with which he spoke communicated itself to all who heard him. He had the art of making even indifferent and worldly topics, and the gossip of the Court, lead gradually to discourses about the soul and to reflections of a higher order. Ever united in mind to God, he found God in everything, and turned everything to his own spiritual profit and that of others. One day, as he was leaving the palace, he came upon a numerous and splendid cavalcade, which was in attendance on a leading duke; and in order to avoid it, he turned back and withdrew into a neighbouring church. There, by one of those sudden impulses which take the reason by surprise, he felt a desire of once more seeing the very spectacle which he had come there to avoid. But no sooner was he aware of the temptation, than he instantly fixed his eyes upon a picture of our crucified Lord, and bursting into a flood of sweet tears, he poured forth his inmost heart in gratitude to God, thanking Him for deigning to admit him to His presence, and saying to himself that there was not in the world so delightful and profitable a sight as that of Christ hanging on the Cross for love of us. Hither should all our thoughts and affections be turned, here may we satisfy all the cravings of our feelings, for the desire of that spectacle infinitely transcends the deceitful pleasures given by all the sensible objects in the world.

Meanwhile, the love and reverence of King John for Father Peter Favre increased daily. His modesty, gravity, humility, prudence, union with God, and all the other singular gifts of nature and grace which he perceived in him, made the King love and regard him exceedingly. All this confirmed him in the determination to use every effort to keep him in Portugal, and to recall the permission to leave which he had inadvertently given at first. Favre, however, had already received orders from his father, St. Ignatius, to go to Spain with Father Antonio Araoz, and to find, in the Court of Prince Philip, some means of introducing the Society into that country. Embracing therefore a favourable opportunity which presented itself, he went into the King's presence, and told him of the order he had received, together with the reasons which dictated it. This was sufficient to induce that prudent sovereign to prefer the good of the whole Society to his private advantage, and to conform his designs to those of St. Ignatius. Indeed, he voluntarily expressed himself most willing to help on the work, by giving to the fathers the most earnest letters of recommendation to his daughter, Doña Maria, to Prince Philip, and to his Ambassador at that Court. Favre thanked him with all possible gratitude, and as his poverty prevented him from testifying it in any other manner, he presented him with two of the heads of companions of St. Ursula, which he had brought from Cologne. The King accepted the holy relics with the greatest delight, and made Favre place them with his own hand in a rich reliquary in the Queen's private oratory.

Favre sent a third head to the College of Coimbra, where it was received with much veneration. As he was not able to make a farewell visit there to those fervent young sons of the Society, he wrote them the following affectionate letter from Evora.

'Dearest brothers in Christ,—

'May the grace of our Lord Jesus Christ and the love of the Holy Ghost be in your hearts! I cannot yet give you positive information concerning our departure. Soon after my coming to this Court, the King gave me leave to go, but after awhile he retracted that permission. Believing as I did that it was God's will that I should go, I set myself to remove the difficulties which were in the way, so by arguments and prayers I have prevailed; and I am free to go to Castile. I pray God, Who is the life and defence of us all, to be my Guide and Protector on the journey. The day of our departure is not settled; we hope it may be next week, but there is still some important business to be despatched. I shall not be able to take your College in my way, as would be my wish and yours also. This is a great disappointment to me; and also, I think, to your charity. Our Lord knows the joy it would be to me to spend a few days among you, and to be thus both consoled and edified by your company. But we must sacrifice everything, as our only desire is the perfect accomplishment of God's will, not of our own. I am therefore obliged to do by letter what I would so much rather do by word of mouth, and beg you to remember me before God, knowing, as you well do, my dearest brothers, how greatly I need your prayers and sacrifices. I do not know how long I shall be separated from you. I am afraid that, on the one hand, it would be rash to say that I will come and see you once more before I die; and, on the other hand, it would be a great want of confidence to despair of meeting many of you again. All this is a great sorrow to me; and I think to you too. As it is, you must take this letter as my substitute, and as a token of my remembrance of you; for you know, dearest brothers, the love that I bear you. So all good be with you. Go on serving Christ our Lord in gladness of heart, and conform yourselves entirely to His divine management. Be steadfast in this, and attach yourselves to no one but Jesus Christ, Who can never be taken from you. From time to time we may enjoy the society of men, but, as it is often rather a hindrance to us than otherwise, let us turn our affections to the things of heaven. Now and then you may converse on earthly subjects, but such conversations must all be ordered to eternal truths. Hence the pleasure which proceeds from conversing with men must be directed to that interior satisfaction that dwells in the heart. And I say the same of all our other feelings and affections, which are only profitable in proportion to the degree in which they are directed to the things of the spirit. And this is understood by all those to whom it is given by divine wisdom to enter into the spirit of Christ's words—*Audi filia, et vide, et inclina aurem tuam.* And let this be said for those who are wont to grieve bitterly at separation from their friends. If it was a desirable thing for Christ's Apostles to be deprived of the Presence of Him Who by His Presence gave salvation to the world, shall it not be useful and necessary for us to be not only separated, but entirely cut off from those in whose society we have always lived? Let it be enough for us that we are always united with God, and with Jesus Christ, Who is the Mediator between the Father and men. He is all things to all. Let us keep ourselves always in His presence; let us rest in Him Who is the source of all good; in Him every one will find both himself and those dear to him. Let us also meet together in prayer to our Blessed Lady. And so, my dearest brothers, I leave you now, with my last farewell, under the protection of God—*Cujus vale dicere et facere est conferre ipsam valetudinem:* beseeching Him *ut de rore ejus, et de pinguedine ejus sit benedictio vestra. B'ne valete, et in eodem Jesu Christo Domino nostro,*

   'Your most loving brother in Christ,

      'PETER FAVRE.'[1]

---

[1] Tellez, *Chronica de C. de Jesu en Portugal*, t. i. p. 207. This author gives March 20th, 1545, as the date of this letter; but probably this is an error, and it should have been the 2nd of March, as Favre in his 'Memorial' mentions that he left Evora on the 4th of that month.

CHAPTER XXIX.

At the Court of Prince Philip.

ON the 4th of March, after taking a last leave of the King and Queen of Portugal, Favre left Evora with Father Araoz; and on the 12th of the same month they reached Salamanca. They remained a few days in that city to rest, but the rest they took was to excite the people to the practice of Christian piety, Araoz by preaching, and Favre by private conversation. There were then in the University two very famous professors, greatly distinguished by their talent in learning: Alfonso di Castro, of the holy Order of St. Francis, and Francis Vittoria, of that of St. Dominic. They had known Favre intimately at the University of Paris, and so received him with every mark of affection, speaking so much in his praise and that of the Society founded by Ignatius, that the weight of their authority induced the citizens to apply for a College. But the fathers, satisfied with sowing these few seeds, and leaving behind them a great deal of regretful desire, continued their journey, and on the 18th of March reached Valladolid, where the Court was. They took up their abode, as usual, in the hospital.

There was not yet a single house of the Society in Spain, and, moreover, many people there had a bad opinion of the Society in consequence of false and distorted reports of the persecutions raised against Ignatius.

and his companions in Venice and Rome, which had spread in that country, and were even repeated from the pulpits of the churches. But a great deal was done towards banishing all these evil suspicions from the minds of men by the presence at Court of Mgr. Pozzi, who was now Nuncio in Spain instead of Germany, and of Doctor Peter Ortiz, who, as eye-witnesses, were able to testify to the sanctity, wisdom, and Apostolic labours of this new Order which God had raised up for the aid and defence of His Church. Another powerful supporter of its interests at Court, as Favre himself says in a letter to St. Ignatius, dated April 14, was Don John Bernal Diez de Lugo, a man of great learning, recently appointed to the episcopal see of Calahorra. By his influence, and still more by the letters of Don John, King of Portugal, and by the active exertions of his daughter, Doña Maria, the two fathers had a very kind and courteous reception from Don Philip, to whom Favre, with that marvellously attractive way of speaking which was habitual to him, briefly explained the object of the Society, the means employed for attaining it, and the advantage which its establishment in any city would secure, in the good of souls and the education of the young.

But, in truth, far more persuasive than his words was the example of the lives of the fathers, and their labours in the Apostolic ministry. Favre, seeing so promising a ministry open to him in Valladolid, gave full reins to his burning zeal in incessant labours. He daily visited, one by one, all the sick in the hospital where he lodged, consoling them, assisting them, and ministering to them in all their corporal and spiritual necessities. In the day-time, collecting the children round him in the public square, he instructed them in the rudiments of faith and Christian piety; and afterwards he taught the people from the pulpits of the churches, inciting them to the love of virtue and hatred of sin. There was no poor soul in the city, who was in want of spiritual help, whom he did not hasten to visit as soon as he heard of him. Many, after having experience of the sweetness of his spirit, confided to him the secrets of their consciences, that he might console them in dryness, counsel them in doubt, and guide them into a safe path in uncertainty. All admired the truly perfect life which he led, and the unbroken union with God which breathed in his every word and action. One morning, soon after coming to Valladolid, he was going to the sermon which was being preached, probably one of the Lent course, in the royal chapel. When he entered the palace, the porter, who did not yet know him by sight, shut the door of the ante-chamber upon him, and would not suffer him to go any further. The holy man did not let him know who he was, neither did he appeal to any of the noblemen about the Court; but withdrew, with great peace and tranquillity of soul, to a retired place, and there, reflecting on himself, he said, 'Alas, how often have I shut the door of my heart against God! And when Thou, good Jesus, camest unto Thine own, Thine own did not receive Thee. Every day Thou knockest at the door of our souls, and we do not open to Thee.' And in such considerations he passed the whole of the time, praying and humbling himself before God.

As all these things became generally known, the Court began to show the two fathers open and daily-increasing favour. They were often sent for to the palace; their discourses about God were gladly listened to, and frequent recourse was made to them for the disburthening of consciences in important matters. The consequence was, that all the grandees, both those in attendance on the Prince and his consort, and those who came on business from a distance, abandoned all the suspicions which they might have had of the Society, and used the two fathers for the arrangement of their consciences. We shall soon see what wonderful changes of life were the result. They were besides encouraged in this by the example and words of the Portuguese nobles who had accompanied the Princess Maria to Spain. They had all made choice of Favre and Araoz for their directors, and spoke in terms of the highest praise both of them and of the Society, extolling the great benefits of which it had been the cause, both to Portugal and the whole of the East Indies. Just then, too, arrived most opportunely the first letters of St. Francis Xavier, with the account of the many idolaters converted to the faith of Jesus Christ. These letters were published by order of the King of Portugal, and distributed everywhere, and exceedingly raised the credit of the Society. Hence, Favre, writing to St. Ignatius, was able to say—

'Our Society has now become known throughout Spain: so that, whereas formerly it had either never been heard of at all, or only by the horrible falsehoods that had been spread here from Rome; now, thank God, there is no place, high or low, palace or prison, Court or hospital, and no persons, rich or poor, gentle or simple, learned or ignorant, even women and children, who are not acquainted with our way of life, our institute and its object.'

And, going on to speak of himself and of the honours which he was obliged, against his will, to receive, he adds, that it was no small consolation to him to be often stared and pointed at, and afterwards to be told that it was reported all over Spain that Ignatius and his companions had been convicted of heresy at Rome, some of them publicly burnt, and others condemned to the same punishment. He would reply, with a sweet smile, that he might truly be said to have been condemned by the Society of Ignatius itself to be exposed, not indeed to flames at Rome, but to shame in Spain, in consequence of the unmerited honours which were paid him there.

In this way the state of things in Spain seemed to pass from good to better, and Favre, instead of taking the glory and merit to himself, ascribed them to the labours and persecutions which his father, St. Ignatius, had formerly suffered there, as has been already mentioned. On the 8th of July there was universal rejoicing for the birth of a son, to whom the Princess Doña Maria gave birth. The whole Court was in festival, but the joy, like most earthly joys, was very short, and soon turned into the deepest mourning; for in a few days after the birth of her child, the Princess died. Feeling her last hour approach, she sent for Favre, received the last sacraments from him, and desired him and Araoz to assist her to her last breath; thus, even in the moment of death, remembering her love for the fathers and the Society, like a true daughter of John III. of Portugal. Favre grieved for her loss, at the same time that he rejoiced at the excellent dispositions with which she prepared for her end. He wrote an account of her death to the Duke of Gandia, Francis Borgia, who replied by an admirable letter, full of the Spirit of God and of that contempt of the world with which he was so thoroughly imbued.[1]

[1] Alcazar, *History of Toledo*, p. 50.

After the solemn celebration of the Princess' obsequies, Philip's deep grief would not permit him to remain at Valladolid. He therefore dismissed his Court, and went to Madrid, ordering the two fathers to follow him. Meanwhile, Favre, having received large contributions from persons of condition, founded, with the Prince's consent, a House of the Society at Valladolid, leaving there, for the work of the ministry, James Mendez, John Consalvo, and Hermes Poen of Flanders, all of whom had recently arrived from Portugal.

CHAPTER XXX.

Valladolid and Cologne.

BEFORE leaving Valladolid, I think it well to record the things which happened there, as instances of Father Favre's prudent method of directing souls into the way of salvation, and of his tenderness of heart in supporting and comforting the persecuted and afflicted.

There was a very illustrious personage belonging to the Court of Prince Philip, a man of the world, and altogether devoted to enjoyment and pleasure, and who, therefore, was in the habit of treating his body with self-indulgent delicacy. This man, hearing many persons speak very highly of the sanctity of Father Favre, introduced himself to him one day, and rather out of curiosity to hear some rare spiritual maxim, than from any desire of profit to his soul, asked the father to give him some short method or rule of life. The servant of God, perceiving what sort of a man he had to deal with, and that his idea was to combine the service of God and of the world, carnal enjoyments and spiritual consolations, said, 'I shall suggest to you nothing more than frequently to repeat in your heart, "Christ poor, and I rich; Christ fasting, and I full; Christ naked, and I clad; Christ suffering, and I living in enjoyment."' Having said this, he was silent. The gentleman, on hearing this, laughed in his heart at Favre's simplicity, and at the still greater simplicity of the numbers who followed him and considered him a greater master of the spiritual life, whereas, when put to the test, he was no wiser than the rest of the world. Then, presently recalling to mind the words he had heard, he said that he found in them nothing extraordinary, nothing but what every one had often heard and knew quite well. But one day, when he was seated at a sumptuous banquet, suddenly, in the midst of the abundant dainties and delicate wines, there darted into his mind, and sank into his heart, those words—'Christ fasting, and I full; Christ suffering, and I living in luxury and enjoyment.' Then, comparing the two terms, he was seized with remorse, horror, and interior commotion, and, by the help of divine grace, he entered thoroughly into himself, and, penetrating into the depths of that short and simple sentence, which just before seemed to have nothing in it, he saw revealed there the deformity of his life. Unable to restrain the overpowering feelings which crowded in upon his soul, he hastily left the company, and, seeking a retired and solitary place, he relieved himself by tears of sorrow and penitence. As soon as possible he went again to Favre, and gave him a full account of his past life. The holy man, in the most tender and affectionate manner, began to instruct him in the spiritual life;

afterwards, making him enter on the Exercises, he drew him on to make a general confession, and to reform his life so thoroughly that he became the mirror and model of a truly Christian nobleman to the whole Court.

It has been already related that Peter Favre, when he went away from Cologne the second time, left there Father Leonard Kessel, and eight more of the Society. All these fervent labourers, and in particular Blessed Peter Canisius, continued to work most vigorously in that city, cultivating the souls of the people by sermons, instructions, and private conversations, and teaching the Christian doctrine to the children. The consequence was that the heretics lost both credit and followers every day; while, on the contrary, the Catholic faith began to rise from its ruins, and good Christians, gaining courage, forcibly opposed the propagation of error. The Lutherans were mad with rage at all this; they had before now determined to strain every nerve to drive the fathers out of Cologne, but they did not venture to take any steps while Favre was there, on account of the high reverence with which he was universally regarded. No sooner was he gone to Portugal than they set in motion the machinations they had devised among themselves, being urged on also by the instigation of the treacherous Archbishop Hermann, who had made up his mind to rid himself altogether of those courageous young men, who, by their holy lives and burning zeal, hindered so effectually the spread of the heresy, of which he now made open profession. Accordingly they presented to the senate a list of horrible accusations against the religious in question, demanding their immediate banishment from the city; and they had contrived to give so fair a colour to their calumnies, and to manage matters so cunningly, that the senators, some of whom were gained over beforehand, and others bribed, acceded to their petition. We have a long letter on this subject from Peter Canisius to Favre, and the sentiments of intense zeal and fervour which it expresses render it very worthy of being perused at length. For the sake of brevity we must content ourselves with a short extract.

'I have undertaken,' he says, 'to relate, by God's favour, and in the best way that I can, the miserable tragedy which is beginning to be acted here—a thing which none of our brothers have yet been able to do; and without being too long I will explain to your paternal solicitude the unhappy condition of your children. After you left us, on the 12th of July, we remained here, united among ourselves in brotherly charity, pursuing our studies tranquilly, and more zealously than ever before. Each one of us attended to himself and his own particular duty, according to the instructions you left with us; and it seemed as though the disturbances against us, which had been excited in the senate, would have the effect of strengthening our cause rather than weakening it. But on the 28th of July the same consul who had before been sent by the senate when you were here, came to us again, and this time he was not alone, but accompanied by a numerous party of senators. Happening to find here Master Peter de Hallis and myself, he began thus: "We have related to the senate what you stated concerning your mode of life; we are aware now that your numbers have increased, and that there are now about eleven of you living together." "That was exactly our number," I replied, "but now there are only nine of us." "However that may be," he said, "I am come to declare to you the sentence and decree of the senate, which is, that you all quit this city immediately, and go wherever you like; and the senators have given no reason for this resolution of theirs." I replied, "Very well, but as we are to leave this city, we must request the noble senators to furnish us with a written testimonial of our good and innocent conduct, in order that we may be able to prove, wherever we may go, that we have not been sent away on account of any fault on our part, which would otherwise be supposed by every one to be the case." They refused this request of mine contemptuously, and said, "As you came here without our consent, you may go away without any testimonial from us." I rejoined, "If will and nothing else is to stand instead of reason, I would beg their lordships to consider how unworthy a thing it is to banish innocent persons, living at their own expense, and engaged on their studies; and next, to reflect more at leisure on the account they will have to render to God of this injustice." At these words they became angry, and said, in an excited manner. "You again threaten us then, do you?" I answered quietly, "I have no intention of threatening anybody. I merely remind you that you will have to answer to Christ, the Judge of all men, for inflicting a very severe punishment on innocent men." The consul then said, "Take care not to oblige us to intimate the will of the senate to you a second time. We give you a week to settle your affairs; in the meanwhile prepare for departure." With these words they went away, and in taking leave of them I said, "We will cheerfully remember to pray to God for you wherever we may go." Happy are we in being counted worthy of so great an honour! For surely it is an honour and glory for us to be so hardly judged, proscribed, and driven away against all right reason, and for no fault of ours.'[1]

Canisius goes on to speak of the insults, sarcasms, and ill-treatment which they were daily receiving, including even threats of imprisonment; then of the arts and cajoleries which many people tried upon him to detach him from the rule of the Society which he had embraced, promising him all sorts of ecclesiastical honours, dignities, preferments, and benefices; and, finally, he gives the history of the persecution, showing how it all emanated from Archbishop Hermann, and how, in the end, the heretics and the senate agreed to their remaining at Cologne, provided they did not live in community, but separate from one another; hoping, by that means, that when once the union which kept them together was broken, it would be easier to dissolve the body altogether, and that they might then, without much noise, be made to go into exile. But they were deceived in their anticipations, for only four of the number, the youngest in the house, went to Augsburg, whither they were summoned by Father Le Jay. The remaining five were enabled, by the help of the Carthusian fathers, to remain at Cologne, parted, indeed, from each other, as Canisius says, as to bodily presence, but all the more closely united in spirit, and full of readiness to endure all kinds of trial and suffering, even to prison, chains, and death itself, for the sake of the faith.

Favre, on receiving this letter and others from Father Leonard Kessel and his companions, highly approved the resolution they had taken, and, writing from Valladolid on the 9th of July, 1545, he exhorted them to patience and endurance.

---

[1] Autograph letter from Cologne, August 21 and September 21, 1544.

'In the packet which I have from Cologne,' he says, 'I find a letter from Master Peter Canisius to me. I have read and read it again, and I cannot say whether it has given me more joy or sorrow of heart. For would not any one be moved to tears on hearing that you, who are so entirely one and the same in the union of your wills, are not allowed to dwell together in one house in that place; that you, who have shown so plainly that you have but one heart and soul, are thought unworthy to live in community? I could laugh for joy and weep for sorrow at the same time, when I think that these men insist on your living apart, and cannot endure you to be together; as if you would be better, separated in this way, than you were assembled in the same dwelling. I would fain say to these men who are disturbing and tormenting you, "If you think the tree good, so also ought you to think the fruit; and if you think the tree evil, in like manner ought you to think the fruit evil." But it is not prudent to tell the whole truth, especially in these troublous times. Our Lord be praised, Who gives you union in the spirit, though you are separated in the body. He will know how to gather together again the scattered remnant of Israel. Do you, on your part, place your whole trust in Him Who is the fountain of all grace.'

And, in conclusion, after exhorting them to constancy, he prays our Lord and God to open the eyes of the minds of those who were the authors of this disturbance, and to make them know what a blessing it would bring upon their city if there were many more inflamed with the same fire of zeal and charity which burnt in the heart of Master Peter Canisius.[2] He also wrote to Gerard Hammond, the prior of the Carthusians,

[2] Valladolid, July 4, 1545.

thanking him for the charity he had shown to our brethren at Cologne, and informing him that he had related the whole of it to Father Francis Xavier, in India, and asked him to give his prayers in payment of the debt which the Society owed to that order. Nor did this satisfy him, for the following year, in replying to a letter from Hammond, he says—

'Do not fear, my dearest father, that I shall ever forget you. Go on making ever more favourable to you that Divine Spirit, Who intercedes for you in the hearts of your friends. He watches over you with special care, and moves me to hold you in remembrance. I am also moved to do so by the benefits you have lavished on me and my brethren, and, above all, in obtaining for our Society a share in the good works of your order. That is reason enough for all our brethren having a very special remembrance of you and your monastery. Last year I wrote to Master Francis Xavier, who is in India, begging him to make mention of you all in his prayers. At this time we are sending out thither ten of our Portuguese brethren, who are well acquainted with the favours we have received from you, and also with the love that I bear to your order, and to all Germany. They are conveying another letter from me to Master Francis, in which I have spoken of you and my other friends in Cologne, begging him further to acknowledge his share of our debt, and to help me with his prayers, that I may not be ungrateful to those who feel and act so kindly to me, beyond any desert of mine.'[3]

'Madrid, March 12th, 1546.'

[3] *Acta Sanctorum*, Julii 31.

This storm which was raised at Cologne was not of long duration, as Favre had predicted in his letter; for the efforts of the Catholics, including several of the wisest professors of the University, succeeded in discovering the machinations of the heretics, and in proving the innocence of our fathers; so that the new senators came to see the mistake, and revoked the decree.

CHAPTER XXXI.

At Madrid.

IN Madrid Philip ordered two rooms to be prepared for the fathers, as they wished, in the Hospital of our Lady del Campo, opposite the palace. Immediately on their arrival they both resumed their ministerial functions. But Favre in particular was not able to undertake much settled work, for from the time that he was first seen publicly he was continually visited by noblemen about the Court, who had already learnt to love and respect him at Valladolid, and who now had recourse to him for confession, and to request him to give them written directions for the spiritual life, and rules of perfection. It was a beautiful thing to see the chief nobility of Spain and Portugal coming to him in the hospital, and saying to each other, 'Let us go to the holy priest.' The most frequent and zealous of those who made use of his ministry were Mgr. Pozzi, the Pope's Nuncio, John di Zugniga, Philip's tutor, and his wife Stefana Requesens;

Bernardino Pimentel, the Marquis of Tavora, and Ferdinand da Silva, Count of Cifuentes, the Secretary of the Court. He had formerly been Imperial Ambassador at Rome, and had been a great friend to the Society in its early days. As he was a man of extraordinary virtue and piety, Favre enabled him to attain a very high degree of perfection, giving him rules and directions for meditating profitably on the eternal truths, and for cleansing his soul by frequent examinations of conscience; and his spiritual profit was not for himself alone, but he made every exertion possible to make the labours of Favre bear fruit in the souls of others also.

He had the charge of the two Princesses, Maria and Joanna, daughters of Charles V. and sisters to Philip, who had had an opportunity four years before, though only for a very short time, of having some intercourse with Favre at Occagna. Now that they were at Alcalà, they were exceedingly desirous of seeing him again, and of having longer conversations with him on spiritual subjects. Don Ferdinand then obtained leave to take him to Alcalà, and in the few days that he stayed there he brought the Court to a regularity like that of a religious house. When he took his leave he left written rules of life with the Infantas and their ladies, and also instructions how to meditate profitably on the eternal truths and the Passion of our Lord. After this the Princesses used to go from time to time to Madrid, under pretext of paying a visit to their brother, and went to the hospital to converse with Favre and give him an account of their state. Their piety was fostered and their holy resolutions strengthened by the example and advice of their governante, Doña Leonora Mascareñas, a very devout lady, and so much attached to the Society that St. Ignatius used to call her its 'mother.' And so, indeed, she was, not merely in affection, but in the protection and continual support which she afforded it She had already largely contributed to the establishment of our House at Valladolid; and now at Alcalà, while Favre was there, she arranged with the Princesses, and got together a sufficient sum to purchase a house and maintain some of our number, whom Father Simon Rodriguez sent for the purpose from Coimbra. Their names were Francis di Villanova, Manuel Lopez, and that Maximilian Cappella whose wonderful conversion has been already related. These were the small beginnings of the College which the Society afterwards had at Alcalà, and which did so much for souls, especially among the young students of the University, as Father Peter Favre foretold from the beginning would be the case.

I am here unwilling to omit to mention a circumstance which reflects great honour and praise on Favre. There were some ill-disposed people, who, not being able to detect the slightest blemish in his way of mixing with people about the Courts, and especially with persons of the opposite sex, spread a report that the fathers of the Society carried about them a certain herb which possessed the property of paralyzing all seeds of concupiscence, and that, consequently, it was not to be wondered at that they preserved their purity. This tale came to the ears of Philip, who, whether he believed it or not, charged his tutor, Don John di Zugniga, to inquire into the truth of the matter. The first of the fathers whom he met was Father Araoz, and to him Don John confidentially imparted the Prince's wish. The father, after a little reflection, replied, 'The report which you have heard about us is true, and I may add, that this herb which, by the favour of heaven, we make use of, not only destroys carnal temptations, but restrains the appetite, checks the tongue, moderates the anger, eradicates all vices and implants all virtues in the soul; and if you wish to know its name, it is called in plain Castilian the holy fear of God, and the Holy Spirit has bestowed upon it the power of producing all those effects which I have mentioned.' The father's reply was repeated at Court, and raised him still higher in the respect and veneration of all.

As the number of illustrious persons who flocked to the hospital increased every day, the Prince had the fathers removed thence, and allotted to them a better place of residence. Favre availed himself of the change to give the Spiritual Exercises more conveniently to many people, who most earnestly desired to make them. Among these were bishops and ecclesiastics of every grade, more than I can tell, besides several gentlemen and nobles of the Court, whose change of life was the subject of general admiration and edification. I will only relate one among many, that of Don Alvaro de Cordova, Grand Master of the Horse to the Prince, whose wife, Doña Maria of Aragon, used to say that before Favre came to Madrid she was the wife of a courtier-noble; but that now, thanks to God and to the father, she was not only married to a Christian nobleman, but to a saint. And this was true, for Don Alvaro, after making the Exercises, adopted a way of life so entirely different from his former use, that he seemed a different man. After discharging the duties of his office at Court, it was his custom to retire to his chamber to pray and meditate alone; and when the Prince went for change and recreation to the Pardo, the royal villa, he would retire apart from the rest, into a grove, where, hidden from the eyes of all, he spent the whole time conversing with God. He was liberal and charitable to the poor and needy of all sorts, and there was not a single act of heroic charity which he did not practise towards the sick, especially those in the hospitals, even carrying on his back their mattrasses, and whatever they required. And all these good works of his were shared and imitated by his son, Don Antonio, who afterwards entered the Society, and became a glory to his country by the lustre of his sanctity.

The fame of the labours of Father Favre, and of the fruits which they produced, spread from Madrid to the different provinces, and the result was that people formed a high opinion of the Society, and greatly desired its establishment among them. Many persons who did not know its name, said that the 'Ignatians' had come to Spain; others called them 'Papists,' in allusion to their vow of obedience to the Pope and the Apostolic See. Some, hearing how much the fathers dwelt on the importance of an amendment of life, and seeing that there was no outward difference between them and the rest of the clergy, called them 'reformed priests or clerics.' There were not wanting some who formed even too high an opinion of them, and said that God had sent out new apostles for the salvation of the world. Several cities requested that they might have colleges of the Society, among these were Toledo, Salamanca, Saragossa, Barcelona, and others. But Favre was unable, from the lack of subjects, to embrace many offers; and for the present confined himself to Madrid, Alcalà, Valentia, Valladolid, and Gandia, in which last place the holy duke, Francis Borgia, this year began the College and University, the first in Spain committed to the Society. It was to supply these infant colleges that Favre received a suitable number of novices, over and above the students who had come from Portugal. He trained them carefully as their spiritual master, and he gave Father Araoz the office of establishing everywhere, and putting in force, regular religious discipline and observance. These were the first seeds of the Society in Spain, which afterwards, by God's grace, sprang up and spread not only in that part of Europe, but throughout the vast regions of the West Indies. A large part of this great work is due to Peter Favre, who was the first to make the Society known and valued by all ranks and conditions of persons.

This is so true that when, a year later, the holy father St. Ignatius appointed Father Antonio Araoz first Provincial of Spain, he said, in the patent from Rome, on September 1—'We are moved to lay this burthen on you by the consideration of the abundant fruit which has been gathered in the last few years in Spain by your labour and industry, and especially also by those of Father Master Peter Favre, now resting in the Lord. For already several colleges have been founded there, and others are either begun or will soon be begun, scholastics have been placed for their studies in different Universities; and a great number of well-disposed persons have been led, some of them, to enter the Society and profess the Evangelical counsels; while others have been roused to change their life for the better by spiritual admonitions and ministrations.'

CHAPTER XXXII.

Favre summoned to Rome.

ST. IGNATIUS had fixed a year as the limit of Favre's stay in Spain. Accordingly, at the beginning of 1546, this good son of obedience reminded his holy father of the order he had received, placing himself in his hands with entire indifference, perfectly ready to remain where he was, or to go anywhere else; or, as he said himself, to have to spend his time in continual journeys, without pausing or reposing, merely in visiting his companions and preparing a habitation for them, without himself having port or home of his own anywhere. I do not see how it would be possible to desire more in the way of most perfect obedience in the face of all that nature could suggest to the contrary. For any one who has the slightest appreciation of spiritual things will see and feel how painful it must be to a man of truly Apostolic mind to break off his labours in the midst, when the fruit is just ready to be gathered, to abandon everything at the call of obedience, and to turn in an entirely different direction, without any certainty, or even hope, of its leading to greater good.

At the same time that Favre was writing on this subject, the question of recalling him for the service of the Universal Church was being agitated at Rome. The first session of the Ecumenical Council had been held at Trent on the 13th of December; and as the difficult subjects of original sin and justification were to be prepared in time for the subsequent sessions, Pope Paul III. had asked Ignatius for three men of the Society whom he might send there in quality of Papal theologians. The holy founder, after commending the matter to God, fixed upon Father James Laynez, Father Alfonso Salmeron, and Father Peter Favre for that office. The first two were at Rome, and therefore would be able to go straight to Trent in May. As to Favre, Ignatius foresaw all the difficulties and hindrances which would be put in the way of his leaving by the Court of Madrid: he therefore wrote to the Prince, Don Philip, humbly laying before him the necessity laid upon him by his obedience to the Pope, of recalling Favre to Rome. At the same time he begged his intimate friend, Dr. Peter Ortiz, to interpose his good offices for the same object. The letter to Ortiz is dated the 17th of February, 1546, and runs thus—

'*May the supreme grace and the everlasting love of Christ our Lord ever be our help and protection.*

'His Holiness has resolved and commanded that some of this least Society, which is as much yours as it is ours, should go to the Council. One of those who are to go is Master Favre. That he may start on his journey with the good pleasure and satisfaction of all, I have written on the matter to the Prince. I entreat you, for the love and glory of God our Lord, to give us the help of your good offices, so far as time and place permit, and to obtain free permission for Father Favre to leave the Court. Not only shall we thus be doing the will of the Sovereign Pontiff, but I hope that, by God's great goodness, everything will turn out to His greater glory and honour; and for our own part, whether we are together or dispersed, we shall always be towards you as we have hitherto been, that is, cherishing you most affectionately in our hearts, and owning ourselves infinitely obliged to you in the Lord. I do not in this letter write at such length about yourself personally as, for the glory and honour of God, I fain would do, because I am also writing to Master Favre something on that subject, as well as on the affairs of the Society—yours more than ours—which God vouchsafes to guide and direct with His hand. I will only add that Peter Ribadeneira is at Padua, and excites universal admiration by his progress, both in studies and in virtue. I am convinced that if God gives him life he will do great things and be a true servant of God. Lastly, I beseech the Divine Majesty, and will not cease to entreat Him, by His great and infinite goodness, to give us grace perfectly to know His will, and to perform it always and in all things.

'Yours in our Lord Jesus Christ,

'IGNATIUS.'[1]

'Rome, the 17th of February, 1546.'

At the very time when Paul III. asked to have Favre as his theologian at Trent, King John III. of Portugal was asking for him as Patriarch of Ethiopia. It must be explained that the Portuguese trading along the western coast of Africa had gradually penetrated into the interior and entered Ethiopia, a vast country extending from Nubia towards the east. They found the Ethiopians all Christians, and in many points very strict observers of ancient religious customs. But, as from very early times they had been in the habit of receiving their 'Abuna,' or Patriarch, from the Church of Alexandria, they were infected with the schism of Dioscorus and the heresy of Eutyches. The good Portuguese merchants, in the course of conversations which they

[1] Alcazar, p. 66.

had with David, the Emperor of Ethiopia, introduced religious topics, and made him desire to reunite his people to the Roman Church. David himself died shortly after; and his son Claudius, who succeeded him in the empire, was at last induced to write to the King of Portugal, begging him to make request for him to the Sovereign Pontiff for a Catholic Patriarch. Don John III., ever most zealous for the propagation of the faith, lost no time in the matter, and soon fixed his choice on Peter Favre, of whose virtue, learning, and sanctity he had been an admiring witness. Accordingly, he wrote to his Ambassador in Rome, with strict injunctions to obtain the Pope's express command, foreseeing that without this nothing would ever induce Favre to accept such a dignity. But God had already otherwise disposed of His faithful servant. It was His will to have him, not as theologian at Trent, nor Patriarch in Ethiopia, but blessed in the enjoyment and possession of Himself in heaven.

Meanwhile, the holy man, having received the letters summoning him to Rome, prepared for immediate departure. He went to Toledo to pay his respects to the Cardinal Archbishop, Don John of Tavora, who had twice committed to him the visitation and reformation of his diocese, furnishing him with ample powers for that purpose, and also Dr. Peralta, canon of the Cathedral, whom he used to know at Paris. After that he went to Galapagar, to see once more and take leave of Dr. Peter Ortiz. He had as his companion on this journey Manuel Lopez, one of our young students, and he insisted on his making use of the horse which some of his friends had lent him, while he himself travelled on foot, entirely absorbed in God. On his return to Madrid he appointed Father Antonio Araoz Superior of all our brethren in Spain, Francis Villanova, though not yet a priest, Rector of the College of Alcalà, and Father Diego Mirone of that at Valentia; and so, after giving his blessing to Philip's son, the little Don Carlos, who was brought to him by Doña Leonora de Mascareñas, he left Madrid as secretly as he could on the Tuesday in Holy Week, which fell that year on the 20th of April. And he had, indeed, to take every precaution in order to get away privately, and to make all possible haste, although he was still weak from an illness which had lasted ten days. At the first news of his approaching departure there was great agitation in the city. Many of the principal inhabitants prepared to make every effort to prevent his going, so high was the esteem in which he was held, so great the love which he had won from all classes of people. 'And well indeed did he deserve it,' wrote Father Araoz to St. Ignatius; 'for no words can say how his Apostolic labours had strengthened and confirmed in Christian piety men who may be called the pillars of this Court. Blessed indeed are the city and people, in Italy or elsewhere, that are to have the presence of Father Favre, for in him they will have a soul full of grace and overflowing with the mercies of God.'

On arriving at Valentia, he took a little rest and comfort among our brothers at the College there. He was asked to make a discourse to the people, who greatly desired to hear him. He did so accordingly, with indescribable fervour, in the pulpit of the parish church of St. Andrew, taking as his subject the works of mercy to the poor. The citizens were exceedingly delighted; and many years afterwards they retained an affectionate remembrance of this sermon, and of the fruit it produced in all classes of persons. They were very desirous to keep him with them a few days longer for their spiritual needs; but the holy man was not able to consent to their wish, as he had to hasten to Gandia, where he was anxiously expected for reasons which must now be related.

CHAPTER XXXIII.

Foundation of the College at Gandia.

ST. IGNATIUS had enjoined Favre to stop at Gandia in his journey through Spain. The saintly duke, Francis Borgia, greatly desired this visit; for, four years previously, when he was Viceroy of Catalonia, he had made the acquaintance of Favre at Barcelona, and was continually sending him repeated and very pressing letters and messages, begging him to come and see him. And quite recently circumstances had occurred which made it, in his opinion, highly necessary to have an interview with the father, and to lay open to him his inmost soul, so as to receive his direction and advice. In the April of this year, 1546, his duchess, Leonora di Castro y Meneses, had left this world for a better, and Duke Francis being thus freed from the marriage tie, had resolved to fulfil the promise which he had made at Granada on beholding the disfigured face of the Empress Isabella after her death, binding himself by a vow to quit the world and enter religion, if he should survive his wife. The only thing that remained was to consider in what particular order it was God's will that he should serve Him. And he expected to find in the prudence, sagacity, and discretion of Father Favre, all the spiritual assistance by which he might be enabled to ascertain the divine will in this important affair.

There was a further reason still. The Duke, not satisfied with having given a College to the Society, meditated raising a new building of regal magnificence, and making it a public University in all the sciences, endowed with privileges equal to those of Alcalà and Salamanca. The foundations were already dug, and he was waiting for the arrival of Favre, in order that he might, as the eldest son of St. Ignatius, lay the first stone of the first University intrusted to the Society. Accordingly, when Favre came to Gandia the ceremony took place; and on the 5th of May, after offering the holy sacrifice in the ducal chapel, he proceeded, accompanied by all the Court and followed by great numbers of people, to the site of the building, where he solemnly blessed and laid the first stone. After him the Duke laid another; then his children, one by one; next the fathers of the College, with the Rector at their head. This was that holy man, Father Andrew Oviedo, afterwards created Bishop of Heliopolis, and successor to Father Joan Nuñez Barreto, who was made Patriarch of Ethiopia instead of Favre.

When the function was concluded, the Duke shut himself up in a retired place to make the Spiritual Exercises under Father Favre's direction. The fruit which this retreat produced was, in the first place, that he formed the determination of definitively entering the Society, and in the second, that he formed so high an opinion of the Exercises when explained by so experienced a master, that he immediately wrote to the Pope, humbly entreating him to condescend to approve and recommend them by his Apostolic authority, that so they might produce more extensive fruit, and the faithful be induced to avail themselves of them the more readily, to the great benefit of their souls. And, in fact, after having them examined by Cardinal John

L

Alvaro di Toledo, Bishop of Burgos, Mgr. Philip Archinto, Vicar of Rome, and Father Giles Foscarari, Master of the Sacred Palace, Paul III. approved them in a Brief dated July 31st, 1548, in which it is expressly said that he was induced to do so by the request of his beloved son, the noble Duke of Gandia, Francis Borgia, and by the great good which results from these Exercises, in proof of which the said Duke Francis adduces not only what was reported in several places, but the experience of what he himself has been an eye-witness to at Barcelona, Valentia, and Gandia. The Duke had already made the Exercises more than once at Barcelona under Father Araoz, and the year before at Valentia under Father Diego Mirone. Now that at Gandia they were given by Father Favre, they seemed to him quite a new system of teaching; and the interior effects they produced were so wonderful and powerful, that he was not satisfied till he had made them generally known and appreciated.

Favre stayed in Gandia about a month, edifying by his holy life not the Court only, but all the inhabitants of the city, who greatly loved and venerated him. This feeling was increased by a wonderful prodigy, the remembrance of which was handed down to later times. There was in the ducal chapel a devout picture of our Lady. It had belonged to a holy hermit at Valentia, who, at his death, left it to Leonora Borgia. One day when Favre was kneeling in prayer before this image, the Blessed Virgin, whose eyes were half closed, suddenly opened them, and turned them lovingly on her dear servant. The miracle was witnessed by many persons who were in the chapel at the time, and the news of it speedily spread through the city; and ever after the sacred picture was known as 'Our Lady of the Miracle.' Doña Leonora Borgia bequeathed it to Sister

Jane of the Cross, first Abbess of the royal Discalced Carmelite Convent at Madrid, and it was taken thither and placed in the chapel of our Lady of Nazareth. The numerous miracles which God wrought there so increased the popular worship and devotion, that every year a solemn festival, with an octave, was observed in its honour, at which the royal family of Spain assisted, and the preachers on the occasion always made mention of this first miracle with which Father Peter Favre was favoured.

CHAPTER XXXIV.

Favre's return to Rome, and death.

FROM Gandia Favre went to Barcelona, intending to sail for Italy from that port. But he was detained there by a tertian fever, which for a fortnight so preyed upon his strength, already so much weakened by the continual and severe fatigues of the last three years of his life. Barcelona was exceedingly devoted to St. Ignatius and to the Society; and as soon as it was known that Favre had arrived, a great many people hastened to avail themselves of his help for the good of their souls. The servant of God, supplying by the vigour of his spirit the strength which his body lacked, gave himself entirely up to Apostolic ministrations, hearing confessions, and even preaching in the churches on the days which intervened between his attacks. And such abundant fruit was the result, that Father Araoz was firmly persuaded that this sickness had been sent by a particular providence of God for the sake of those many souls who were assisted by his charity in the concerns of their salvation.

When the news of his illness reached Rome, the holy Father Ignatius began to think it better not to risk the life of such a man at that season of the year, which the excessive heat already made very dangerous ; and he was on the point of writing to tell him to put off coming till the end of the summer. But the other fathers, who longed exceedingly to see Favre again, and to enjoy his holy conversation, prevented his doing so, thinking there was no cause for alarm. The servant of God, not having received any contrary order, firmly withstood his friends at Barcelona, who advised him to delay ; and he persisted in his determination to fulfil his obedience by hastening as quickly as possible to the feet of the Sovereign Pontiff, who had sent for him, even though it should be at the cost of his life. As soon, therefore, as he was in some degree recovered from his sickness, he left Barcelona on the 21st of June, and on the 17th of the following July, when it is usually dangerous even for persons in strong health to enter Rome, he arrived unexpectedly in the holy city. We must say that all this was ordered by God, Whose will it was to crown the labours and to reward the merits of His faithful servant, and to leave us in him an example of that heroic obedience which our holy Father Ignatius wished to be the distinguishing characteristic of his sons. And, indeed, we have the testimony of an express revelation from God Himself, as we shall see presently, that this judgment is quite in accordance with the truth.

Words cannot tell the joy and consolation of the fathers at Favre's arrival in Rome. It was seven years since they had seen him, during which time they had heard and read most wonderful accounts of his Apostolic labours. And now they had the incomparable delight of hearing from his own lips the story of the good and ill fortune which had befallen him; of the beginnings and progress of the Society in Germany, Flanders, Portugal, and Spain; of the sufferings he had undergone in God's service; of the methods he had employed for the spiritual profit of his neighbour, of the hopes that existed of the extirpation of heresies, the reformation of morals, and the sanctification of souls. Favre, on his part, was quite beside himself with the joy of finding himself in the midst of so many brothers who had lately embraced the same rule of life; and, above all, of being able to converse personally with, and open his whole soul to, St. Ignatius, whom he so tenderly loved.

All these mutual joys were very short-lived. A week after his arrival, on the 24th of July, the good father was suddenly attacked by a violent double tertian fever, which, coming as it did, when he was already worn out by fatigue and debilitated by his late sickness, very soon became malignant. Every remedy in use at that time for such cases was tried, but it was impossible to save him. While all besides himself were struck with consternation, he alone was calm, tranquil, and serene in mind and countenance. Banishing every thought of this world, he fixed all his desires and affections on heaven; and, impatient to be set free from the bonds of the body, he panted to be for ever united to God, and to enjoy that supreme blessedness, on the possession of which it almost seemed that he had already entered. He addressed sweet words of consolation to his brethren, who were clinging round him in tears, exhorting them to give infinite thanks to God, Who was pleased to take him out of this life with the merit of obedience, and let him die, as he had always desired, in the arms of his dearest father, St. Ignatius. On the morning of the 1st of August, which that year fell on a Sunday, he received the holy Viaticum with the utmost piety and devotion, and, soon after, Extreme Unction. Then, with his whole soul fixed on God, and his heart filled with the tenderest love, he died most peacefully, between noon and evening, in the presence, not only of St. Ignatius and the brethren in Rome, but of others who had hastened thither to witness the precious passage to a better life of a man of such high merit and repute for sanctity. He was three months and a half more than forty years old. John Codure was the first, Favre the second, of the first ten fathers who were summoned to transplant the Society to heaven, while the rest were still labouring to spread it on earth; and it was remarked by many that the blessed deaths of those two fell each on a day on which a special feast of their name-saints is celebrated: Codure dying on the Decollation of St. John the Baptist, and Favre on the feast of St. Peter's Chains.

Inconsolable was the grief for the loss of such a man in the full vigour of his age. He was regarded with universal admiration as a model of consummate perfection, an indefatigable labourer in the Lord's vineyard, an Apostle burning with zeal for God's glory and for the eternal salvation of souls, and possessing all those gifts, both of nature and of grace, all those virtues, moral and divine, which are essential in forming a character of perfect sanctity. Considering in the seven years, which were the short term of his Apostolic ministry, how many journeys he had taken, how many dangers and sufferings he had encountered, how many heretics and sinners he had converted, how many good Christians he had led to a stricter and holier life; and, besides all this, in how many lands he had planted and propagated the Society, and raised it very high in credit and reputation, what might not have been expected from him if he had been allowed for a longer time to continue labouring with the same strength and energy of spirit? Lastly, seeing what remarkable prudence and unequalled skill he possessed in directing souls, in discerning spirits, and carrying through the most important affairs, every one had reckoned on seeing in him a worthy successor of Ignatius as the head of the whole Society, in case of his surviving him. The fathers at Rome were filled with such deep grief at seeing all these hopes cut off in a moment, that St. Ignatius' found it necessary to encourage and console them by making it known that another would shortly join the Society, who, as regarded his services to it and the Church, would compensate for the loss of Favre. He referred to Francis Borgia, Duke of Gandia, whose vow to enter the Society, taken a month before, the last time he made the Exercises, Favre had confided to the saint.

We find, however, that as soon as they had recovered from the first shock of grief, not only those living at Rome, but all wherever the death of Father Favre was made known, shared in one and the same feeling of joy and consolation, which arose from the confident belief that he was without doubt already received into heaven, and in the hope that now that he was with God his intercession would be so much more powerful for the protection, support, and spread of the Society, and that he would transfuse into his brethren the same spirit of charity and zeal for the propagation of the faith and the conversion of souls which had been in his own heart. And this assurance was opportunely strengthened by a letter received at this very time from Father Andrew of Oviedo, Rector of the College at Gandia, in which he mentioned a divine revelation made to a devout person greatly favoured by God, in which the soul of Favre was seen in great glory, like that of the saints, and in which he had spoken many times with the person who saw the vision, and said great things concerning Christ's obedience and his own, expressing the greatest happiness at having died by obedience; and, lastly, promising never to cease to pour forth supplications to God for His Church.[1] Father Oviedo does not mention the name of the person who had this vision of the glory of Favre, but it is certain that it is the holy duke, Francis Borgia. Father Daniel Bartoli had already expressed his opinion in his *Historical Memoirs of the Men and Deeds of the Society*, in these words— 'No one was greatly surprised at what Father Andrew of Oviedo wrote at that time from Gandia to Rome, concerning a person of well-known sanctity, perhaps St. Francis Borgia.'[2] But what Bartoli in his time conjectured, was positively affirmed afterwards by Father Philip Ghisolfi, and still more strongly by Father Alvaro Cienfugos, afterwards a Cardinal, in his copious Life of the Saint, which was in great part taken, as he says in the Preface, from the manuscript accounts of Father Dionysius Vasquez and of Father Peter Domenech, the former of whom was the confessor, the latter the companion of Borgia. The following is the statement of this exceedingly accurate writer—

'The death of Favre at Rome was known at Gandia so speedily, that it seemed as though his last breath had been borne thither on the air. For at the moment he died the holy Duke saw him surrounded by a bright cloud, and in the company of many saints of heaven.

[1] Original letter from Gandia, October 13, 1546.
[2] *Memorie Istoriche*, lib. i.

He saw that Favre enjoyed a special glory by reason of having lost his life from starting immediately on his journey, and exactly following the painful course pointed out to him by obedience. Father Andrew of Oviedo wrote an account of this glorious vision to St. Ignatius, saying that it was revealed to a person of eminent holiness, from whom he heard it; and Father Philip Ghisolfi, in his biography of St. Francis Borgia, says that he was the person referred to. And it was very fitting that he should be a witness of the glory of the holy man whom he succeeded on earth, in order that he might be encouraged to imitate his spirit and his zeal by the spectacle of so splendid a triumph. It is certain that on seeing this vision the Duke felt his heart on fire within him, and a great eagerness to enter the Society, and to put on the victorious armour which that departed soldier had left behind him; and in Gandia this death was hailed with every mark of triumph and jubilation. All this is related by Father Domenech.'[3] So writes Father Alvaro Cienfugos, and we now see why it was not possible for Father Oviedo, who was the Duke's confessor at the time, to speak more plainly, or to reveal the name of the holy person to whom the vision concerning Father Favre's glory had been granted. For the rest, it is true that Borgia was most anxious to hasten on the time of his entering the Society; that, immediately after the death of Favre, he despatched one of his people to Rome with letters to St. Ignatius, begging him to receive him as one of his sons; and not only did the saint consent to do so, but, soon after, he obtained leave for him from the Pope to bind himself by solemn vows, and, notwithstanding this, yet to continue to govern his States in the secular

---

[3] *Life of St. Francis Borgia*, bk. iii. ch. v.

habit till such time as he should have arranged his private affairs.

Besides Borgia, it seems beyond a doubt that the glory of Favre in heaven was revealed to St. Ignatius. There is extant a copy of the circular letter sent to the Houses of the Society, bearing date August 7th, 1546, and having these words written on the margin, *De morte sancti Patris Petri Fabri*—'Concerning the death of the holy Father Peter Favre.' This letter says that Peter Favre died on the 1st of August, the feast of St. Peter's Chains, as John Codure had died on that of the Decollation of St. John the Baptist; and that '*their souls are together in heaven, as their bodies are in the Church of Sta. Maria della Strada.*' Then, without giving any directions for Masses and prayers to be offered up for the soul of the deceased, as is done in every other instance, the letter goes on to say expressly, that, '*as we have need of the intercession of friends and saints on our behalf, we must all hope that Favre will not help us less powerfully in heaven than he could have on earth.*' St. Ignatius then asserts, not conditionally, but absolutely, that the soul of Favre is in heaven, together with that of Codure. Now all his biographers are agreed that scarcely was Codure dead before God gave Ignatius the consolation of seeing him enter heaven, surrounded with light, and accompanied by angels who had descended from Paradise to conduct him thither. In the same way, therefore, it is fair to say that he saw the soul of Favre also received into the company of the blessed in heaven; and that, for this reason, instead of prescribing the usual suffrages, he enjoined on the Society confidence in him, in that, as a friend and a saint, he will intercede for us unto God.

CHAPTER XXXV.

Testimonies to Favre's sanctity.

IT has been seen from time to time in the course of this biography, how every one who knew and conversed intimately with Peter Favre considered and esteemed him as a saint. We shall, therefore, here only add a few facts which have reference to persons who, by his means were brought to God, and entered the Society. No words can describe the affection and reverence which they always professed and manifested towards him on every occasion, writing to him wherever he might be, and asking for his advice and direction in everything. We may give the first place to Blessed Peter Canisius, who, writing from Cologne, after telling him that he is cherished in the undying remembrance of all the principal citizens, and that they begged his prayers to God for them, adds these words—

'And if they commend themselves to your prayers, how much more earnestly should we do so, who have been trained in your school to acknowledge Jesus Christ as our Father in this holy Society of God's children? It remains therefore, Reverend Father, that by your prayers to Christ you help us your children, whom you have so happily begotten to Him. Without you, we are indeed orphans, but we shall be full of joy and gladness if our weakness is helped by your prayers with God and the saints. Oh, if you own as your children those who will never cease to claim you as their father, behold them one and all kneeling before you with clasped hands and prostrate bodies, and their eyes bathed in tears; listen to the words with which they implore you, by your tender and fatherly affection, to have pity on them, left here as poor and orphan children in need of food and clothing. But why do I ask bread for one who still requires milk, and who is unfit for stronger diet till he is more advanced in age? No, I am mistaken in my judgment to suppose others to be like myself; they indeed have abundance of bread in the house of our Heavenly Father, where they are more highly esteemed than hired servants. No, it is only Canisius, I confess, who is perishing of hunger, and there is no one to take pity on his misery but you, my dear father and my support, in whose hands is my fate. Hasten then to help me; rejoice the heart of your servant; say to my soul that God is my salvation; say to me, "Take courage, my son, and fear not: may blessing and peace be upon thee, day and night: I will be with thee always in all thy ways." Ah, yes, my father, if you are at my side I shall indeed have nothing to fear, and my confidence will be firm and constant, if only you bless me from your heart in the name of our Lord, by the merits of the saints, and by the charity, simplicity, patience, fortitude, and salvation, which are in Jesus Christ our Lord.

'Your meanest servant and son,

'PETER CANISIUS.'[1]

'Cologne, December 30th, 1545.'

Another of his children, Hermes Poen of Rotterdam, whom Favre had gained to God and the Society at Louvain, and afterwards sent to study in Portugal, as soon as he heard that Blessed Favre had arrived at

---

[1] Autograph letter of Canisius.

Evora, wrote to him from Coimbra, on the last day of September, a very affectionate letter in which he says among other things—

'It would be difficult to express our joy at the news of your arrival in this country. As loving children, we longed ardently to see our father once more. Grant us the happiness of having you amongst us one day. The soul of your Hermes is pining for you, as a son tenderly desirous of seeing his father. For indeed you are my own father in Christ; you have begotten me, you have saved me from the storms of a treacherous world by the help and grace of Him Who draws all things to Himself. You have snatched me from the jaws of the devil, and fed me with the Word of Life. Do not cease to train and guide the son to whom you have deigned to give birth. I am ready to bear the sweet yoke of our Lord in everything. Do you dispose, form, direct, command me. There is nothing, however hard, which I am not willing to undertake with the utmost cheerfulness. I will venture to say that I am ever more ready to obey than you are to command. Do you then direct, instruct, teach, and guide your son in the way of salvation. You have subjected him to your rule, you have numbered him amongst your children. Do you act a father's part towards me, and never, by God's grace, will I fail in the duty of a son.'

Of the same tenor are the letters of other young men, either belonging or about to belong to the Society, which he received while he was in Spain, from Coimbra and from Cologne. The letters show, not only their affection and reverence for him, but the spiritual fervour and solid virtue which the holy man had known how to transfuse into his disciples.

After his death this general opinion and veneration of his sanctity increased rather than diminished. In

Upper and Lower Germany, in Flanders, Portugal, Spain, and Italy, no sooner was his happy passage from this life known, than his virtues found as many to praise them as had before admired them. The grandees of the Court of Madrid could find no better way of expressing their sentiments than by saying that the Society would soon fall to pieces, now that it was deprived of the pillar which supported it. At Galapagar, Dr. Ortiz and all the inhabitants celebrated, instead of funeral solemnities, solemn festivities of jubilation and triumph. At Gandia things went still farther. The excitement throughout the city was such that, as we learn from Father Andrew of Oviedo, an eye-witness, there was a public festival held to honour the heavenly birthday of Blessed Peter Favre, and for many years after the anniversary of the day of his death was kept like that of a canonized saint, and all felt their souls strengthened by invoking him. As long as Father Oviedo was at Gandia, it was his custom to send a candle to St. Ignatius to burn before the tomb of Favre, whom he called 'Blessed.' The Carthusian fathers at Cologne preserved some letters and other writings of his as relics, and never spoke of him but as 'Blessed.'

It would take too long to quote the testimony of his religious brethren one by one, and so to prove to every one their high opinion of the virtue and holiness of Favre. 'They were all firmly convinced,' writes Orlandini, 'that he had gained the glory of heaven and the honour of being in the number of the Blessed, and therefore there was an end of sorrow and of weeping. All feelings were merged in those of joy and consolation because he who on earth had been a teacher and pattern of perfection was now gained as a patron and advocate in heaven.'[2] The first fathers, whose intercourse with him

[2] *Vita B. Petri Fabri*, cap. ult.

had been the longest, could find no words or phrases for expressing what they had come to think of him. Father Simon Rodriguez, in the History which he wrote in the year 1577, on the origin and progress of the Society down to the period of its confirmation, says—

'The first who joined our Father Ignatius was Master Peter Favre, a Savoyard, who was moved by the confidential and holy conversation and the saintly life of the Blessed Father to lead a truly wonderful life and to consecrate himself to God. He burnt with an incredible desire to visit Jerusalem and the other holy places of Palestine, and to spend his life in labouring for the salvation of men and bringing them from darkness to the light of the truth, from death to life. Not to speak of a great multitude of other virtues, there was in this father a rare and sunny grace and sweetness in his intercourse with others, such as I confess I have never seen in any one else. I am at a loss for words to express the way in which, by his amiable and pleasant manners, he gained every one's goodwill and affection, and won all with whom he had intercourse to the love of God.'[3]

Equally strong is the testimony of Father Ribadeneira, who, from his youth, had known Favre, both at Rome and at Louvain. He says—'Father Favre was a man of great learning and virtue, possessing a wonderful gift of knowledge and discretion of spirits, and also of healing the sick. He practised himself much in continual prayer and meditation, and his abstinence was such that sometimes he neither ate nor drank anything for a week. He was most obedient, and a great despiser of himself. His zeal for the Church and for the salvation of his neighbour was very great. When he spoke of the things of God, it

---

[3] *De origine et progressu Societatis Jesu usque ad ejus confirmationem.* Roma, 1869. Typ. *Civilta Cathol.*

seemed as though he held the keys of men's hearts on his tongue, so powerfully did he move, and so strongly did he attract them; and the affection he inspired them with was fully equalled by the reverence which they felt for the sweet gravity and solid virtue which shone in all that he said. Our Lord God favoured him with many communications of Himself, and filled his soul with sweetness by marvellous lights and divine revelations.'[4]

But the holy Apostle of the Indies, St. Francis Xavier, went even farther than Ribadeneira in showing, both by word and deed, his high estimation of the virtue and merits of Favre. These two great souls were always very closely united in heart and mind from the time when they shared the same room in the same College in the University of Paris. They were the first two who made acquaintance with Ignatius, to whom he gave the Spiritual Exercises, and who offered themselves to him as companions and fellow-helpers in the great work which he was projecting. There was a very great similarity in their characters: the same rectitude of life, the same charm and sweetness in words and manner, the same burning zeal, and the same generosity in undertaking, and constancy in carrying through, the most difficult and arduous projects, at the cost of great sufferings and the risk of life itself. Both were sent by the Pope, one to convert the heathen, the other to reconcile heretics. They had a great love and reverence one for the other; and, as a proof of this, it will be remembered that their conscientious judgment led them to give their votes each for the other, after Ignatius, as General of the Order. When Xavier, who was in India, received news of the death of his beloved Father Favre, he was so firmly convinced of his beatitude in heaven, that he began at once to invoke him in his greatest

[4] *Vita di Santi Ignazio,* lib. iii. cap. xi.

dangers. 'In returning from Malacca to Goa,' he writes to the fathers at Rome, 'I met with great perils. For three days and nights the ship was exposed to the most fearful storm I ever remember to have witnessed. When the tempest was at its height, I turned to God and pleaded with Him the intercession of our fathers, our spiritual friends, and all faithful Christians, between us and the impending danger. Then, invoking all the spirits of the Blessed, I particularly appealed to Peter Favre.'[5] And from that time he began the practice of inserting in the Litany of the Saints, which he was in the habit of reciting almost every day, *Sancte Petre Faber, ora pro nobis*—'Holy Peter Favre, pray for us.'[6] So, by the providence of God, hardly was Favre dead before he was venerated at Rome by St. Ignatius, at Gandia by St. Francis Borgia, and in India by St. Francis Xavier.

[5] *Epist. S. Franc. Xav.* lib. iv. cap. 8. [English edition, *Life and Letters of St. Francis Xavier*, vol. i. p. 419.]
[6] Bartoli, *Mem. Istor.* lib. i. cap. 20; Cienfugos, *Vita di S. F. Borgia*, lib. i. cap. 18.

CHAPTER XXXVI.

Veneration of Favre in Savoy.

BUT the place where the veneration and worship of Blessed Peter Favre spread and increased more than anywhere was Savoy, and above all his native town, Villaret. On the 1st and 2nd of October, in the year 1596, D. Peter Critan, the curé of Thonon, D. Justus Balliat, the curé of Sixt, and D. John Fournier, curé of the Great Bornand, drew up a little process, in which they summoned five witnesses who had known Father Favre, to give their testimony as to the childhood and the reputation for sanctity of the servant of God. All of them in their depositions invariably speak of Favre as 'the Saint,' or 'Blessed,' and desire that this fact should be noted as having been a thing constantly done for some time throughout the Great Bornand and the neighbourhood.

Together with the title of 'Blessed,' and the veneration appertaining to it, various kinds of public *cultus* were introduced, with the cognizance of the bishops and ordinaries of the diocese. The Blessed Father had only been dead sixteen years, when the little room in which he was born was made into a chapel, and the Vicar General of the Bishop of Geneva granted faculties for the celebration of Mass there. The original decree of the Episcopal Court is still extant. The following is a literal translation from the Latin—

'We give permission for the holy sacrifice of the Mass to be celebrated in the chapel of Villaret, in the parish of St. Jean de Sixt, lately built by the Rev. John Favre, priest, and by the honourable John Favre, doctor of medicine, in honour of God and of the holy Apostles Peter and Paul, and in memory of the Reverend Father Peter Favre, companion of the founder of the Society of Jesus, who was a native of the above place: provided that the altar be a portable one, and that nothing be done to the prejudice of the curé of the place as to the feast of St. John the Baptist.

'S. DECOMBA, Vicar-Substitute.[1]

'Annecy, August 16th, 1561.'

The chapel was dedicated as stated in the document, in honour of the Apostles St. Peter and St. Paul, and in memory of Father Favre, for, at that time, it was the custom in Savoy to dedicate chapels and altars to more than one saint. But as a matter of fact, thenceforward down to the present day, the title of the Apostles was altogether dropped, and it never was nor is it known except as the chapel of the Saint of Villaret, or of Blessed Peter Favre.

One of the two founders, the Dr. Favre, left his own country and settled at Janville, a city of the province of Champagne, in France. He there heard that God was working many miracles by the intercession of His blessed servant, and learning that the room at Villaret, which had come to be venerated by his means, was in a very bad condition, he resolved to return, after an absence of thirty-nine years, to his native place, in order entirely to rebuild and beautify the chapel. Accordingly, in the year 1600, he undertook that journey of eighty leagues, which is the distance from Janville to Villaret, and immediately on his arrival he and that other relative of his again met, and having obtained possession of the

[1] From the original.

site of the poor cottage where Favre was born, they built upon it in his honour a little church, or public chapel. This is the statement of one of the witnesses in the Process of 1626—

'He says, moreover, that after the death of Father Favre, a chapel by the title of St. Peter was built in the village of Villaret, by Dr. John Favre, priest, and the paternal uncle of the deponent, and by the honourable John Favre, physician, both natives of the same place, on account of the great and daily increasing reputation of the Reverend Father Peter Favre. The said John Favre began building the chapel in the year 1600, he having returned from the province of Champagne, in France, where he had lived for thirty years without once revisiting his own country; and while the building was going on, the witness has frequently heard his uncle, John Favre, say that nothing would ever have brought him back to this country but the desire he had to build that chapel in honour of Blessed Peter Favre (for by that title he called him), because he saw that he was esteemed Blessed, and wrought great prodigies in every place he had visited.'[2] From which words we infer that as early as at that time, Father Favre was considered and venerated as Blessed, and believed to have worked numerous miracles, not only in Savoy, but in France and elsewhere.

After the rebuilding of the chapel, the devotion of the villagers and neighbouring inhabitants to the Blessed Father went on increasing. Great numbers of persons were induced to visit the oratory by the fame of the many graces by which God honoured the merits of His faithful servant, and these were not only people of low condition, but personages of noble birth and high rank. Antony Favre, the famous lawyer, President of the Senate of Chambery, and the intimate friend of

---

[2] Process of the year 1626.

St. Francis of Sales, paid several visits of devotion to the chapel, and had a Latin inscription of his own composition, in praise of the Blessed Father, carved thereon. But the person who most distinguished himself in this way was the noble Don Honoré d'Urfey, Marquis of Val Romey, Baron of Castle Morand, and lieutenant of the Duke of Mayne. We will hear him tell in his own words how and why he went from Thonon, where he commanded the forces of the Duke of Savoy, to visit the chapel of Villaret and to venerate the memory of Blessed Favre, to whom he was tenderly devoted. He writes thus to the Father Rector of the College of Chambery—

'I had read in the Life of the Blessed Ignatius that his first companion, the Blessed Peter Favre, was a native of a place called Villaret, in the diocese of Geneva, and being at Thonon I was smitten with a great wish to render the honour due to the birthplace of so great a saint. I was told that it is very near to this, and this morning I went there with the curé of this place, who is much attached to your holy Society, to hear Mass in the devout chapel which has been built in the house of the servant of God. On my arrival, I reflected how holy a place that must be which had witnessed the birth of this great friend of God, and my conscience so smote me that I felt unable to enter that holy house till I had been eased of the burden of my sins; and thus, by the help of God and the holy patron of the place, I confessed and communicated, returning thanks to the Reverend Father for all the favours and benefits which I have received from that Society, of which he is the second founder. At the same time, I made a resolution to have a picture of that blessed saint painted, and placed on the altar. Now, as I cannot do this without your help, as I have no portrait of him, I have recourse to your Reverence, begging that you will get it painted by some good painter, and I will send the requisite sum immediately. I think the best way of representing him would be in an ecstasy, lifted in the air before the Blessed Virgin holding the Infant Jesus, for I have read in a deposition made by a pious lady, the mother of the curé I have mentioned, that she had frequently seen him in that state, and in this very place. I wish to say, however, that this is only a notion of my own, and that I leave it entirely to your choice. I also wished to have a lamp made to burn before the altar, and to make a permanent fund for keeping it up. But the aforesaid curé thinks it would be better to establish a solemn High Mass, which the priests from Thonon shall be bound to go every year in procession to sing. I do not like to determine anything on the matter without your wise counsel. But it is not so much for that reason that I am writing to you, as to congratulate all your holy Society for the consolation which I have received from visiting this holy place, and which no words can describe unless they are inspired by God. Will you then let me know which of these two plans you prefer? because if you incline to the Mass, I should think it ought to be said on the day of St. Peter's Chains, both because the Blessed Father's name was Peter, and because he passed from this life to everlasting bliss on that day. And since, in course of time, the remembrance of almost everything wears out, I will get an instrument drawn up before I leave, which I will sign, so that there may not be any doubt hereafter that this chapel is built on the site of the house of this great saint, and I hope that this will be an additional stimulus to the devotion of those who in future shall venerate this great servant of God. I will also, if you approve, have an inscription made on brass, to be placed over the entrance of the chapel, and all this shall be for the glory of God, Who delights to be honoured in His saints, and also as a testimony of the affection which I bear to this Blessed Father and to all your holy Society. And so, with a heart filled with gratitude for the benefits I have received therefrom, I kiss your hands, and commending myself to your prayers, of which I pray God that I may never make myself unworthy,

'I remain,

'Your most devoted servant and son in Christ,

'HONORE D'URFEY.[3]

'Thonon, the vigil of the Epiphany, 1618.'

All the Marquis' intentions, as regards the picture to be placed over the altar and the inscription in front of the chapel, were punctually carried out; and as to the Mass, he founded not one, but two High Masses, for which he contributed eight hundred florins. All these things were deposed on oath in the Processes by Dr. Peter Critan, the curé of Thonon, the same who went to Villaret with the Marquis. 'The illustrious lord, Honoré d'Urfey,' he says, 'being quartered at Thonon with the troops in the service of his Serene Highness, and hearing that there was at Villaret a chapel built upon the site of the house in which Father Favre was born, had a pious desire to go there to hear Mass; and he begged me to accompany him and to say it. On our arrival, just as the Marquis was in the act of entering the chapel, he experienced a movement of intense awe, so that he did not dare to go further till he had made a general confession to me. Having done this, not only did he feel no return of that fear, but after assisting at Mass and communicating, his heart was so filled with consolation and devotion to Father Favre, that he called him Saint, and always continues

[3] Process at Annecy, 1869.

to call him so. Afterwards he gave eight hundred florins, currency of Savoy, to the aforesaid chapel, and on this foundation two Masses are solemnly sung there every year; one on the 1st of August, the day on which the Reverend Father Peter Favre died, and the other on Whit Tuesday. He also sent to the said chapel a large brass plate, which cost a hundred ducats, on which was engraved an inscription in gold letters, stating that it had been the house of the Blessed Peter Favre, for by that title he speaks of him. Lastly, he presented an oil painting representing the Blessed Virgin with her Divine Child in her arms, and Father Favre kneeling at their feet, in the act of taking a lily from the hand of the Infant.' The following is the inscription put up by the Marquis d'Urfey, according to the style of the times—

D · O · M · VIRGINIQUE · MATRI
HIC · QUONDAM · DOMUS · HUMILIS
DOMUS · NUNC · SANCTISSIMA
NE · MIRERIS · VIATOR
JAM · TUNC · DOMUS · ERAT · DEI · SANCTISSIMA
CUM · IN · EA · NATUS · EST · B · PETRUS · FABER,
FABER · INQUAM · ILLE
QUI · NON · SOLUM · B · IGNATII · LOYOLÆ
PRIMUS · SOCIUS · FUIT
ET · PRIMUS · PRÆDICATOR
ITA · UT
PETRUS · ISTE · FABER
ET · PETRA · ET · FABER
SOCIETATIS · JESU · VERE · DICI · POSSIT.

In this inscription it may be seen by every one that there is no mention made of the title of the Apostles St. Peter and St. Paul, but it is simply intimated that the chapel is dedicated to Blessed Peter Favre. And so, also, no picture was exposed on the altar for the veneration of the faithful but that of Blessed Favre.

This increase of worship was a great means of rekindling the devotion of the people to the Blessed Father. And indeed, far from slackening as time went on, it kept on increasing, and was propagated for more than two centuries throughout Savoy and elsewhere. Not only did the neighbouring parishes begin and continue the custom of going in procession from time to time to visit the chapel, but pilgrims and devout people came at all times of the year from a distance to venerate the Blessed Father and to fulfil vows made in thanksgiving. In the Processes the witnesses make deposition that the peasants of Villaret never go out in the morning to their work in the fields till they have knelt at the door of the chapel to pray and to ask the saint to bless them. Besides the perpetual Masses founded in his honour by Dr. Favre and the Marquis d'Urfey, the records of pastoral visitations prove that there were others to the number of several hundreds, and that the founders were not all inhabitants of the small village of Villaret, but also of neighbouring parishes. A great portion of these foundations was lost at the end of the last century, during the French Revolution, and the church itself, with all its sacred contents, was utterly destroyed by sacrilegious hands. In the year 1826, however, thanks to the exertions and piety of M. Etremont, the curé of St. Jean de Sixt, it was rebuilt, and restored to the devotion of the faithful. This venerable priest, with the assistance of a few other benefactors, contributed as much as he was able to the restoration of the building, the erection of the altar, and the purchase of the vestments necessary for divine worship; and thus the veneration of the people for the Blessed Father once more flourished. Masses were once more celebrated, and the pilgrimages from the neighbourhood and elsewhere resumed.

All this is amply proved on oath by the witnesses in the last Processes drawn up by the Bishop of Annecy in 1869; the first of whom says—'I have always heard that there was a great veneration for this chapel, and I have seen it with my own eyes. I have seen the faithful in the neighbourhood come there to pray and to hear Mass. I have now and then seen some foreign priests who came there to say Mass; and I have heard that these marks of devotion were paid to Father Favre as "Blessed."' And the second witness, who is the curé of the parish, adds—' From the time of my being appointed to St. Jean de Sixt I have always heard that there has existed a constant veneration to this chapel; and I am led to believe the truth of this from what I have seen myself. There is a pilgrimage to this chapel, but it is not habitually practised except by the faithful of the place and of the adjoining parishes. From the observations I have been able to make since I have been here, I am led to believe that the object of these visits is to testify a special devotion to the Venerable Father Favre. I myself, personally, have often received offerings from the faithful of the parish for Masses to be celebrated in the chapel of Villaret, or elsewhere, in honour, as they said, of the Blessed Peter Favre.'[5]

In 1699 a second chapel, or, more correctly speaking, an entire hospital with a chapel attached, was dedicated to Blessed Peter Favre in the same city of Annecy, where the bishops of Geneva resided. M. Christoval Joseph Gautier, a citizen of Annecy, bequeathed a valuable inheritance for the foundation of a hospital, stipulating, among other dispositions, that the chapel and the entire hospital should be dedicated to the most Holy Trinity, the Blessed Virgin, the Blessed Amadeus, Duke of Savoy, St. Gautier Abbot, and Blessed Peter

[4] Process at Annecy, 1869.   [5] *Ibid.*

Favre of the Society of Jesus, and that a picture should be painted and placed on the altar of the chapel, and two on the credence tables, representing their figures; and concluding with the request that the Bishop of Geneva, or his Vicar General, would ratify and confirm this deed. The testator's written document, drawn up by a notary, is preserved in the archives of Annecy, together with the recommendation of the bishop's pro-curator-fiscal and the ratification and approval of the Rev. D. Joseph Falcaz, doctor of the Sorbonne, canon and vicar general of the diocese of Geneva.[6] Here, then, we see two public oratories consecrated, with the approval of the bishops of the diocese, to the honour and worship of Blessed Peter Favre, one at his native place, Villaret, and the other at Annecy; in both of which his picture was exposed for public veneration.

CHAPTER XXXVII.

St. Francis of Sales and Peter Favre.

WHAT greatly aided in the propagation and increase of the honour and worship of Blessed Peter Favre throughout Savoy, was the example of the saintly Bishop and Prince of Geneva, Francis of Sales. He had a very great devotion to Favre, and not only did he honour him with the title of 'Blessed,' but he exerted himself in every possible way to make others know and venerate him. In the year 1604 he was unable personally to visit the parishes of the Great Bornand, and therefore he sent Dr. Peter Critan, the

[6] Positio de Cultu Summ. addit.

curé of Thonon, to Villaret, to visit and arrange, in his name, everything belonging to the oratory, or public chapel, erected in honour of Blessed Favre. The authentic record of this visitation is still preserved at Villaret. It is as follows—

'On the 15th of January, 1604, I, Peter Critan, a citizen of Thonon, did, by commission of my lord and father in Christ, Mgr. Francis of Sales, Bishop and Prince of Geneva, visit the chapel of St. Peter founded by the MM. Favre in the village of Villaret, on the identical spot where once stood the house of the Reverend Father Peter Favre, one of the first founders of the Reverend Jesuit Fathers. This chapel is excellently well built, and furnished with chalices, missals, vestments, and very precious relics. Before leaving, I charged the above-named gentlemen, the founders, in the name of my lord the bishop, to set about the completion of whatever they considered remained to be done in the aforesaid chapel. To preserve the memory of so great a father in his native place, we purpose representing in the chapel the life of the said father, of the first Jesuits, and of the first founders of that holy Society;[1] and also providing everything requisite for the divine sacrifice, and I attest this by affixing my signature and seal to this paper.

'JUSTE BALLIAT, curé of Villaret.
'PETER CRITAN, citizen of Thonon, and deputy of my Most Reverend Lord Bishop.'[2]

[1] It seems that M. Critan intended having the events of Favre's life and those of other saints of the Society painted on the walls of the chapel. It was, indeed, the custom in Savoy at that time to represent on canvas in the churches the acts of the saints most venerated there, as St. Francis of Sales himself bears witness, in a letter of his dated September 16th, 1609.
[2] Proc. fol.

Three years later, when the holy bishop was at Thonon, he experienced great consolation at reading the Process, made in 1596, on the life and reputation for sanctity of Favre, and, as it was not of sufficient authority (having been made by three curés without competent jurisdiction), he heard the witnesses again himself, and approved of the deeds. Then, making his visitation at St. Jean de Sixt, he determined to consecrate the altar of the chapel at Villaret, where his predecessor had only allowed a portable altar. The function was very solemn, and lasted three hours. The Lords of Alex, and all the parishes of the valley of the Great and Little Bornand assisted at the procession. After the consecration the saint preached to a large congregation, dwelling, with the tenderest affection, on the virtues, merits, and holy life of Blessed Favre; and he has left a brief notice of all this in the sixteenth chapter of the *Introduction to a devout life*, which he published in the July of the following year, 1608, where he says—' It was a great consolation to me last year to consecrate an altar in the birthplace of that blessed man, the little village of Villaret, situated among our wildest mountains.'

This visitation of the chapel of Villaret is also mentioned by Charles Auguste de Sales, in his Life of his saintly uncle, in the seventh book of which he says—' On the 9th (of October, 1607) he visited the parishes of our Lady in the Great Bornand, and of St. Jean de Sixt, and the chapel built in honour of the Blessed Father Peter Favre, the first priest, theologian, and companion of St. Ignatius of Loyola, the founder, of the Society of Jesus; he would also see his relations, and the house where he was born, and he said many beautiful things in praise of that truly great man.'[3]

[3] Process, 1869.

Father Nicolas Polliens, the Rector of the College of Chambery, had sent the holy bishop a copy (as I believe) of the 'Memorial' written by Blessed Favre, and the saint, after he had read it, returned it with a letter, which was submitted to the appointed judges, and by them acknowledged in due form as authentic, and inserted in the Process of 1626. It breathes a spirit of the tenderest devotion to the Blessed Father, and we here give a translation of it.

'*To the Reverend Father in our Lord, Father Nicolas Polliens, of the Society of the Holy Name of Jesus.*

'Very Reverend Father,—

'It is high time for me to return you the little book concerning the holy life of our Blessed Peter Favre. I have faithfully refrained from copying it, as, when you sent it to me, you spoke of it as being, for the present, a thing exclusively reserved for your Society. I should very much like, however, to possess a copy of so holy a history, and that, too, of a saint to whom I am—as for many reasons I am bound to be—greatly attached, for my memory is not sufficiently good to retain the details of what I read; I only carry away a general impression. I cannot but believe that the Society will resolve to gain for this first companion of its founder the honour which it has already secured for the rest, for although his life cannot furnish such copious matter to the biographer as those of some others, both from its shortness, and because in those days they did not take note of all that passed; still, what we do possess is full of the sweetest honey of devotion. The good M. Favre, our doctor in this city, has lately discovered in the Chartreuse of the Sepulchre, an autograph letter of this Blessed Father, which I have had the happiness of seeing and kissing. In conclusion, I thank you for your charity in kindly communicating to me what you have done, and I beg you to continue to remember me in your prayers, for I am, with all my heart, your humble and very affectionate brother and servant,

'FRANCIS, Bishop of Geneva.[4]

'January 10th, 1612.'

In the year 1612 the *Life of Favre*, written in Latin by Father Nicolas Orlandini, was published at Lyons. The printer, Pierre Rigaud, well knowing the affection with which the Bishop of Geneva regarded the servant of God, dedicated it to him. It was soon afterwards translated into French, and the saint procured a great many copies, which he dispersed through his diocese. Lastly, we must not omit a circumstance, which clearly shows how far the holy bishop went in his respect, veneration, and devotion towards Father Favre. There was at Thonon a congregation or society of priests, called Altarians, all devoted by their rule to their own sanctification, and to the spiritual culture of the people by Apostolic ministrations. Each lived in his own house, and they met, from time to time, for the purpose of consulting together as to their method of working. St. Francis of Sales persuaded them to live in community, and gave them rules and laws for preserving and increasing their spiritual fervour, and in order to encourage them still more in their labours for souls, he not only put Blessed Peter Favre before them as a model, but declared him patron of their holy society. These rules, placed under his protection as titular patron, and sealed by St. Francis of Sales, and confirmed by his successor, were laid before the judges

[4] Process, 1626.

in the Process of 1626, by Dr. Peter Critan, as he himself affirms in these words—

'The said respondent then added, in further proof of the reputation for sanctity enjoyed by the said Reverend Father Favre, that the late Blessed Mgr. Francis of Sales, of happy memory, and also the present Most Reverend John Francis of Sales, his brother, and most worthy successor, gave their approbation to the laws and rules for the good performance of the cure of souls, and of the divine offices, which are established in the said parish church of Thonon, under the patronage of the Reverend Father Peter Favre, which laws and rules he has laid before us, and shown us to be signed by the aforesaid most reverend bishops, and sealed with the great seal of the diocese.'[5]

All the successors of St. Francis of Sales in the episcopal see of Geneva and Annecy followed his example. Not only did they tolerate the many marks of public worship paid to Blessed Favre, but they greatly kindled the devotion of the people by personally visiting the chapel of Villaret, and praying before the picture of the Blessed Father. In 1626 Mgr. John Francis of Sales ordered an authentic Process to be drawn up, in which all the acts of public worship and veneration paid to the Blessed Father are deposed to by many witnesses. When Mgr. Michael Gabriel de Rossillon visited the parish of St. Jean de Sixt, in 1705, he gave his approbation to the vow which the inhabitants of Villaret had made to keep the 1st of August as a day of abstinence from work and a high festival, and that, not on account of the feast of St. Peter's Chains, which is very little known in that

[5] Process, 1626.

part of the country, but for the greater honour of Blessed Favre; all the more because, for more than a century, it had been the custom to sing High Mass on that day in the chapel of the Blessed Father, according to the foundation made by the Marquis d'Urfey.

To be brief, all the witnesses examined in the last Process of 1869 are agreed that the bishops of the diocese not only did not prevent, but constantly promoted the public and ecclesiastical *cultus* paid to Blessed Peter Favre, both before and after the decrees of Urban VIII. We will quote but two. The first says—

'I never heard of any opposition on the part of the diocesan authority to these tokens of public and ecclesiastical veneration paid to the Blessed Father by the faithful, either before or after the decrees of Urban VIII. in 1634.'[6]

And the second adds—

'I know of no act proceeding from the diocesan authority condemning the various marks of public and ecclesiastical *cultus* paid to the Reverend Father Favre. Prior to the decrees of Urban VIII., both St. Francis of Sales and his brother and successor, John Francis, had implicitly approved of the said worship by placing the association of the priests, called "Altarians," under the patronage of Blessed Favre. After the decree of Urban VIII., the said veneration seems to have been implicitly approved by the visits of devotion successively made by the bishops in the course of their pastoral visitations, as I have already said in my replies to former questions.'[7]

[6] Process at Annecy, 1869. [7] *Ibid.*

Not only the bishops, first of Geneva and then of Annecy, but the other bishops in the neighbourhood, united in proclaiming and venerating Father Peter Favre as Blessed. Mgr. John Peter Camus, Bishop of Belley, the intimate friend and associate of St. Francis of Sales, preached a course of sermons during the octave of St. Ignatius, in 1622, in the Church of the Society of Jesus, at Chambery; and on the 1st of August, taking his subject from the feast of St. Peter's Chains, and the anniversary of the death of Favre, which both occur on that day, he combined the praises of St. Peter the Apostle, of St. Ignatius, and of Blessed Favre in his discourse. 'On this same day,' he said, 'another Peter was loosed from the chains of this mortal life, on whom, after St. Ignatius, the Society of Jesus may be said to have been founded. He was a son of thine, O Savoy, a fellow-citizen of yours, my dear hearers; at once the honour and glory of the diocese of Geneva. I speak of the Blessed—yes, I will call him so, for his virtues entitle him to the honour—the Blessed Peter Favre, the first priest, the first preacher, the first theological professor of the Society of Jesus, and the first companion of its founder, St. Ignatius.'[8] And he continues, all through the sermon, to combine the praises of the three, according to his thesis, describing the labours endured by Father Favre in defence of the Church, which is founded on the Apostle St. Peter, and in propagating and making glorious the Society of Jesus, instituted by St. Ignatius, and exalting the many virtues which raised him to so high a degree of sanctity, by which he finally merited the glory of the Beatified.

[8] *Panegyrics on St. Ignatius of Loyola*, Panegyric vii. Lyons, 1623.

CHAPTER XXXVIII.

The last Process.

In conclusion, all that remains for the completion of this subject is to quote the minute testimony recently given by the best-informed inhabitants of Villaret as to the antiquity, publicity, and legitimate character of the worship rendered by them and their ancestors to Blessed Peter Favre.

'We, the undersigned inhabitants of the village or the neighbourhood of Villaret, in the parish of St. Jean de Sixt, in the diocese of Annecy, having just heard the holy Mass in our chapel by the Rev. Silvain Vittoz, curé of the Little Bornand, in the same diocese, give the following testimony, which we are ready to confirm by oath—

'I. We declare that there is, in the village of Villaret, a public chapel which has always been called, by our fathers and ourselves, the chapel of St. Peter Favre, the Jesuit. A constant and unanimous tradition fixes the date of its building at twelve or fifteen years after the death of the aforesaid Saint, or Blessed, Peter Favre. The same tradition has always witnessed, that it was built by the relations of the saint on the ruins and the site of the house in which the said Blessed Peter Favre was born. This chapel having been plundered, and almost destroyed, by wicked men during the French Revolution of 1793, it was rebuilt by the care and the offerings of our families in 1826.

'II. We are also able to declare, having heard it from our ancestors as well as from persons not belonging to our country, that a Mass, founded by bequests made in this and neighbouring parishes, is celebrated weekly in this chapel. The same tradition also relates that after the building of this chapel—that is to say, after more than three centuries—some of the faithful, at a great distance from Villaret, among whom were residents in the episcopal city, more than seven leagues off, very often came to have Mass said in this chapel, both to implore the protection of our saint, Peter Favre, and to thank him for blessings which he had obtained for them.

'III. Our ancestors always declared that this devotion was begun immediately after the building of the chapel by those who had known the saint either in his childhood, or in a visit of a few days which he paid to his native place when he was a holy priest, before whom they fell on their knees and prostrated themselves, as they always related.

'IV. We declare openly and most positively, that there has always been a very lively and fervent devotion to the aforesaid Blessed Father in our village; in proof of which, we have heard by oral tradition, that our fathers never used to go to work in the fields in the morning without first kneeling in the chapel, or on its threshold, to recite some little prayer by which to dedicate the day to him.

'V. There is a constant tradition that a great number of pilgrims, men and women, priests, nobles, lawyers, soldiers, &c., have been seen thronging from all parts both of our own and of the neighbouring dioceses, to venerate the chapel and picture of Blessed Peter Favre. Many of them went to confession before hearing Mass, in order that they might communicate in the said chapel.

'VI. We have heard, both from the lips of foreign pilgrims and from the witness of our fathers, that during the episcopate of St. Francis of Sales, and that of his immediate successors, processions of whole parishes, carrying blessed banners, were seen to come to the chapel of Villaret.

'VII. We feel it our duty to declare that not only in Villaret, but in adjoining villages and parishes, the name of "Saint" and of "Blessed" has always been bestowed on our fellow-citizen, Peter Favre. This public opinion acquired additional strength from St. Francis of Sales having given him the title, in his work on the *Introduction to a devout life*. After reading the sixteenth chapter of this book, which is to be found in all our households, it was not possible for our fathers to give Peter Favre any title but that of "Blessed." We have, all of us, from our childhood, read or heard read those words written by St. Francis of Sales more than two centuries and a half ago—"Last year I had the consolation of consecrating an altar in the little village of Villaret, the place where it was God's will that this blessed man should be born."

'VIII. We declare that a great number of prodigies, and especially of miraculous cures, have at all times been ascribed to the intercession of the saint invoked in the chapel. Our fathers have assured us that the sacrilegious hands of the Iconoclasts of 1793 destroyed many *ex voto* offerings, among which were the crutches left in the chapel by a peasant as evidence of his cure; and that the same profane hands took down and tore the picture of the Blessed Father, which had been over the altar for two centuries.

'IX. We affirm that ever since St. Francis of Sales, the bishop of this diocese, preached the panegyric of the saint, previous to consecrating the altar, all the bishops of the diocese, when making a visitation of our parish church, have come to pray in this chapel, which is a league distant from the Church of St. Jean; and many of the undersigned, since the restoration of the chapel in 1826, have seen four of our bishops in succession come to pray before the picture of St. Peter Favre.

    'JOHN BAPTIST ANTHOINE,
    'CLAUDE CHOVEX,
    'DOMINIC FAVRE,
    'ISIDORE FAVRE,
    'FRANCOIS MISSILIER,
    'JOSEPH LARVAZ,
    'AUGUSTE LETHUILLE,
    'JOSEPH FAVRE,
    'MAURICE DUPONT,
    'N. DUPONT,
    'N. LAMBEL, Secretary of the Commune.

'Villaret, feast of SS. Fabian and Sebastian, January 20, 1872.

'And I, the undersigned Maria Bernard, parish priest of St. Jean de Sixt, declare that the preceding signatures are authentic and original; and likewise that all the undersigned witnesses are honourable and religious men, some of them of much piety. And hereto I add my signature.

           'MARIA BERNARD.

'Villaret, 1872.'

CHAPTER XXXIX.

Graces and Miracles.

God Himself was pleased to add fresh lustre to the sanctity and worship of Blessed Peter Favre, by working many miracles through his intercession. Some of these were sworn to on oath in the Processes, others were related by credible witnesses, and in quoting them we shall frequently make use of the simple and truthful language in which they are reported in the original depositions.

Dr. Peter Critan, being questioned whether he ever knew or heard of any one who had recourse to the prayers and intercession of Father Favre after his death, and whether by these means graces had been obtained and miracles wrought, makes answer and deposes, 'that as he was returning, on the 15th of February, 1625, from Annecy, where he had been to learn from the Most Rev. Mgr. the Bishop of Geneva, when he would be pleased to make his general visitation at Thonon, he was riding past the place called Les Peirasses, near Thonon, when the night was pretty far advanced, when he suddenly remembered a dream which he had had the night before, in which dream he seemed to see a religious of the Society of Jesus, whom he believed to be the Blessed Father Peter Favre, to whom he has always been greatly devoted, following in this the example of his mother, Madame Wilhelmina d'Arenthon, who used often to tell him that she obtained many graces by the merits and intercession of the said father. Now, as he was thinking on this dream of his, his horse fell with him, and struck violently against some sharp points of a rock. In falling he invoked Blessed Favre, and it seemed to him that he fell close to him. Certain it is that he was in no way hurt by the fall, although his head and side struck against those hard rocks, and he remained lying there for some time head downwards. There were travelling with him from Annecy, M. George Gerface, Maurice de la Thullie, and Mdlle. Claude Fournier, all of whom thought he was dead, and were utterly amazed at seeing him safe and sound, with no other harm done but the fright. And he believes that he was preserved in this danger by the merits of Blessed Peter Favre.'[1]

The Marquis Honoré d'Urfey, who has been mentioned several times, suffered, after his first visit to Villaret, from so severe an inflammation of the eyes, that he was on the point of losing his sight altogether. He had recourse with all confidence to the help of Blessed Favre, and the result was a complete cure. Being very grateful for the benefit he had received, he resolved to return as a pilgrim, on foot, to the chapel of Villaret, there to offer due thanks to his benefactor, and to pay his vow, as is attested by M. André Trombet, citizen of Thonon—

' He says further, that about three years ago, the Lord Marquis d'Urfey came on foot to this city of Thonon, accompanied by some gentlemen and pages, and by a hermit father, that they were all on foot, and that the Marquis had his lodging in the house of the deponent, who was much surprised, and asked some of his suite the reason of his coming. They told him that the Marquis had come there, as a pilgrim, to visit the chapel of Blessed Peter Favre, as an act of thanksgiving for a favour which he had received through the intercession of

[1] Process of 1626.

the said Blessed Peter Favre, which was his being cured of a bad inflammation of the eyes. Afterwards, deponent heard all this from the said lord marquis, who gave him the account that night after supper. Next morning, the Marquis, with all his suite, went to the chapel of Villaret, accompanied by the curé and some of the other principal persons of Thonon, who related on their return, that all these gentlemen had confessed and communicated in the said chapel.'[2]

Peter Vacheran declares, 'That he had gone one day to cut wood on the mountain of Thonon, to which place he belonged, when, finding a part of the road very much broken up, he set about making it level by filling up the crevices with stones and earth. Whilst he was digging out earth under a large mass of what he believed to be solid rock, it chanced that this mass, which measured about eighteen feet square and more than two high, burst up from the surrounding earth, falling upon him, so that only his head and left arm were free. He lay five hours in this condition, crying aloud on God and man for help. At the end of that time some comrades of his came by that way, and quickly removed the stone and carried him home, with all his body bruised and in pain. He was three weeks in bed, and when he left it he found himself unable to move, except by supporting himself on crutches. He was advised by the priest, Peter Critan, to go to Villaret, and to hear the Mass said on the 1st of August in the chapel of Blessed Favre. He managed as well as he could to go there on horseback, and recommending himself to the Blessed Father with his whole heart, he found himself cured by the end of the Mass; and as a perpetual remembrance of the miracle, he left his crutches hanging in the chapel.'

[2] Process of 1626.

Pernette de la Motte declared that she had a little daughter named Claude, two years and a half old, who fell into the fire, and was much injured in the eyes and face. The poor mother, fearing that Claude would become quite blind as she had not been able to open her eyes once for nine days, betook herself with great confidence to the intercession of St. Peter of Villaret, making a vow to have a thanksgiving Mass said in the chapel of Villaret. No sooner had she made the vow than the little girl was cured, and recovered her sight. When the mother was asked what St. Peter she meant when she spoke of making a vow to St. Peter, she replied that she meant that St. Peter who had been a native of Villaret and a religious of the Society of Jesus, whom she had often heard that he was 'Blessed;' and she is convinced that her child's cure was owing to his merits and his prayers to God.[3]

The miracles which we have here described are those the reports of which are given in the old Processes. We will add some others which have happened lately and are inserted in the Process of 1869. A young man of St. Jean de Sixt, named Auguste Larvaz, had fallen desperately ill. He was given over by the doctors, and his death was expected from hour to hour. His father, who was in the greatest affliction, reanimated his faith and invoked Blessed Favre, promising to have a Mass said in the chapel of Villaret. The grace followed close upon the vow, and the young man was cured at that instant.[4]

A lady, Josephine Dubourial by name, belonging to the parish of St. Jean de Sixt, deposed on oath that a married sister of hers in Paris, who was on the point of death, was cured at the moment when she made a

---

[3] Process of 1626; eighth witness.
[4] Process of 1869, part iii. fol. 16.

vow to have a Mass said in the chapel of Blessed Favre.⁵

Rose Perillat Charlat, of Villaret, a woman of sixty, had lost the use of her limbs from incurable paralysis. Not being able to support herself on crutches, she was compelled to remain helplessly sitting, or lying in bed. At length she was conscious in her heart of a firm conviction that, by invoking the intercession of Blessed Peter Favre, she should be cured. She accordingly began a novena of prayers, and determined to go each day to hear Mass in the chapel of the Blessed Father. Her neighbours, knowing her pious intentions, willingly offered to carry her to the sanctuary in their arms, but she refused, and insisted on going by herself, though with the greatest difficulty, crawling on her hands and knees. On the last day of the novena, after having renewed her supplications to the Blessed Father, she rose up perfectly well and with the free use of her limbs, and as long as she lived she never had any return of her malady. The miracle was attested in the presence of witnessses by her nephew, John Paul Perillat.⁶

Another member of the same family, Frances Mary Perillat, a child of six, paralyzed from her birth, was carried by her parents to Blessed Peter's chapel, and there she said with a loud voice, ' My blessed St. Peter, give me the use of my legs.' On the 1st of August the mother had a Mass said in the chapel, and at that very time her daughter was cured, and was seen walking and running about like other children of her age, to the great astonishment of all.⁷

In the parish of the Great Bornand, about half an hour's walk from Villaret, a woman, forty-one years of age, named Frances Suize, told the Abbé Antoine Perret, the principal priest, that from twelve years of age she

---

⁵ Process of 1869, part iii. fol. 16.   ⁶ *Ibid*.   ⁷ *Ibid*.

had been almost entirely blind, and had her eyes constantly bandaged, not being able to bear the light. Her mother made her pray to Blessed Peter Favre, and took her to the chapel of Villaret, where she entirely recovered her sight, which ever since continued to be excellent.[8]

Euphrosyne Blanchet, whose maiden name was Perissin, and so descended, on the mother's side, from the family of Blessed Favre, had a son named Joseph, whose legs had been strangely deformed and contorted from his birth. When he was an infant she took him to the Carthusian Monastery of the Sepulchre, where she recommended him to God's mercy, and the result was a degree of improvement in his condition. At the age of five, however, the boy was still in very poor health. His nerves were in a very weak state, and he suffered so severely from pains in the loins, that he could not walk without great discomfort. The good mother, accompanied by her sister and sister-in-law, took her child to Entremont, where many precious relics are exposed for veneration. She did not, however, receive the grace she desired, and the party returned towards the Great Bornand. As they were passing the chapel of Blessed Peter Favre at Villaret, the child stopped and asked to go in; but the women, who were anxious to get home before dark, paid no attention to him and went on. Little Joseph, however, sat down on the steps of the chapel, declaring that he would not stir till the door was opened. His mother then turned back, and taking him in her arms, showed him the altar and the picture of Blessed Peter through the window; but the child was not satisfied with this, and kept saying most positively, 'No, no, I will go in; I want St. Peter to cure me.' There was nothing for it but to get the key of the chapel.

[8] Process of 1869, part iii. fol. 16.

And no sooner had the child entered and remained for a short time before the altar and picture, than he sprang to his feet, exclaiming joyfully, 'This time I am really cured!' He then went out, and running before his mother and the other two women, he was the first to reach his home, full of glee and delight, and entirely healed of all his maladies.[9]

The same Euphrosyne, soon after her son's cure, fell dangerously ill, was given over by the doctors, and had received the last sacraments. Nevertheless she had recourse with great confidence to Blessed Favre, and recovered her health, contrary to all human expectation. She also declared that she had often heard her brother, Michael Perissin, who was a priest, say that he had never asked any favour in vain of Blessed Favre. And out of gratitude to his benefactor, he contributed largely to the restoration of the chapel built in Blessed Peter's honour at Villaret before setting out for India, where he went as Apostolic missionary.[10]

---

[9] Process of 1869, part iii. fol. 16. [10] *Ibid.*

CHAPTER XL.

The Immemorial 'Cultus.'

FOR more than three centuries, therefore, the servant of God had received in Savoy a public and ecclesiastical veneration, supported by the testimony of saints, by the sufferance and permission of the bishops, by the devotion and visits of great numbers of the laity, and, moreover, divinely confirmed by constant and numerous miracles wrought by the invocation of his name. Little or nothing of all this was known beyond Savoy, and the only ancient writer who makes any special mention of it is Father Daniel Bartoli, who gives a short *résumé* of what he had read in the Process, drawn up in 1626, by Mgr. John Francis de Sales, the immediate successor of his brother, the saintly bishop.[1]

It was the reading this very History of Bartoli's that kindled in me the desire of seeing and reading the ancient Process from which he quotes, and having, after a long search, happened to find a copy of it in the archives containing the acts of the Causes of God's servants belonging to the Society, I perceived, after reading it, that it contained sufficient proof to show that the Cause of Blessed Peter Favre ought to be reckoned in the number of those which are excepted from the decrees of Urban VIII., and therefore that it would not be difficult to obtain the confirmation of his veneration from the Apostolic See. All that remained to be proved

[1] Bartoli, *Istoria della Compagnia di Gesù, l'Italia*, lib. i.

was, that from that time to the present the fervour and devotion in the veneration paid to the servant of God as 'Blessed' had not failed. This could not be done without a new Process, in which the depositions of the witnesses and the documents referring to them should be collected. A request to this effect was made to Mgr. Claude Marie Magnin, Bishop of Annecy, who, having always had a great devotion to Blessed Peter Favre, very gladly furthered the desire, which he cherished as ardently as ourselves. Accordingly, he gave orders that a Process concerning the veneration paid to Blessed Peter Favre in Savoy should be immediately drawn up, and the acts were begun on the 23rd of June, 1869. Eight of the most credible witnesses were examined, and several documents collected by grave and learned persons.[2] The two ancient Processes of 1597 and 1626 were again acknowledged to be authentic, and lastly, all necessary care and diligence having been previously taken, Mgr. the Bishop solemnly published the following decision on the 23rd of July, 1869—

'In the name of Christ, we say, affirm, declare, pronounce, and definitively decree, that it is evident that from time almost immemorial there has been veneration, together with the title of Blessed, paid to the Venerable Father Peter Favre, priest of the Society of Jesus, and that from his death to the year 1634, in which the last decrees of Urban VIII. were published, only twelve years of the prescribed century are wanting, and it is also evidently among the cases excepted by Urban on two

---

[2] We must mention, as especially devoted to Blessed Favre, the Rev. D. Silvain Vittoz, curé of the Little Bornand, who had been occupied for many years in collecting and collating, with unwearied care, the most credible documents relative to the origin and continuance of the veneration, and we have to thank him in a great measure for the successful issue of the Process.

other grounds, namely, the writings of the saints, and the knowledge and sufferance of the ordinaries, which are proved from a very early period down to the present time. Wherefore we declare that this Cause is among those cases which are excepted by the said decrees concerning the absence of *cultus;* and, therefore, that there is in this case no infraction, but rather compliance with the aforesaid decrees,' &c.

It is impossible to describe the joyful excitement which pervaded the diocese of Annecy during the completion of the Process on the veneration of Blessed Favre, by the appointed judges. Father Antonine Maurel, who was appointed Vice-Postulator of the Cause, was received at Villaret, whither he went to collect accurate information, with so many and great demonstrations of joy, that I cannot describe them better than by quoting the original narrative inserted in the Process—

'On the 28th of June, 1869, Father Antonine Maurel, and M. Silvain Vittoz, the curé of the Little Bornand, had hardly begun to mount the hill, on the top of which is situated the Church of St. Jean de Sixt, when the ringers began to peal the bells, and the workmen to fire salutes, which were echoed far and near by the mountains. The curé and the mayor, together with the members of the council-general of the department, came to meet them, while, at the same time, the little bell of the chapel and the petards of Villaret answered those of St. Jean de Sixt, and bonfires were kindled on the crests of the neighbouring mountains. The chapel of Blessed Favre, which had been decked with flowers and garlands during the day, was illuminated all night, and all the village kept gala. The next day, the 29th of June, the bells were again rung, and salutes fired at daybreak, both at St. Jean de Sixt and at Villaret. The mayor and municipality conducted the two visitors into the chapel of Blessed Favre, which was completely filled, and surrounded by a crowd of at least five hundred persons. After the celebration of Mass, which was preceded and followed by other Masses, Father Maurel spoke to the assembled multitude, who were overflowing with joy and fervour, wishing in this manner to express their devotion to Blessed Favre, and their delight at the reopening of a cause so dear and so glorious to the whole country. In the evening, the father and the curé went to pass the night at the Great Bornand, after having made an excursion to Thonon. Everywhere there was a repetition of the same marks of piety and rejoicing, and the discharge of small mortars. On the following day, the 30th of June, the father was again obliged to preach in the parish church to a very numerous audience. It would be difficult to recount all the honours paid during these three days to the holy memory of Blessed Favre, and all the manifestations of hope and rejoicing made by all the parishes of those valleys.'[3]

At this time, a hundred and eighty-seven priests of the diocese were assembled at Annecy for the purpose of making the Spiritual Exercises, and they all signed a humble petition, which they sent to the Sovereign Pontiff, and which I will here quote, as a proof of their piety and devotion to Blessed Favre—

'Most Holy Father,—

'A Process has recently been drawn up, in the episcopal court of this diocese of Annecy, on the subject of the veneration paid from time immemorial to the servant of God, Peter Favre, of the Society of Jesus, a native of this diocese. And although we have

[3] Process of Annecy, part iii. fol. 14.

good hope, as this Process has been sent to the Sacred Congregation of Rites, that your Holiness will shortly enable us, by your approbation, to pay public veneration to the Venerable Father Favre, nevertheless we, the undersigned canons, parish priests, arch-priests, and priests, here assembled to make the Spiritual Exercises, prostrate at the feet of your Holiness, implore you, with all humility and earnestness, to lose no time in declaring, by Apostolical authority, that the aforesaid servant of God is numbered in the company of the "Blessed." We entreat you, most Holy Father, graciously to receive this our pious and most earnest request; and to grant to the diocese of Annecy, so devoted to the Holy See, the favour of being at liberty to invoke with all confidence this new patron so pleasing to God, the Father of all mercy and consolation. All we priests of the diocese of Annecy greatly wonder that this man of God has not already been placed in the list of saints; he who was the first companion of St. Ignatius of Loyola, the first priest and preacher of the divine word and the corner-stone of the Society of Jesus, the unwearied labourer in the Lord's vineyard, who was called and honoured as "Blessed" by St. Francis Xavier and St. Francis of Sales, and other men remarkable for sanctity, following St. Ignatius; who has always been so regarded, and publicly invoked and worshipped by the people, especially those of the valley in which his native place, Villaret, is situated. We entreat your Holiness to deign graciously to grant our petition, and by your supreme authority to approve of the veneration hitherto rendered to the servant of God, Peter Favre; and lastly, to give your Apostolical benediction to the undersigned priests, whose pride it is to declare themselves your Holiness' most devoted and affectionate sons.'[4]

[4] Summ. n. 14.

The Process, together with the documents collected in Savoy, having been sent to Rome, the Cause was laid before the Sacred Congregation of Rites on the 31st of August, 1872. Their Eminences the Cardinals, after having fully discussed the matter, declared that the case was one of those excepted by the decretals of Urban VIII. All this being related to his Holiness, Pius IX., he, on the 5th of September, confirmed the sentence of the Sacred Congregation of Rites, and sanctioned the public and ecclesiastical veneration paid to Blessed Peter Favre, as is shown in the decrees here annexed as the conclusion of this Life.

CHAPTER XLI.

Decree Approving and Confirming the Cultus.

DIOCESE OF ANNECY.

Confirmation of the Cultus paid to the Servant of God, Peter Favre, Professed Priest of the Society of Jesus, and first companion of St. Ignatius, commonly called 'Blessed.'

' IN Villaret, a village of Savoy, in what was formerly the diocese of Geneva, was born Peter Favre, one of those Apostolic men who shed a lustre on the beginnings of the glorious Society of Jesus. His childhood was passed in tending a small flock of sheep in his native place: afterwards he was the first of those companions in the University of Paris who devoted themselves to following Ignatius of Loyola in the way of perfection: the first, also, who, by command of the Sovereign Pontiff, Paul III., went to Germany, and there defended the pure doctrine of the Catholic faith and the divine authority of the Church, both by word of mouth and by his writings. He then traversed nearly all the provinces of Belgium, Spain, and Portugal; everywhere gathering abundant fruit in labouring in the field of the Gospel, and in keeping it free from the infection of heresy. At length, having, in the brief space of his life accomplished many great things, he rested from his labours by a blessed death, at the age of forty, on the 1st of August, 1546, at Rome, whither he had gone shortly before, out of obedience, although broken in health and worn out by labours. The marks of sanctity which he left behind him were so evident, and God Himself so plainly pointed them out, as has been credibly attested, by signs and miracles, that he began at once to be honoured, especially in his native place, by popular devotion and ecclesiastical veneration; and, shortly after his happy death, a public chapel was canonically erected at Villaret, on the site of the very house in which he was born; and in it the worship openly rendered to him from the beginning, continued to be vigorously kept up and propagated up to the present time. There was, also, not only the sufferance and permission of the bishops, but the testimony and authority of St. Francis Xavier and St. Francis Borgia, and most especially that of the holy Bishop of Geneva, St. Francis of Sales, who not only declared both by word and deed his very high opinion of Peter Favre's sanctity, but did all he could to promote his public veneration.

'In proof whereof, important and appropriate documents having been collected from different places, at the request of the Rev. Father Joseph Boero, Postulator-General of the Causes of God's servants belonging to the aforesaid Society of Jesus, the Very Reverend Bishop of Annecy, in whose jurisdiction the village of Villaret now is, drew up a legal Process, and having considered the various reasons therein specified, gave judgment on the case as one excepted from the prescriptions of the General Decrees.

'All these facts having been communicated to the Sacred Congregation of Rites ; at the request of the aforesaid Very Reverend Bishop and of the Clergy of Annecy, as also of the Postulator, and of the entire Society of Jesus, the undersigned Cardinal, Prefect of the said Sacred Congregation and "Relator" of this Cause, did at the ordinary meeting held this day at the Vatican, propose the following doubts, *i.e.*, *Whether the judgment delivered by the Most Reverend Bishop of Annecy on the veneration paid to the aforesaid Servant of God, as being a case excepted by the decree of Urban VIII. of holy memory, should be confirmed in the case and for the object in question ?* Whereupon, the Very Eminent and Reverend Cardinals of the Sacred Congregation of Rites, after having with mature deliberation weighed and discussed each and all of the circumstances adduced in this Cause, and after hearing the Rev. Dr. Lorenzo Salvati, Coadjutor of the Promoter of the Holy Faith, returned the following rescript, that, *All things considered, this was one of the cases excepted from the decrees of Pope Urban VIII. of blessed memory.*

'August 31, 1872.

'All which, having been faithfully reported to his Holiness, Pope Pius IX., by the undersigned deputy of the Secretariat of the Congregation of Sacred Rites, his Holiness ratified the rescript of the Sacred Congregation, and confirmed the public and ecclesiastical veneration paid to Blessed Peter Favre, confessor.

'5th of September of the same year.

'✠ CONSTANTINE, Bishop of Ostia and Velletri, CARD. PATRIZI,
'*Prefect of the Sacred Congregation of Rites.*

'By Rev. D. Dominic Bartolini, *Secretary.*
'Joseph Ciccolini, *Deputy.*'

PART THE SECOND.

'MEMORIAL'

OR

SPIRITUAL DIARY OF BLESSED PETER FAVRE, OF THE SOCIETY OF JESUS.

BLESS the Lord, O my soul, and forget not all His benefits, Who redeemeth thy life from destruction, and crowneth thee with mercy and compassion, Who filleth thy desire with good things, and Who has forgiven and daily forgiveth all thy sins, and healeth all thy diseases, giving thee good hope that thy youth will be renewed as the eagle's. Give thanks ever, O my soul, and never forget the many benefits that our Lord Jesus Christ both has done thee and doeth thee every moment, through the intercession of His Blessed Mother, our Lady, and of all the saints of heaven, as well as of all who pray for thee in the Catholic Church. Adore, O my soul, the Heavenly Father, ever honouring and serving with all thy might, and all thy wisdom, Him Who with His love and mercy is so continually helping and strengthening thee. Adore thy Redeemer, our Lord Jesus Christ, Who, as the Way, the Truth, and the Life, with His grace alone teaches and enlightens thee. Adore the Person of thy Glorifier, the Holy Ghost, the Paraclete, Who by His kindly communication of Himself, renders thy body, soul, and spirit, pure, right, and good in all things.

In the year 1542, in the octave of Corpus Christi our Lord, I had a certain notable desire of doing for the future what up to that time I had omitted solely out of negligence and sloth; I mean, of noting down, with a view to their remembrance, some of the spiritual lights with which the Lord had favoured me, whether they tended to my improvement in prayer or in understanding or in any way of working, or to any other kind of spiritual help. Before, however, speaking of the future, it seemed good to note some points in my past life up to this hour, just as it presents itself to me now, and as I can recall my feelings in those days, together with any notable sentiments of thanksgiving, contrition, or compassion, or any other spiritual emotion raised within me by the Holy Ghost, or from admonition on the part of my own good angel.

1506—1509.

The first benefit, then, which I have noted with thanksgiving, was that in the Easter of 1506 our Lord brought me into the world, in the village called Villaret, in the diocese of Geneva, which was then very Catholic, that He vouchsafed me the grace of baptism, and that of being brought up by good, Catholic, and pious parents. Although they were peasants they had enough of this world's goods to aid me in all that was requisite for the salvation of my soul, conformably to the end of my creation. For they so brought me up in the fear of the Lord, that from my very childhood I began to have great understanding; but, what was a sign of still greater preventing grace, even in my seventh year I several times experienced special instincts of devotion, so that from that time forth our Lord on His part wished to take full possession of my soul as its Spouse. Oh, that I had been wise! Oh, that I had then been wise enough to welcome Him and to follow Him, and never to separate myself from Him!

1516—1517.

When I was about ten years old, I felt a certain desire to study, and being a shepherd, and intended by my father to live in the world, I could not rest, and I wept so much in consequence of the great wish I had to go to school, that my parents were obliged, contrary to their intention, to send me there; but when they saw plainly the fruit and the progress I made in my studies, they did not like, nor indeed were they able to prevent, my continuing them, especially as the Lord permitted that I was not fit for worldly affairs. My master was Peter Veillard, a man whose learning and life were so Catholic and holy, that he may be said to have made all the heathen poets and authors Christian, because he applied everything to the edification of youth in the holy and chaste fear of God.

1518—1524.

Hence it was that all we, his scholars, by means of the teaching and example of such a master, grew in the fear of God, and so, when I was twelve years old, I had certain stirrings of spirit to offer myself to the service of God; so that one day, in holiday time, when I was in a joyful mood, in a pleasant open country, feeling in my soul a great desire of purity, I promised to our Lord perpetual chastity. Oh, great mercy of God, Who wast my leader and guide, and wast pleased, from that time, to draw me to Thyself! Ah, why did I not know Thee well? O Holy Spirit, why did I not know at that time how to detach myself from all things to seek Thee, and to come to Thy school, since Thou didst invite me, preventing me with Thy blessings? Nevertheless, Thou hast made me Thine: Thou hast signed me with the indelible mark of Thy holy fear. And if Thou hadst permitted this, together with Thy other gratuitous gifts, to be taken from me, I should have shared the fate of those of Sodom and Gomorrha.

I went to that school for nine years, growing in age and in knowledge, but not so constantly in goodness of life and in custody of the eyes. And here I have to grieve greatly for the sins which I committed every day against my God, and I should have committed many others if the divine goodness had not permitted that, together with His fear, there should be aroused in my heart a certain inordinate desire of knowing and learning. For it was by this means that He removed me from my native place, where I was not able to serve Him wholly and duly. Blessed for ever be Thou, my Lord, for so great a kindness as Thou didst then show me, taking me away from the flesh and from my corrupt nature, and gradually drawing me to know and enjoy Thy Divine Majesty.

1525—1528.

In the year 1525, and the nineteenth of my age, I left my native place, and went to Paris. Call to mind, O my soul, the spiritual spurs with which the Lord pricked thy conscience in His fear, that is to say, the scruples and remorse with which the devil tormented thee, that thou mightest seek thy Maker, and without which neither would Father Ignatius have been able to move thee, nor wouldst thou have sought assistance from him, as it came to pass.

1529—1533.

In the year 1529, and the twenty-third of my age, on the 10th of January, I was made bachelor, and, after Easter, licentiate under Master John Pegna (now a doctor of medicine), in the College of St. Barbara. And now, may the divine goodness grant me a grateful memory to acknowledge His many corporal and spiritual favours which He bestowed on me in various ways in the course of these three years and a half, giving me such a teacher and such a companion as I found in that house, namely, Master Francis Xavier, who is now one of our Society of Jesus. In the same year Ignatius of Loyola, a Spaniard, came to be admitted into the aforesaid College of St. Barbara, and into the same room with us, as he intended to begin the course of philosophy by the next feast of St. Remigius, when I was to begin to lecture. For ever blessed be the Divine Providence, Who so ordered it for my good and salvation, that, having to teach the holy man I have named, I had first exterior and then interior intercourse with him, and living together, as we did, in the same room, at the same table, and of the same purse, he was my teacher in spiritual things, showing me the way to rise to the knowledge of the divine will. And in this way we became altogether one in our desires, and in the firm resolution to choose this life which we now lead in this Society, of which I am not worthy. May the divine clemency give me grace to remember and well consider the benefits which He granted me at this time by means of this man! —and especially of having first enabled me to know my conscience, and the temptations and scruples in which I had been for so long a time entangled, without finding a way to escape from them. These scruples arose from the fear that I had not, for a long time, made a good confession of my sins, and I was so tormented by these scruples that, to cure them, I would willingly have chosen to dwell in a desert and always to live on roots and herbs. As to the temptations, they consisted in vile and impure thoughts which were suggested by the evil spirit of fornication; which things I did not then know by spiritual light, but only by learning and letters. Ignatius then advised me to make a general confession of my whole life to Dr. Castro, and afterwards to confess, and receive the Sacrament of Communion, every eight days. He also gave me a daily examen of conscience, and for the present would give me no other spiritual exercises, although I had a great wish for them.

About four years passed in this way, and every day I made spiritual progress, to my own profit and that of others. During nearly all the time that I was at Paris, I was assailed in different ways by various temptations, sometimes of vainglory, sometimes of gluttony. As a remedy for the former, our Lord gave me a great knowledge of myself and of my defects, permitting me to search into them deeply with interior anguish; and thus, by His grace, He gave me great peace in this respect. As to the other temptation, of gluttony, I was never able to find rest till I made the Exercises, when I tasted nothing for six days, except when I received Holy Communion. I had many other temptations besides, such as dwelling on the faults of others, false suspicions, and rash judgments, in which also I was assisted by the Holy Spirit, my Comforter, Who was leading me to the highest degree of charity towards my neighbour. I also had scruples about almost everything, and many imperfections which I did not know till I was leaving Paris. The Lord then instructed me in various ways, giving me a remedy for much sadness which sprang from these causes, all which it would hardly be possible for me to recollect. This I can indeed say with truth, that I was never in any affliction, or temptation, or scruple for which I did not, either at the time, or shortly after, find the true remedy by the grace of our Lord, Who gave me grace to pray, and beg, and supplicate (which is a source of countless blessings), and made me know the diversity of affections and of spirits. For our Lord had left in me certain impulses which did not allow me to be tepid. But with regard to the knowledge and discerning of evil spirits and affections, as also with regard to those things which concerned myself and my neighbour, our Lord, as I have said, never, so far as I am able to judge, permitted me to be deceived, but always delivered me at the right time from those delusions by the illumination of the Holy Ghost, and of the holy angels. Having come to the end of the four years I have spoken of, and finding myself fixed in the resolution that I had made more than two years before, to follow Ignatius in poverty of life, and waiting for nothing but the end of my studies, and those of Ignatius, and Master Francis Xavier, and other companions who were of the same mind, I went to my native place to visit my relations, and stayed some months with my father—my mother having died before this time.

1534—1535.

In the year 1534, and the twenty-eighth of my life, having returned to Paris to finish the theological course, I made the Exercises, and received all the sacred Orders. I then said my first Mass on the feast of St. Mary Magdalene, my patroness, and that of all sinners. Herein are contained innumerable benefits which the Lord granted to my soul, in calling me to so high a rank as that of the priesthood, and giving me the grace to do all my actions for love of His Divine Majesty, and not from the worldly motive of acquiring temporal goods and honours, which had influenced me before I applied my mind to the rule of life given to me by our Lord by means of Father Ignatius. At that time I sometimes had a wish to be a physician, sometimes a doctor of laws, or of theology, now a master of a school, now a private priest, at other times a monk, according as I was moved by various affections. From all of which being, as I have said, delivered by the Lord, I resolved to be a priest wholly dedicated to His divine service in this high and perfect vocation, of which I acknowledge myself unworthy, and with which I shall never be able worthily to correspond with all the strength of my spiritual and corporal powers.

On our Lady's feast in the August of the same year, all of us, except Master Francis Xavier, having made the Exercises, we all went with one accord to the Church of St. Mary, at Montmartre, to make a vow there to go to Jerusalem, at the right time, and after our return to offer ourselves in obedience to the Sovereign Pontiff, and at once to begin to abandon our relations and everything but what was needful for the journey. The names of those of us who were together this first time, were Father Ignatius, Master Francis Xavier, and I Favre, Master Bobadilla, Master Laynez, Master Salmeron, and Master Simon (Master Le Jay had not yet come to Paris, and Master John and Paschase had not yet joined us). On the same day in the following year and the year after that also, we all went again to the same church to confirm the same determination, feeling every day greater spiritual profit; and on this last occasion of renewing our vows there were present Master Le Jay, Master Codure, and Master Paschase.

1536.

On the 15th of November, 1536, all we nine above-named left Paris, Master Ignatius having done so a year and a half before, and having gone to Venice where he was waiting for us, and where we arrived after Christmas. In this journey the Lord granted us so many favours that it would never be possible to write them down. We went on foot; we passed through Lorraine and Germany, where there were already several Lutheran and Zuinglian cities, such as Basle, Constance, and others. The season was winter, and very cold; and the war was still going on between the Kings of France and Spain: and from all these dangers the Lord delivered us. We reached Venice in good health and spirits, and four of us went to the Hospital of SS. John and Paul, and five to the Hospital of the Incurables, waiting till the season of Lent to go to Rome to ask permission of Pope Paul III. to make the journey to Jerusalem.

1537.

After Easter, in the year 1537, having obtained the Pope's permission, but not being able to start then, in consequence of certain hindrances, we dispersed ourselves in various places of the Venetian territory, determining to live there retired for three months, without attending to others, in order that such of us as were not priests might be better disposed and prepared for so great a ministry. Master Ignatius, I, and Master Laynez went to Vicenza, Master Francis Xavier, went with Salmeron to a place twelve miles from Padua, Master John and the Bachelor Hosius to Treviso, Master Le Jay and Master Simon to Bassano, Bobadilla and Paschase to Verona. After this time we were summoned, in the month of October, to Rome, where we three, who were at Vicenza, went.

1538.

In the year 1538, all our other companions having returned to Rome, and as we saw for that year the way was not open for us to go to Jerusalem, we obtained faculties from the Pope, empowering us, as Apostolic missioners, to preach the Word of God and to hear confessions everywhere. The patent was granted in the month of May by the Cardinal of Naples, who was then Legate of Rome. Would to God that I knew how to acknowledge, on my part, the very many favours which

He granted us all in that year, in which also we endured much opposition to our good intentions, principally from the Inquisition, which we ourselves induced diligently to take informations, and make known the truth. And, in effect, it did give a definitive sentence in our favour, notwithstanding many obstacles. It was also a notable favour, and as it were a foundation of the whole Society, that on our presenting ourselves in that same year to the Sovereign Pontiff, Paul III., as a holocaust, that he might see in what way we could serve Christ to the edification of our neighbour in perpetual poverty, being also prepared to go, in obedience to his Holiness, even to the farthest parts of the Indies, he graciously accepted us, and congratulated us on our good resolutions. For which I and the whole Society shall be ever bound to return thanks to Jesus Christ our Lord, for His having vouchsafed to declare by the mouth of His Vicar on earth (which is a very evident vocation), that He is well pleased with our service, and is willing to employ it for ever.

1539.

In the month of May of the year 1539, Master Laynez and I went, by order of the Pope, with Cardinal S. Angelo to Parma, and remained there till the month of September of the year 1540, gathering much fruit. Remember, O my soul, the favours thou didst receive in that city from God, Who produced so much fruit by our means, and that of Dr. Jerome Domenech, that is to say, by confessions, sermons, and other spiritual exercises. Neither will I be silent concerning my sickness which lasted nearly three months, beginning on the 25th of April, 1540, from which thou knowest what great fruits I was enabled to gain, according to the knowledge given to me by the Lord. Remember also how greatly I am indebted to Master Laurence and to Master Marino, in whose house I lay sick, and where so fair an opportunity was offered to me. Remember, too, how greatly thou wast stirred to devotion on the feast of SS. Peter and Paul, of St. John the Baptist, and of the Visitation of our Lady, to whom thou art so greatly indebted, and oughtest to preserve eternal remembrance of and gratitude to them.

1540.

In the same year, 1540, when I was by commission from his Holiness to go to Spain with Dr. Ortiz, he received a summons from the Emperor, and took me with him to Germany to the Diet of Worms, where we arrived on the 28th of October. Remember, O my soul, the remarkable devotion which our Lord gave thee on that day to the life of Christ and that of the Blessed Virgin, so as to commemorate them daily at the canonical hours; that is, the life of Christ beginning from the Incarnation to the Ascension, and that of our Lady from her Conception to her death. Remember also the notable consolations which our Lord gave thee at Worms in thy prayers, and the great light in discovering different methods of prayer, and of asking graces for thyself, for the living and dead, and especially for Germany. This year the Society of our Lord Jesus was founded, and confirmed by a Bull of his Holiness.

1541.

In the month of January of the year 1541, we went to Ratisbon, where the Imperial Diet was held. During the journey we had great consolations in various prayers and contemplations, many methods and much matter for prayer suggesting themselves to me while travelling, seeing, and hearing; such as asking of our Lord the grace that the archangel guardian of that province, together with all the guardian angels of its several towns might be propitious to us, and that the true Guardian, Jesus Christ, might assist us and provide for all the necessities of the inhabitants of each place, of the sinners there who were at the point of death, of the souls of the departed, and of those in any sort of affliction and tribulation. Again, while passing by mountains, fields, and vineyards, various methods suggested themselves to me of prayer with reference to the variety of these good gifts, so that they might be multiplied, and of rendering thanks in place of the owners, or of asking pardon for those who do not know how to acknowledge in spirit these goods, nor God from Whom they come. In like manner I invoked the saints who have the care of those places, begging them to do what the inhabitants do not know how to do, namely, to beg pardon, and give thanks for them, and to ask things necessary for them.

That same year I received countless other graces at Ratisbon. The first of these was that the Lord granted to me to effect great things in His service, especially as to the confessions of the nobility of the Imperial Court, and of the Duke of Savoy, my prince, who chose me for his confessor; which confessions produced much fruit, and were the beginning of much more, which was the result of the Exercises that were made by Spanish, German, and Italian personages, by means of whom nearly all the good which afterwards followed in Germany was accomplished. Besides, I also received other methods of prayer, as on the litanies, on the mysteries of Christ, and the Christian doctrine, in which I asked different graces answering to each of these methods. I also went over the three powers of the soul, the five senses, and the principal parts of the body; and the temporal benefits received, not only by myself, but also by other persons, living as well as dead, and I applied, moreover, the holy sacrifice of the Mass for that intention, that the aforesaid benefits might have their effect more perfectly. I also fell in with a book of the holy virgin, St. Gertrude, in which some of her particular devotions were written, and from them I learnt various methods of prayer to my very great profit.

In the same year our Lord granted me another very memorable favour, that is, that on the octave of the Visitation of our Lady, I made my solemn vows of profession at Ratisbon, before the high altar of the Church of our Blessed Lady, which is called the Old Chapel. I did this with great spiritual consolation, and with a great increase of strength to my soul in renouncing the goods which I had already renounced, in leaving the pleasures which I had already left, and in placing under entire subjection my own will which I had already made subject. The vows which I made were of poverty, chastity, and obedience to the Superior General of the Society, besides the vow of obedience which we all render to the Supreme Pontiff as to the missions. This profession I made before the Blessed Sacrament, just as I was about to communicate, according to the following form, a copy of which I sent to Master Ignatius, who had been elected General.

'I, Peter Favre, promise and vow to God our Lord, and to the Blessed Virgin, and to all the saints of heaven, to observe with their aid perpetual chastity, and perpetual poverty, and perpetual obedience to the Superior General of the Society of Jesus, and likewise to observe perpetual obedience to the Supreme Pontiff as to the missions; and all this I promise to observe in conformity to the constitutions and rules of this Society aforesaid. And this is my profession, and so I have made it, and such is the truth, and I make it again to our Lord God, and to the Blessed Virgin, and to you,

Master Ignatius of Loyola, as vicegerent of Christ and Superior General in the said Society, and in confirmation thereof I subscribe this with my own hand.

'Peter Favre.

'July 9, 1541.'

The 27th of July in the same year, Dr. Ortiz and myself, with his whole family, set out from Ratisbon, passing through my native country and France, where we were detained and imprisoned for seven days. Wherefore be not unmindful of the great benefits of our Lord, Who set us at liberty, and granted us the grace of conversing with our captors and producing fruit in their souls, to such an extent that even their leader made his confession to me. And things so fell out that the desires which our Lord granted us to do good towards the whole world, were not interfered with, or disturbed by this accident. Nevertheless, I felt some temptation to diffidence and fear lest we might not escape thence without some delay and great expense to Dr. Ortiz; but I also received from God, on the other hand, much consolation and good confidence as to everything that happened in our liberation.

On the feast of St. Elisabeth, Queen of Hungary,[1] I felt great devotion, and a desire of keeping certain persons in my memory to pray for them, not looking to their defects. These were the Supreme Pontiff, the Emperor, the King of France, the King of England, Luther, the Grand Turk, Bucer, and Philip Melancthon; and the occasion was that I had felt in my soul that the aforesaid were having judgment passed upon them by many, whence there arose within me a certain holy compassion proceeding from the good spirit. The same day I promised Christ, and I made a vow, never to receive anything for confessions, Masses, or sermons, nor to live on any income, even if it were offered to me, except it were in some way which I cannot with a good conscience set my face against, and of this vow it behoves me to be very mindful, as of a singular benefit from Christ our Lord, Who thus aids me to keep the better my vow of poverty.

On the day of the Presentation of our Lady,[2] with the help of the Holy Spirit, I made a vow of perfect chastity, and, the better to keep it, God granted me a certain feeling of special reverence towards that most pure infant, our Lady. In testimony and memory of which reverence I resolved to refrain for ever from, and to be on my guard against, putting my face near any child of either sex, even with any lawful intention whatsoever. So much more may God protect me from doing the same with more grown-up persons.

This same year, on entering Spain, I felt remarkable devotion and spiritual tenderness in the invocation of the principal archangels, guardian angels, and saints of Spain. I felt specially moved towards St. Narcissus, who lies at Gerona, also to St. Eulalia, in Barcelona, towards our Lady of Montserrat, our Lady of the Pillar and of Guadaloupe, St. James and St. Isidore, St. Ildefonsus, the holy martyrs, Justus and Pastor, and St. Engrazia, who lies at Saragossa; beseeching all these saints graciously to favour my journey into Spain, and to help me by their prayers to produce some good fruit, as really happened, more through their intercession than from my diligence. This, too, I resolved to do in every kingdom or province where I might happen to be—namely, to commend myself to the principal angels, archangels, angels guardian, and saints whom I knew to be chiefly honoured in such province or kingdom; whence also my

[2] November 21.

devotion was confirmed to certain saints venerated in Italy, whom I have noted and entered in my Roman Breviary, and to others whom I have seen venerated in Germany, especially to the Three Kings, and to the eleven thousand virgins, more particularly to St. Ursula and St. Pinosa, whose head, along with the very arrow by which it was transfixed, I saw with my own eyes in a monastery of St. Benedict, as well as to St. Helvetus in Nuremberg, and St. Maximin at Trèves. In France, also, I took up a devotion to St. Genevieve and St. Marcellus, Bishop of Paris, whose bodies are a great protection to the city; as well as to St. Denis the Areopagite, whose body is in the Church of St. Denis, in France. Likewise in Narbonne to St. Paul Sergius, at Marseilles to St. Mary Magdalene and Martha, her sister, and to St. Lazarus. In Savoy, also, I felt a devotion that I must not omit, to St. Bruno, the founder of the Chartreuse, to St. Amandus, who belongs to Nancy, where we were imprisoned, and to St. Claude, to Brother John of Burgos, to my professor, Master Peter Veillard, whom, though not canonized, I regard as saints. Many other saints I marked down at this period, taking them for my advocates. I resolved never to forget them, but to invoke them for myself, for the living and dead, and especially for those who are either living or dead in the places were such saints were born, grew up, or died. I invoked, also, the Apostles and other saints who had produced fruit in divers parts of the world, to engage them to take particular care of our Society, and of all its members dwelling in such countries or provinces, for which they once applied their charitable exertions. This is the plan I adopt, as often as I wish to pray specially for any place or kingdom, namely, to invoke those saints and angels who have, and have had, special care of such souls of the living or dead.

About this time I began a devotion vouchsafed me from God, for the better reciting of the canonical hours, namely, of saying between the psalms, for the renewal of spirit, this short prayer, which I found very useful—*Heavenly Father, give me Thy good Spirit!*

Another devotion I took up, to be prefixed to each of the seven canonical hours, applying each to some intention. That is, to say ten times, *Jesus! Mary!* at the beginning of each hour—(1) For the honour of our Lord; (2) the glory of His saints; (3) the improvement of the good, that they may advance in every good intention they may happen to have in this hour; (4) for the conversion of those who during this hour shall be in mortal sin; (5) for the increase of the Catholic Church; (6) for peace amongst Christian and Catholic princes; (7) for those who during this hour shall be in tribulation of body; (8) for those suffering tribulation and affliction of spirit; 9) those that are at the point of death; (10) those that are in purgatory, that during that hour and at the time corresponding to the office I am then reciting, they may receive some relief from their punishments and labours.

Observe here, O my soul, how the Lord freed thee from so many and such grievous perturbations of spirit, and from the distress and temptations I underwent from thy defects, from the disturbance of the spirit of fornication, and from my negligence in advancing in good. Remember what clear light thou didst receive on the occasion of such temptations, and that thou scarcely ever hadst a notable temptation in which thou wast not consoled, not only by a clear knowledge, but also by a spirit opposed to sadness, to fear, to pusillanimity, the world, the flesh, the devil, and all inordinate affections. Thou didst receive also from the Lord a great desire, together with good hope, that thou mightest be the dwelling-place of the Holy Spirit, and that the malignant spirits might not dwell in the animal or vital spirits of the body. For this end I used to make various enumerations of the powers, senses, and principal members of the whole body, beseeching our Lord that He would deign wholly to cleanse me. I had also much light and feeling as to the virtues of sobriety, chastity, and diligence, and, on the other hand, of humility, patience, and charity. I received many gifts in thought and feeling, our Lord inspiring me with many prayers concerning them, together with many affections of faith and hope; may He be blessed for ever and ever! Amen.

I likewise received many lights regarding the Catholic doctrine, conformably to the Roman Church, regarding its constitutions and ceremonies, pious pilgrimages, vows, fastings, the worship of the saints of both sexes, of the angels, and of our Lady, and of the souls in purgatory, feeling in all great relish and great devotion in the approving of such things.

1542.

In the month of January, in the year 1542, I set out from Spain and returned to Germany, by order of the Pope. During this journey the Lord conferred on me innumerable favours, especially by satisfying the great desire I felt that I might be granted some one to keep me good company for His service, and so I had with me Master John Aragonio and Master Alvaro Alfonso; also by freeing us during so long and perilous a journey from all temporal evils, contrary to all human hope; for instance, in Catalonia from robbers and imprisonment, in France from soldiers, and on entering Switzerland, on the borders of Savoy, from heretics, in Germany from plagues and pestilences, and finally a greater deliverance than all, from temptations to discord, that is, from the spirit of division. Many were the feelings of love and hope, regarding heretics and the whole world, which the Lord granted to me during this journey, and had granted me before, but especially a certain devotion, to be continued till my death, for the good of these seven cities, namely, Wittemberg, in Saxony, and the chief city of Sarmatia, whose name I do not know, Geneva in the duchy of Savoy, Constantinople and Antioch in Greece, Jerusalem and Alexandria in Asia or Africa. This resolution I determined to keep ever in memory, with the hope that I, or some one of the Society of Jesus Christ, might at some future time be able to say Mass in each of the said cities.

In the octave of Corpus Christi, as I was desiring to have a conversation with the Dean of Spires, for his benefit, and could not in effect attain my object, but only by prayer, I conceived a devotion which I had not felt hitherto, namely, to invoke first, his Heavenly Father, secondly, his loving Mother and Lady the Mother of God, thirdly, his teacher, and as it were, tutor, the angel guardian, fourthly, the saints of both sexes who particularly felt towards him like brothers and sisters. This seemed to me a good plan of canvassing to secure any one's friendship, and it occurred to me to recite for the first of the said persons the *Pater noster*, for the second the *Ave Maria*, for the third the *Deus qui miro ordine angelorum*, and for the fourth the *Omnes sancti tui quæsumus Domine*, and it presented itself to me as very necessary for gaining any one's good will (besides what may be done by deeds) to have a devotion to all the guardian angels, who have it in their power to predispose persons, and to check the violence and temptations of our enemies.

And here note, my soul, and be mindful, that our Lord hath given thee in the past an abundance of knowledge about the temptations and annoyances of the demons, whence thou hast sometimes made reflections in prayer about the lives of the saints, or about the mysteries of Christ or the Christian doctrine, or about the members of the body, asking for grace against the enemy and especially against the spirit of fornication, that he might lose all power against thee, nor ever molest thy intellect, memory, or will. And for this I prayed with much devotion of spirit, and had much firm confidence that so it might come to pass before my death. And the Holy Spirit would suggest that I should earnestly beseech of His divine goodness and purity to dwell in my body as in His temple and in my spirit as well, and that the angels might, as it were, find a corporal habitation in me, driving away our enemies. Of gaining this purity I had great hope, and I determined again (as I had done for a long time before) to observe much temperance in eating and drinking, and much modesty in all exterior acts, in order to prevent the bad spirits from having such great power to dwell in me, or influence my flesh, not finding my heart weighed down with meat or drink. Bless therefore the Lord, O my soul, for so great a desire granted to thee, with such a wish for corporal sanctity and spiritual cleanliness, together with the hope of obtaining it. Being, too, specially devoted to my own angel, I experienced an abundance of aid from him, praying that he would defend me from the evil spirit, chiefly from the spirit of fornication.

On St. John the Baptist's day[3] I had and felt in my spirit, a notable sentiment of reverence towards St. John, and I felt great spiritual grief that here in Germany his feast is not made so much of or cared for so much as it is in other countries. And therefore I longed with great affection to have it in my power to move those who possess authority and spiritual rulership to have his feast rendered more solemn.

[3] June 24.

On the feast of SS. John and Paul,[4] I received a certain help towards the better saying of office. It was this—to notice that four limits and bounds should be marked out, beyond which there was to be no exit in time of office: first, the place where it was being recited; second, the persons or saints occurring in such prayer; thirdly, the words, and fourthly, the external actions that occur in such office. This is useful for the better resisting of the wanderings of the memory, intellect, senses, or desires, to other places, persons, conversations, or external actions that occur.

Another help too I noted, which I had often before found to be useful to the same end. It consists in this, that before saying office, each principal part of such office or hour should be thought of, however remote it be, with a great desire of being engaged in it, as if a person were to say to himself, See, you have to recite first this psalm, then that psalm, or prayer; and with such consideration to enter upon and begin office. Likewise at the end of office to take care that the mind does not wander elsewhere, but retains as far as possible the same holy thoughts. It is useful too, for whoever is occupied in other things, to withdraw the mind as far as can be, before beginning office, from all other matters, often directing our desires to things that tend and belong to the office, or fixing on a certain time for saying it, before which time all business is to be got through, so that we may be then free from other cares, and so have nothing else to think of, and be able to remain awhile quiet with the mind raised to God. Otherwise, one who only forms a desire to pray at the moment when he is to begin, can have no well-founded devotion, except by a miracle. For this, then, it is well to have our time well arranged, and often to remember our prayer and desire it; and also, when distractions of

[4] June 26.

mind come, to grieve and be sorry for them, and to keep up this sorrow till the time for the next exercise comes. This sorrow, moreover, must be for the love of God, and out of devotion to the words of the office, and not only for the disagreeable character of such distractions. For there are many who are sorry rather because they hate the distractions, than from pure love of prayer. This way, however, is good to lead us to love prayer, and when once we love it, we next come to desire to attend to what we recite, and this not with the attention of the mind alone, but with intent affection also, for the pure love of God.

At the same time, within the octave of St. John the Baptist, I observed something very necessary for the direction of our own affairs, our desires and cares, and in brief the whole tenour of our life, and for the obtaining of tranquillity in spiritual and corporal occupations. It was to follow that injunction of Jesus Christ, *Nolite curare de crastino*; that is, in spiritual desires and cares it is proper as far as possible to have no care for the morrow, but a man ought to dispose of his hours and of the time of that day in such a way as not to allow himself to be distracted, or to think or care with too much joy or sorrow of what is afterwards to happen. For when the attention is thus divided by thoughts of many and different matters, the present cannot go on well, or be attended to as perfectly as it might if the mind were more collected.

Another petition likewise occurred to me, to be presented to the most Holy Trinity, namely, for grace, that when I have any good desire, all my faculties might work together in such a way as to be no obstacle one to another, but that, on the contrary, whenever any of them happened to be distracted, the others might never concur, but rather be a hindrance to the distraction.

On the day of the Visitation of the Blessed Mary,[5] in connection with the subjection and the humility we owe to those over us, and to every creature for the love of our Lord, I had a certain good feeling about the humility of our Lady who went to serve her cousin St. Elisabeth, humbling herself to her as being the mother of the precursor of our Lord Jesus Christ. Hereupon I felt a desire within my spirit that all who live in any way under obedience should exercise themselves till they obtain perfect humility, patience, and charity, supporting and honouring those placed over them, good and bad, looking at and being affected towards what is good alone and not what is bad, and that how much soever the Superior might seem less good in his degree, by so much the more the inferior might be perfected in his own, which is to be an obedient, diligent, and faithful servant for the fear and love of our Lord. For one who served in this way would merit to be afterwards Superior, and to have good subjects, and on the other hand, one who had been a bad Superior would deserve to become subject and have a bad Superior over him, and one who has been or is a bad subject does not deserve a good Superior.

On a certain day that fell within the octave of the Visitation of the Blessed Virgin, I felt certain interior desires, in which I besought of God the Father that He would be to me, though unworthy, a Father in a special manner, so that He might make me His obedient and dutiful son. Of the Son I begged that He would deign to be my Lord, and to give me grace that I might be His faithful servant. From the Holy Ghost I begged that He would be my Master, and teach me to be His good disciple. To obtain all these petitions I implored with great devotion the help and intercession of the

[5] July 2.

chosen daughter of God the Father, of the handmaid and Mother of Jesus Christ, and of the pupil of the Holy Ghost, that is, the Virgin Mary, for whom it is easy to obtain with God the above-mentioned favours. I desired, too, that she herself might teach me the true mode of being a son, a servant, and a disciple, after her own example and as she herself is; and that as Jesus Christ was her Son, servant, and disciple, so I too should be in the same way humble as He was, and such as it becomes me to be in each of the said three characters. Entering still further on this subject, I came to see how necessary it was that this humility should be practised, for when subjects have arrived at the condition of true obedience, humility, subjection, and reverence towards those placed over them, they would deserve that our Lord should give Himself to them, and grant them also a Superior according to His own Heart. On the other hand, it may be said that one who is indisposed to receive a favour, deserves to be deprived of it, and he who has not yet become a true subject does not deserve to have a Superior given him whose goodness he may enjoy. Whence also it is to be hoped, that when subjects have attained such humility, patience, and charity, as suffice to enable them to honour, serve, and bear with any Superior, however bad, not losing their goodwill, but rather increasing in it, with the resolution of persevering thus even to death, then I say there is ground for hope that our Lord will be moved to grant other and better Superiors. Not so if the contrary be the case, that is, if the bad are seen to grow worse every day as regards obedience.

On another day, also during the same octave of the Visitation, as I wished to begin as usual my meditations on the mysteries of the life of Christ with the Annunciation, I was considering how the Blessed Virgin offers her whole self to be the Redeemer's handmaid, and then there came to me great and most excellent desires that whatever I was destined to do I might first rightly understand, as it were, by the grace of that Annunciation. And in the same way that all women before they conceive might even then direct their intention that their children might be in all things obedient to the will of the Lord; and in the same way of corporal fathers and spiritual fathers, who have spiritual sons or disciples that obey them. I desired too that whatever profit I may have derived from my past good works, or labours, or studies, should be directed to the good and advantage of this nation of the Germans.

In my meditation on the Visitation, considering the grace of the Virgin who was so pleasing to the Most High, I desired that as she was able to obtain the sanctification of St. John the Baptist, she might also obtain for me the sanctification of my habitation, my body, and of whatever I had done of good works, and that they might be pleasing to God, and if there was anything impure, that it might be cleansed away. On the passage about the shepherds coming to Jesus at His birth, I begged the grace that the Lord would deign to raise my heart to higher things, as He raised the shepherds; and to humble it to lowly things, as He humbled the Magi.

The same day, during Mass, I was considering how God is compassionate and merciful, and how all things are present to Him; and I asked Him to deign to have mercy on this German nation, and to compassionate it in the evils which I foresaw will come upon it if it does not return to the Catholic faith and to its devotion to the Roman Church.

On the octave of the Visitation,[6] I was considering that that was the day on which I had made my

[6] July 9.

profession. I felt a great devotion for my vows, asking grace from God the Father for perseverance and a continual increase of chastity against all carnal concupiscences. To the Son I committed the care of my obedience even unto death. To the Holy Ghost I commended my poverty, praying that He may always of His goodwill keep me well affectioned towards poverty, so that I might never give up my love for it. I also begged that my three powers might ever increase in knowledge, memory, and desire, conformably to the aforesaid vows, and that for this end the Father would infuse His power into each one of them, taking special care of my memory, that the Son might in like manner infuse wisdom and light, and might take care of my intellect, and that the Holy Ghost might infuse His gifts, and take care of my will. I also prayed the most Holy Trinity (One in Essence) to reside in my heart, diffusing in Its goodness the Personal attributes through my three powers. And my Lady I begged to be my advocate for everything, seeing that she is such a true example of chastity, obedience, and poverty, having flesh the most pure, and a soul the most undefiled, and a most holy spirit, each of these graces being wrought out in her with such power of the divine virtue, and such wisdom and goodness, that each of them would suffice of itself to keep the other two in its purity; that is, her flesh so perfectly undefiled, that it would suffice to prevent any defilement from actually or possibly approaching or reaching the soul or the spirit, and in like manner her spirit so full of gifts that it would suffice to detach the soul in such a way that nothing which was not most pure could enter either it or the flesh. In the same way, her soul possessed such great perfection as sufficed to shed lustre on the spirit and the flesh.

On the day of the Division of the Apostles,[7] I had certain great desires that a feast like this should be celebrated with great veneration everywhere. I had also in my prayer great consolations and desires that the Apostles might follow Jesus Christ into my soul, since they knew better how to honour Him, minister to Him, and understand His will, conversations, and words, making excuses for my ignorance in the like duties. Several recommendations to be made on behalf of my dispersed brethren also occurred to me.

On St. Alexius' day,[8] certain considerations occurred to my mind as I was going through the mysteries of Christ and the Three Kings, and I felt a great desire that the pilgrimage of Dr. John Aragonio should represent the pilgrimage of the Three Kings coming to adore Christ; and I saw that it was very fitting they should be visited in their relics, as having so much honoured our Lord. Whence, too, certain reflections occurred to me as to the pilgrimages of St. Alexius, St. James, St. Roch, of Jesus Christ, our Lady the Blessed Mary, and the Apostles; and from all I felt great hope that such pilgrimages would be very acceptable to our Lord and to all the saints, especially in these times and in these countries, where now so few pilgrimages are made, on account of the heresies which turn men away from valuing and esteeming works of this kind, which are of so great moment.

On a certain day, when the Annunciation of the Blessed Virgin Mary had come into my mind, and I was desirous of having some visits from my companions, I came to know how much it pleased God in that respect to give me a certain degree of sadness and bitterness, for three reasons—first, that I might know that this was not pleasing to God and His saints, on

---

[7] July 15.   [8] July 17.

account of my imperfections and defects; secondly, that I might think myself very far from the Lord; thirdly, because I produced so little fruit in the service of His Divine Majesty. Hence I felt a vehement desire that the Virgin Mary herself, as being full of grace, might render me pleasing to God; secondly, that seeing that she had Christ always with her, she might unite me to Him; thirdly, since she is blessed amongst all women, that I might not deserve to be accursed amongst men. And since the fruit of her womb is blessed, that she might obtain grace for me to produce some fruit in the service of Christ our Lord.

On a certain day, namely, when Don John was about to make his pilgrimage to Cologne, I felt certain great desires that it might be very acceptable to God, to our Lady His Mother, to all the angels, and all the saints, but especially to the Three Kings, and to St. Ursula and her companions; all this for the advantage of Don John himself, for the extinction of war, for peace in our time, as a recompence for the pilgrimages which the Germans formerly made in Spain, visiting St. James in Galicia, our Lady of Montserrat, and our Lady of Guadaloupe, and also for the safety of his journey from robbers and all other dangers, and to appease our Lord and His saints for the insults offered them for some years past, in the contempt shown for pilgrimages and other pious and holy works undertaken in the spirit of penance and for the honour of God and His saints, and for all other good works whatsoever.

At the same time an inspiration presented itself to me to do every kind of work of piety purely for love of God and to the glory of His saints; and I felt a keen pang of sorrow in seeing that the works of the saints are not considered, and that the acts of the life of our Lord Jesus Christ are not pondered and meditated on. I grieved especially that the pains and sufferings of the martyrs are not more deeply considered; and here I noted four points, from which we may easily perceive whether a work was well done. The first point is to consider what the work is; whether it is for the glory of God, the honour of the saints, or the advantage of one's own soul, or for the benefit of our neighbour. The second point is, why it is done, looking to the end and intention of the doer. The third is, the spirit in which it is done, that is, whether from a servile or a filial fear of God, from love of God or our neighbour, or from some pious and proper motive that stirs the will; or, in fine, from the dictate of right reason which the will obeys. The fourth is, the order in which it is done, that is, whether it is offered in union with the merits of Christ, for He it is Who makes our good works of any value.

On the feast of St. Praxedes,[9] as I was pondering the mysteries of Christ's life, it occurred to me to petition for graces from God through the merits of the Annunciation, the Incarnation, and the Visitation, and to pray God to make known to me the practical way how to praise Him, honour Him, know Him intimately, love Him, desire Him, and serve Him, applying to this all my faculties, and this in a way that was conformable to the ordinations and practices of His holy Church, and to the true and Catholic teaching, both as to the holy sacraments, as to prayers and invocations of the saints, and as to good works in remembrance of and suffrage for the souls in purgatory.

During Mass another pious desire came into my mind, namely, to do all my future good works under the direction of the good and Holy Spirit. I also desired that no reform should be made in accordance with the desire

[9] July 21.

of heretics; for, although they, like the demons, profess many truths, still they do not profess them in the spirit of truth, and therefore are not pleasing to God.

Lastly, after Mass, on not perceiving within myself that delight which I felt before, and which I intensely longed for, the thought came to me to ask our Lord Jesus Christ to cause me thoroughly to know the faults of my intellect, memory, will, and other faculties, and also to have the virtues and gifts which I lack and of which I am in need.

I had also another desire, namely, that our Lord would deign to guide me according to His own good will in all things that, with the grace of the Holy Spirit, I sought for myself and others; for I am wont to say, write, and do, much without that fervour of spirit with which I began. For example, I sometimes give utterance, in a calm and joyous frame of mind and with external signs of pleasure, to thoughts which I had previously conceived in a penitential mood and with a kind of spiritual groaning. Hence it results that the hearer gets less good from these things, because they are not given forth in the same good spirit as that by which they were first suggested by God. I prayed therefore that our Lord would deign to give me the grace of having the same fervour in the progress as in the beginning of the work, the same fervour in speech or writing as in the conception; and this will be the case when the same spirit reigns over the feeling and thought, the word and work. From this I saw a special sense and meaning in that passage, *Ductus est Jesus in desertum a Spiritu,* and of that other, *Venit in Spiritu in templum,* in which a special 'spirit' is intimated, which moves a person to act or to speak, and does not leave him in his own human and proper feeling.

On the feast of St. James,[10] in the introit and beginning of the Mass, feeling myself enchained by my faults and imperfections, as I said the verse, *Quare tristis incedo dum affligit me inimicus,* this sort of interpretation seemed to me as if the Spirit said to me, 'Why are you sad on account of your troubles and the suggestions of the enemy? You would have reason to be sad if our Lord Jesus Christ was the Person Who afflicted you, or if you thought this affliction came to you because you are not according to His will.'

The same day a thought occurred to me which I had often had before, that if a man wishes to purify his soul more and more, he should keep his first intention always directed to God, and in this consists his profit. Hence we must not fix our chief attention (as I have often done up to this) on the remedies of troubles, temptations, and sadness. For he who sought our Lord solely and chiefly in order to be free from temptations and sadness, would not seek devotion principally for itself, but, on the contrary, would seem to show that he would little esteem it, unless he were suffering; and this is seeking love from a fear of imperfection and misery, and in order to escape evil. For this reason God, in His justice and mercy, allows you to be troubled for a time, because your affections were not directed to Him; and in order that you may shake off tepidity and idleness, He sends you these pains and distresses as goads and spurs to urge you to walk on in the way of the Lord without seeking rest, until you repose solely in God Himself, our Lord Jesus Christ. Nay, even though you were not to feel any trouble from the enemy, or any temptations, or evil and vain feelings, or imperfections, you ought never to remain inactive, as do the tepid and idle, and all those who care only not to fall or go back. For not to make progress in the way of

---

[10] July 25.

the Lord, is to go back. Do not then be content with merely not falling or going down the hill, but 'lay up in your heart ascensions,' increase, and progress towards interior perfection; and this not from fear of any fall, but from the love of holiness. Desire and thirst after spiritual things, not as if they were remedies against bad or vain feelings, but on account of what they are and contain in themselves. Thus you will at length attain to the perfect love of God, and so you will no longer think of things vain and idle, nor fear sins, which are the hindrances which impede our attaining to God and being intimately united with and at rest in Him.

On the feast of St. Martha,[11] the hostess of Jesus Christ, while praying for the soul of Lady Tullia, the news of whose death had just reached me, as well as of that of Doña Antonia, who had been an attendant of the Marchioness de Pescara, I felt great devotion, and on reading certain prayers which are commonly said in the church at the burial of the dead, I felt a great devorion towards these pious recommendations. These prayers often came back to my mind with a deep feeling of faith, and I desired that now, even more than ever before, they should be recited at the burial of Catholics, even supposing that we knew for certain that their souls were in heaven. For I felt that these prayers for the resurrection of their bodies were pleasing to God, and that from them we might gain some knowledge of that supreme wisdom by which the wondrous resurrection is to be wrought, and the dust which we now see in the tomb is to be one day so beautiful a body, to the glory of each one of us. God should be thanked also, Who by means of these relics, so humble in appearance, has often wrought great good. By these and such like thoughts, Christians may not only be invited to remember the souls of the dead,

[11] July 29.

and to thank God if those souls are now in heaven, and to pray for them if they are in purgatory, but also to increase their own faith in the article of the Creed on the resurrection of the body.

On the day of the Dedication of the Portiuncula,[12] which is the feast of our Lady of the Angels, I had many spiritual feelings, and felt a great devotion in the desire that my soul and body might now be dedicated as a living temple to the Lord, to receive and keep within it the spiritual gifts of God. I also had an intense longing that everything which I had up to this received from God, in words, acts, or holy inspirations, should be noted by me and all men with great consideration and attention. Also, that all which had been established in the church by our holy and pious predecessors, should be considered with great thankfulness and fear, lest it be taken from us as unworthy and ungrateful.

I also gave thanks to God during Mass for all the public corrections which had been inflicted or permitted by God up to this time on peoples or provinces or states or persons, with the view of an amendment of life; and I grieved that such matters were not noticed, as for example, plagues, earthquakes, wars, floods, droughts and other such like temporal evils, from which we may know the most high and dread Judge, Who by these methods puts before us the memory of our last end, desirous that we should return to the way of penance, that so we may recognize the gifts of His goodness and mercy, and brings before us His second coming when He sees that we have lost sight of His first and lowly coming. He also wishes to impress us with the Day of Judgment and the coming of the reign of His majesty and justice, seeing the Gospel of His Kingdom despised and rejected by us.

[12] August 2.

On this day I also noted how I ought each night to make the sign of the Cross with great attention, and also the versicles—*Dignare me laudare te, Virgo sacrata : da mihi virtutem contra hostes tuos.* These enemies are those of faith, humility, chastity, and purity, of meekness and charity. Also—*Procul recedant somnia ; Noctem quietam et finem perfectum ;* and *Hostem repellas longius, pacemque dones protinus,* adding a *Pater noster,* an *Ave Maria,* a *Credo,* and I must do this after the litanies and the examination of conscience, and after having set in order the duties which I have to do on the following day. In the morning, on rising from bed and before my work, I must say these same versicles or others according to the time, as well as *Pater noster, Ave Maria,* and the *Credo.*

The same day, going over in my mind the text, *Omne quod calcaverit pes tuus, tuum erit,* considering how the holy fathers had been strangers in the land which afterwards belonged to them, I conceived in spirit a great hope to be able to arrive at the spiritual kingdom and the inheritance of the Lord, holding myself always as a stranger on the earth.

On the day of the Invention of St. Stephen[13] the protomartyr, while thinking of the bodies which were found at the same time with his, I began with a pious desire to ask Christ our Lord to grant me by and bye to see with these eyes those glorious bodies, whose relics I had already seen, and in general the bodies of the Blessed.

While saying office, I felt some distractions which I wished removed from me. I heard within me a voice which said that I should have tried out of prayer time to discover the causes of distractions, with a desire of having my mind in peace at the right time, if I wished

---

[13] August 3. The bodies mentioned are those of SS. Gamaliel, Nicodemus, and Abibon.

during prayer time to enjoy the sweets of conversation with God.

In the same way during Mass, as I was longing to adore devoutly the Body of Christ, I observed that I did not gain that grace because I neglected to exercise myself out of the time of prayer in such like desires, whence it was that I did not then deserve any grace, like a person who might grieve when at table at not having any appetite, when he had not taken the trouble before dining to get an appetite; or as if a man who was to receive some precious liquor from another, if he brought at a fixed time to the house some clean vessels to hold it, were to forget to wash the vessels, and so not be ready at the time of the distribution, and have to wait for another occasion to receive the precious liquor.

Once, when grieving that I could not adore Christ as the Three Kings did, nor weep like Magdalene, nor find grace to hear the many words of consolation which Christ spoke in this world, I felt this answer within me—that I had not prepared my soul as the Three Kings did, who had abandoned such wealth, and left their country so far away, and all their goods, and had brought their offerings themselves; and thus I arrived at the knowledge of the dispositions in which those persons were to whom Christ granted similar graces; and it seemed to me that I should have rejoiced very much if I heard those words—*Remittuntur tibi peccata*, and also those others—*Hodie mecum eris in Paradiso*, not considering how far I am from the state of soul in which those persons were; and that I have never desired to come to that state in which the good thief on the cross was, or the weeping Magdalene at the banquet; and how I have never felt such pain at my spiritual blindness, as the blind man possibly felt for his corporal blindness, although I have no lack of faith as to obtaining the grace of spiritual sight. Thus too with regard to my other spiritual weaknesses, I compared them to the corresponding corporal ills which Christ our Lord (Who takes account of the toils and suffering and faith of those who suffer in sympathy with Himself) used to cure, and daily cures, considering the wants of every one with His eyes of kindness and His Heart full of charity.

On the feast of our Lady of the Snow,[14] I saw how our Lord had kept me for several days past in constant weariness of spirit, because I do not find devotion in prayer and meditation. He stirred up also within me a great desire to recover it, and it appeared to me to be a splendid boon not to have to experience again the disgusts and troubles which disappointed my desire of finding devotion in my soul towards my God and Lord Jesus Christ. And in this I saw that I had received grace better to govern my soul, so that my heart's first wishes and cares might be centred in what is of chief and primary importance—that is, seeking and finding God by means of my spiritual exercises, which are the way to Him : I mean prayer, meditation, and, above all, the Mass.

On the feast of the Transfiguration,[15] feeling great sadness at not having experienced any devotion, I consoled myself in the knowledge that this trouble which had lasted for some days, had not been able to distract me or drive me away from God. For I found myself full of affection and anxiety to find God again, and yet I had allowed myself to be carred away by some other desire or grief, longing for the edification of my neighbour, or the increase of God's worship among others. Or, when I was grieving over my temptations or imperfections, grief of this sort had taken away the better sorrow which came from the longing after God. On that day, then, I saw clearly that

[14] August 5.   [15] August 6.

God conferred on me more abundant favours in proportion as my griefs had been caused by desires and longings after Him, which could not be cancelled by any grief of an inferior kind.

Here, too, I observed another grace to my soul, which ought to be valued much, namely, that I had never felt so much lifted above all rejoicings or sorrows which from time to time visited me from the temporal profit or loss of souls: I mean profit which depended on me. I had been wont to rejoice or grieve very much in this matter, according as things went well or ill. But it now seemed to me that no good fortune in any matter could console me unless our Lord gave me an overflowing devotion to Himself and the saints, and that no sorrow could enter my soul that arose only from the fewness of the occupations offered me in working for Him.

Blessed be the Lord, Who has so many ways of leading us to perfection, according to the many kinds of fear, of grief and hatred, which reign over these lower creatures in which there is no peace. And yet they are the means of man's rising to the love of God, and enjoying Him. For if a man's union with God has begun by the way of fear, he can always return to it by the way of love. But if it has begun by the way of pure love, he can always go on increasing therein, and penetrating still more deeply the things of God, and at the same time he can come down from Him more securely in order to busy himself with the salvation of his neighbour.

May God grant such love to me and to all my brothers, yea, and to all men. For I confess that I am as yet far from this charity of the perfect; nevertheless, I believe I am not altogether out of all charity, as I am not altogether out of the grace of Christ. And here we must note that Christ is the way, the truth, and the life.

Now there are three ways: the purgative, the illuminative, and the perfective. In the first are beginners, in the second proficients, in the third the perfect. Although all may be in charity, still to be in charity and to live and abide in charity are different things. Beginners have charity, inasmuch as they know and hate sin. Proficients have charity, inasmuch as they act from desire of charity, in which they endeavour every day to increase. The perfect have charity, inasmuch as their only motive for action is the love of God, and they seek His most holy will in everything. In beginners, their charity produces the result that they detest and lay aside their sins; in proficients, that they give themselves to the acquisition of the virtues that they desire to have; in the perfect, that they grow to the knowledge and close love of God, directing thereto all their thoughts, affections, and actions. And as the beginners who hate sin endeavour to lay aside the old man, so also the proficients who desire virtue, strive to put on the new man and adorn him ever more and more, while the perfect aim at appearing clothed on all sides with the marriage garment. And we should also consider that in each of these three degrees there are three orders, that is, in each there is beginning, middle, and end, so that we may say that among the perfect there are beginners and proficients, and others who are altogether perfect.

On the day on which I celebrated the feast of the Patriarch St. Dominic,[17] while I was communicating in the Mass, I felt a great desire that Jesus Christ might enter my heart and dwell in the midst thereof, and that at the same time all my vicious propensities might melt away as the wax before the fire. Before Mass I was reflecting as usual on the mysteries of the life of Christ, and I asked through the intercession of St. Dominic that God

---

[16] August 4 (it seems to have been translated).

would give me grace to relish and understand each mystery in the way in which that great saint relished and understood the same when he was alive.

The same day I was going along the street, and I found no joy in the things which I saw there, but rather sadness, distractions, and temptations to vanity and evil thoughts, and then I had this answer made to me interiorly—You ought not to be displeased because you do not find peace in vain things, you should rather rejoice thereat, and give thanks for this to God. You should rather be sorry because you do not find consolation in prayer, in holy exercises and in heavenly conversation. Many would not care for these things, if they found peace in the things of this world. Raise therefore the eyes and ears of your mind, and all your interior senses, to heavenly things, and then you will never hear or see anything that does not edify and console you. Here on earth if thou wast to desire, like a man at full liberty, to see everything that might meet thee, thou wouldst see nothing but things pleasing to the senses, laughable or shameful; thou wouldst hear nothing but vain and scandalous words, nothing, in short, serious or grave, nothing that can conduce to the praise of God. Let him then who is withdrawn from these things, and who is moved to seek those things that are true and eternal, thank God for that He wills not that he should lose his time in thoughts so low.

On the feast of SS. Cyriacus, Largus, and Smaragdus,[17] I desired that our Lord would grant me by the merits of His blessed life, Passion, and glory, that my Mass might as efficaciously assist the souls of purgatory, as if I offered it with all the desires, prayers, sighs, anguish, and thanksgivings which are felt or made by each soul in purgatory which cannot assist itself. I desired also that

---

[17] August 8.

our Lord would give me those same feelings which the souls in purgatory have as to their own sins and the benefits which they have received from God. And as I did not deserve such grace, I prayed that my deficiency might be supplied by the divine sacrifice and by the intercession of these glorious saints.

On the same day it came to my mind that it would be a thing very helpful to the souls in purgatory, if when I prayed for them I were to represent and offer to Christ that charity and compassion with which He said, *Hodie mecum eris in Paradiso.* For it may be said in general that a faithful soul that is in purgatory is in greater necessity than the thief to whom those words of Christ on the Cross were said. It also occurred to me that those souls might repeat the seven words of Christ on the Cross, praying, that is, for their enemies whom they have left behind in the world, and for their friends and debtors, grieving over the sins and ills which they commit; or again, showing their heartfelt charity to them, and especially to those who are most united to them in blood, for whose prosperity and salvation they would do all kinds of good if they could. And in the same way these holy souls would desire to be able to say, *Consummatum est,* that is, to be delivered from those torments which can never be described, and go forth thence to the glory of heaven.

On the vigil of St. Laurence,[18] which is the feast of St. Romanus, martyr, it came into my mind before Mass to ask for grace against all distraction, so that I might be master and ruler of all my passions, for I felt myself then much distracted. I found good help in reflecting on those sufferings which our Lord underwent when His Soul was in agony, and when He was on the Cross, saying, *Deus meus, Deus meus, ut quid dereliquisti me?* and

---

[18] August 9.

especially in making my petition, through the most holy grace of Christ which was in the hypostatic union. In the Mass I desired to communicate with great devotion, and I besought our Lord to deign to receive me a sinner and to pardon me my sins. After Mass, I went home through a certain street, and there I felt great devotion as to what had happened to me, and each part of the Mass came back to my mind. I prayed our Lord that as it often happened to me that my memory was distracted about various business, thoughts, or considerations of matters which were not immediately directed to God, He would grant me that in the time of meditation I might have my affections so thoroughly in order according to true charity, that I might not feel any disturbance in mind, understanding, or will. This grace I hoped to obtain, because those affections of which I speak were not altogether disordered, but only wanting in perfection, inasmuch as they did not unite me to God with all my heart and soul and strength. But to have them in that higher state, that it is in which consists true charity, and consequently true peace and tranquillity of soul, never disturbed either in the memory, the understanding, or the will. But that supreme perfection belongs properly only to that home of the Blessed to which we now aspire.

On that same vigil of St. Laurence, after compline, Don John Aragonio came back from his pilgrimage to Cologne. The Lord gave me such consolation thereat as I had never felt before, and moreover, He gave me grace not to be above measure excited in spirit by the joy of his return and the desire I felt to converse with him, as at other times had happened to me with some damage to devotion and fervour in meditation. On this account I gave many thanks to the most Holy Trinity, the Blessed Virgin, the Three holy Kings, and St. Ursula, praying for all those people who had done any kindness to Don John, and also for all those who had been cause of his suffering any ill.

On St. Laurence's day,[19] as I was meditating in the morning on the holy mysteries, according to the matter before me, I felt an indescribable desire that the Mass might supply and avail for all the labour that it would cost me to go over the several calendars of particular dioceses, in order specially to honour the saints that are contained therein. I also felt the strongest faith that could be as to the great aid which our Lord would never fail to give to me and to the Society by means of His saints. If a single saint can do much more towards the bringing back of the heretics to the Christian faith and the practice of good works than an Emperor can do, how much more will all the saints together be able to do to help me and the Society!

I experienced great devotion on reciting that verse which says—*Adjuva me et salvus ero, et meditabor in justificationibus tuis.* At the *Pater noster* in the Mass, when I said, *Panem nostrum quotidianum da nobis hodie,* I felt an interior desire that the Heavenly Father might make me feel how it is that He gives bread both for the soul and for the body, and I said within myself, Lord, let me feel how it is that Thou givest to me that Bread which is Thine own Son.

On the feast of SS. Tiburtius and Susanna,[20] I was considering how St. Tiburtius reproved with so much fervour of spirit Fabian the judge, because he took delight in carnal things, and gloried in them alone, and desired so much to be pleasing to others, and especially to women; and there came to me a desire to pray this saint to obtain for me the grace never to desire to please myself or to glory in myself, and also not to desire to please others, but only God, before Whom and in Whose

---

[19] August 10.   [20] August 11.

sight we ought to stand in such guise as worthily to please Him only and His saints.

When I was making my *memento* before Mass, I thought of all those persons who had been kind to Don John Aragonio on his journey, and I devoutly prayed our Lord that with His liberality and mercy He would recompense them for the good which they had done, both in giving him alms and in showing him his way, and also in welcoming him to their houses and treating him with charity. And I did not omit to pray for those also who had behaved to him in a different way, since our good Lord Jesus is wont often to permit such things, in order to try the humility and patience of His servants, and to rouse them to pray for those who have treated them ill.

As I was praying in a certain oratory dedicated to St. John, I felt a desire that everything that I asked for the benefit of that house and of the persons who dwelt in it, might, by the mercy of God, happen also to all the houses and other people in the city. May our Lord in His goodness grant this, as if I were dwelling in each one of them.

On the same day, I felt a great movement of devotion, to ask that when I begged any grace from God for myself, or for the living, or for the dead, His Divine Majesty might deign to grant it me, as if our Blessed Redeemer Himself were to ask it, or the Blessed Virgin Mary, or the saint whose feast I that day celebrated. This kindled my devotion to say Mass, since Mass is of so great value in itself, on account of the victim and sacrifice that are offered therein, that there is nothing that we can ask, if it be just, which may not be granted to us by virtue of that same sacrifice made upon the Cross, especially if we have great confidence in our Lord.

On the feast of St. Clare,[21] while I was saying Mass I had a distraction from a desire to give edification to the people present, and to feel devotion in order that I might do so; and I did not know that it was a temptation, and even if I had known it I did not then know how to get rid of that desire, as it has since been granted me to know, His Divine Majesty granting me light to seek always purely the glory of God, and not to feel any more such imperfections.

On the Sunday within the octave of St. Laurence,[22] I had certain remarkable spiritual feelings as I was saying the matins of the Sunday, and so I prayed most earnestly to the most Holy Trinity that, for the sake of the glory of the Resurrection, I might have special grace given to me in reciting all the Sunday offices, to such a degree that the help which I had received on that day might be preserved to me for all the other offices during the week. In the same way I prayed at the Mass.

The same day I prayed our Lord, with great confidence, that for His bounty and patience He would supply all my defects, delivering me from all confusion that I might have deserved by my negligence, and not allowing me to suffer such except in such degree as was for the glory of His Divine Majesty and for the good of my neighbours. Then I prayed that the evil spirits might never, because of me, have any power over any who might see or feel my defects. And here take note, my soul, how many manifest defects thou hast committed, in so many places, and in the presence of so many men; which defects of thine have nevertheless not been remarked or considered as in rigour and justice they deserved. And therefore thou art under great obligations to thy Lord, Who, out of His own goodness, and by the prayers of His saints, and the

---

[21] August 12.   [22] August 13 (1542).

ministry of His holy angels, does not permit thy actions to be looked into or judged hardly, especially when they are so manifest. And how many things thou hast done and said which might and ought to have been taken amiss, and yet nevertheless no notice has been taken nor memory preserved thereof!

As the eve of our Lady's feast in August[23] was approaching, and I was saying the office of St. Hippolytus and his companions, and was reading about St. Concordia, whose body was thrown into the sewer and then taken from thence by Irenæus, to the great consolation of St. Justinus, I felt great compunction of spirit at the thought that in doing so lowly an office he was performing an action so holy and pleasing to God. And on this I made an earnest prayer to the Blessed Mother of our Lord, to obtain for me grace to know and be able to serve her Son with a perfect will in my office as priest, since he in the discharge of his humble office had found an opportunity of doing a thing of so much moment in the service of His Divine Majesty. I prayed, likewise, for men of all conditions, that our Lord might give them grace that in the work that they do they may be able to do something for the praise of His Divine Majesty, the salvation of their souls, and the good of their neighbours, living and dead.

As I was saying lauds after matins, and when I came to the psalms *Benedicite* and *Laudate*, I felt in myself great confusion, considering that all the creatures serve man effectually, to his comfort, his use, his healing, or the supply of his necessities, as the sun giving him light, the water refreshment, the fire warmth, and so on with the rest, and that I, on the other hand, was doing no good to the honour and glory of Him Who had created all things for man. I thought over the many excellent and

---

[23] August 13.

noble results which the Blessed Virgin saw in the Nativity, Annunciation, Visitation, and Assumption; as for instance, in the Nativity of her Son she saw the shepherds raised to so great a knowledge of divine things, and the kings so deeply humbled, and upon this I prayed her to obtain for me grace to produce some fruit, as her loving servant. And it seemed to me that at that moment I felt within me the affection of one who desires to serve some great prince, and who begins by serving other servants of his Court, and so seeks to make himself known to the prince as worthy to serve him.

At the first vespers of our Lady's Assumption, I was in the Church of St. Mary at Spires, and all the ceremonies, lights, organs, chants, relics, and decorations moved me to an extent of devotion that I do not know how to describe. And in that spirit I blessed the man who had lighted the candles, the man who had left revenue for that purpose, the organs also and the organists, the music and the singers, the relics and those who had discovered them and placed them in that place, and also the vestments and decorations which I saw there. And then I seemed to feel that God had great bounty and mercy for all those who apply some part of what is theirs to His external worship and that of the saints, whether it is by giving of their riches, or working with their hands, or in any other manner.

When the feast of the Assumption came, and as I recited matins and said Mass, I felt that I was altogether as it were, in myself, that is, without any motion of the spirit, good or bad, and this made me know my own frailty, being left alone by our Lord. And then I prayed Him to give me grace to grow daily, and become a vessel of larger capacity and greater purity, always well prepared to receive good inspirations only. And I remembered that almost always on the most solemn feasts I found myself without devotion, and also how the interior moving of the spirit is wont to change a man from his own being into another that is better, and so it seemed to me a great gift of God that a man should often find himself left in his own life, as it were, with the grace that is essential to him, in order that he may learn better how to discern his own spirit, which belongs to his common mode of acting, from that which comes from without, good or bad, and to understand the ups and downs that belong to each state, as well as the increase and decrease that may happen in whatever state he may be—as, for example, in one state we may say, with a good meaning to the words, not excluding God's grace, *Vivo ego, et jam ego*—' I live, it is I;' in the second, *Vivo ego, et jam non ego, vivit vero in me Christus*—' I live, but it is not I that live, but Christ liveth in me;' and in the third, *Vivo ego, jam non ego, vivit vero in me peccatum aut malus spiritus*— ' I live, but it is not I, but sin or the evil spirit liveth in me.'

After Mass, as I was giving thanks to God and to the Blessed Virgin, I considered the singular perfection which she possessed in her own nature, and that though she was always full of grace, and our Lord was always with her, and she was always blessed above all women, nevertheless it was possible, as I think, that she should not always have the same amount of sensible consolation and the same sensible fervour of the spirit, in order that there might be room in her for more perfect humility, and greater hunger and thirst, and desire to be pleasing to the Most High, and fear lest she might not always be as useful as God willed. And I prayed her to obtain for me grace that I might be so reformed and strengthened, that when it happened to me that the actual motion and cooperation of the Holy Ghost were withdrawn from me, I might not become disordered or unmindful of the gifts of God, and so become tepid and negligent in the spiritual life. May it please the goodness of God that I may so cooperate with His essential grace that I may become every day more strong, more wise, and better in the work which I do, and that in my soul and body and spirit there may be such habits of good, that when the fervour which I ordinarily feel in my actions fails me, I may still be able ever to grow in God's grace!

The day after the Assumption I made commemoration of St. Roch, and resolved to do so every year, because so it is done in Paris.

In the Mass I had great devotion and feeling on those words, *Gloria in excelsis Deo*, and those others, *Mariam sanctificans, Mariam gubernans, Mariam coronans*, and I prayed our Blessed Lady with great faith and hope to obtain for me, first, the grace of chastity and purity both of body and spirit, then the grace to be able to regulate and order well my life in the service of her Son, and lastly, peace in all things, so as to acquire virtue in this world and glory in the next.

I was afterwards before the Blessed Sacrament, and wishing to pay to it devout adoration, I remembered how the Blessed Virgin Mary is placed above all the choirs of the angels, and that she it is who pays more reverence to the Divine Majesty than all other creatures, and that her favour and protection over men is much greater than that of the angels and seraphim. For she not only is Queen over all creatures, but also more than all she magnifies, praises, and serves her Son and the most Holy Trinity as Queen, Virgin Mother, and advocate for the renewal of all creatures who as yet have not arrived at the knowledge of their own perfection, essential and accidental, and so she procures daily new gifts of grace to men on earth, and fresh gifts of accidental glory to the Blessed.

On the feast of St. Bernard,[24] I had infinite devotion and many tears at Mass, as I considered the diminution of the honour due to the most Holy Sacrament which is the results of the tepid lives of Christians, and of the loss which is caused by men who leave the Church. I considered also the loss that befalls the souls in purgatory on account of these false opinions, and also the irreverence which is done to prelates and to the things of God, and also the many faults of evil speaking against men's neighbours which prevail, and how no one can bear another unless he does as he himself does.

The same day I felt a great devotion in offering myself to St. Bernard, praying him to be willing to accept me for his disciple, because he himself was so entirely pleasing to the Blessed Virgin Mary.

On the feast of St. Louis,[25] bishop and confessor, I had much devotion, thinking that I would apply my Mass, among other things, for all my negligences committed as to examining and attentively noting down the benefits which are offered to me every day by means of the works of God, and His words interior and exterior, and also by means of His own Body, which every day I have in my hands and before my eyes. From this there rose in me a great clearness of understanding, and a great desire which I ought always to retain in my mind, as to that verse, *Revela oculos meos, et considerabo mirabilia de lege tua.*

In like manner, I had often a certain feeling of marvel which occurred to me as to the changes which follow in a mind which at one time is disconsolate and at another joyful, considering at the first the reality of its own defects, and at the other the mercy of our Lord, and on this subject an interpretation came into my mind of that verse of the offertory, *Veritas mea et misericordia*

---

[24] August 20. [25] August 19.

mea cum ipso, that is, that our Lord at one time sets forth His truthfulness, showing justice ; at another, His mercy, giving signs of peace; and in these two ways He exercises His servants.

On the octave of the Assumption,[26] I received an excellent light as to the Passion of our Lord, which made me recover my devotion in the office and in my prayers. It was chiefly about these words, *Tristis est anima mea usque ad mortem. Transeat a me calix iste. Deus meus, Deus meus, ut quid me dereliquisti ? Mulier ecce Filius tuus!* and *Pater, in manus tuas commendo spiritum meum,* understanding all with relation to the Assumption, that it was by means of the compassion of the Blessed Virgin which she had for the Passion of her Son (that Passion being the direct and perfect road to go to heaven by), that she was raised above all the choirs of angels. And so it appeared to me a proper means for contemplating the Assumption of our Blessed Lady, to contemplate first the Passion of the Son, and then the compassion of the Mother.

In the Mass, before and after the consecration, and after my communion, I reflected on three things, or times, that relate to Christ—(1) before the Incarnation; (2) while He was in the world; (3) after the Ascension. In like manner there are three other times as to our Blessed Lady—(1) up to the conception of her Son ; (2) up to His death and Ascension; (3) from the time of His Ascension to her death. And on this a desire occurred to me that new graces might be communicated to me that I might be able better to know and love Christ by means of His Mother's intercession, so that I might have given me, in accordance with what I have said about the Mass, (1) some gifts that answer to the time before the Incarnation, which is

[26] August 22.

represented to me by the part of the Mass before the consecration; (2) some gifts which belong to the time between the Incarnation and the Passion; (3) others that relate to the time after the Passion up to the Judgment.

I also desired, for the great devotion which I have towards the Blessed Virgin, that each year, according to the time which intervenes between one of her feasts and another, our Lord might grant me grace, like to those of which she was full, taking (1) the time from the Conception of our Lady up to her Annunciation, to be therein continually prepared, so that I might truly say, Behold the servant of the Lord, already become the Tabernacle of the Most High; (2) for the time between the Annunciation and the death of her Son, to feel Christ always present with me, by means of my compassion with and imitation of Him; and (3) for the time after that up to her Assumption, to bear therein His absence, with holy desires of following Him into glory, after having here on earth done His holy will.

On the same day I reflected that the Passion of Christ and the compassion of the Blessed Virgin, are as it were two ladders by which to ascend straight to the knowledge of the mysteries of the Ascension and the Assumption, and I felt great devotion in offering to our Lord that little amount of knowledge that I possessed of these eathly things, as well of heavenly things, and I desired that He would give me grace never to let myself either be sad or rejoice except in accordance with the sadness and joy which Christ shared with His Blessed Mother.

On the feast of St. Bartholomew,[27] among other things, I applied the sacrifice of the Mass for the labours, not only present, but past and future also, of our fathers and brothers, adding all due thanksgiving to our Lord, asking

---

[27] August 25.

pardon also for all negligences committed, and begging the graces which are acquired by means of such toils. I wished also that I could be present at the execution of the martyrs, and be able to say to each one of them—*Exaudiat te Deum in die tribulationis. Tribuat tibi Dominus secundum cor tuum et omne consilium tuum confirmet. Impleat Dominus omnes petitiones tuas et holocaustum tuum pingue fiat!*

On the same day I was trying to say compline, and I felt a certain sadness of mind and distraction on account of my defects, such as I could not have wished to have felt on a day like that. But there came over me after that a certain feeling of consolation, inasmuch as it pleased our Lord, on days of that sort more particularly, to discover to me my own imperfections, in order that those saints seeing it might pray for me and might deliver me from them. So I gathered much hope from all this, and prayed that not only our Lord, but His Mother also, and the Apostles, St. John Baptist, St. Anne, St. Mary Magdalene, and all the saints, might thus come to know my spiritual necessities.

On the feast of St. Louis, King of France,[28] I felt much devotion in saying Mass for a certain cardinal, and in praying for the whole of France, in which so many good deeds have been done and so many sins pardoned, and for all the kings, dukes, counts, and other nobles, for the archbishops, bishops, abbots, and parish priests, and for the universities and cities, in which there are so many necessities both of body and soul.

On a Sunday, as I was saying office and reciting the words of the psalm—*Diligam te Domine, fortitudo mea, Dominus firmamentum meum et refugium meum et liberator meus, Deus meus adjutor meus, et sperabo in eum, protector meus et cornu salutis meæ, et susceptor meus*—I went on

[28] August 25.

pondering these things with great faith and hope and desire to love my Lord, but considering the frailty of the flesh, and that the soul is so blind and the spirit so perverse in judging of its own wants, I felt arise within me a strong feeling of devotion, suggesting to me to commend to the Almighty Father my body, praying Him to strengthen it, and my soul to the Son, that He might deign to enlighten it, and my spirit to the Holy Ghost, that He might bless and improve it so much that it should never forget its duty. By the soul I mean the sensitive part together with the lower portion, that faculty which deals with those things which are made known by the senses. By the spirit I mean that higher part which is engaged with divine things. I also asked the Son that He would grant me these gifts in the receiving of His most precious Body, Soul, and Divinity present in the Sacrament.

On the feast of the Decollation of St. John,[20] finding myself somewhat distracted, and seeing my difficulty in recollecting myself, I had much devotion at the thought how the most Holy Sacrament is peculiarly that source from which grace is found for such recollection, as our Lord therein is ever longing to enter into us and enlighten us.

I prayed St. John Baptist to teach me the manner of preparing the way of the Lord, since he is the voice crying out in the desert, *Parate viam Domini*, and I considered three ways of receiving and finding Christ —one in ourselves, because *regnum Dei intra vos est;* the second in heaven, whither He has ascended to draw us after Him ; the third in the Blessed Sacrament, wherein He has left Himself as the food of our soul, in which way we can draw Him to ourselves, according to that saying of His—*Ad eum veniemus et mansionem apud*

---

[20] August 29.

cum faciemus, and that other—*Si quis aperuerit mihi januam, intrabo et cœnabo cum illo, et ipse mecum.*

Whilst saying the office of St. Sabina,[30] martyr, a feeling of devotion arose within me to bear in mind at the same time during all the hours, St. Serafia, virgin and martyr, who whilst frequenting the house of St. Sabina was converted and instructed in the faith by her.

On the same day, considering how almost all sins are committed with much application of mind, as men speak and listen willingly about their subject-matter, I had a certain train of thought which led me to pray God to deign to prevent the evil spirits from tempting men so much, as for example, to the sin of gluttony, in which people plunge nowadays with as much affection and thought, as if they were thinking of nourishing their soul itself, which seeks other food; and so also as to the sin of carnality, in which men are so unbridled in fulfilling all their evil desires, and so have no taste for spiritual and divine food. Whereas, on the other hand, the body should rather be drawn to the spiritual tastes of the soul, and this cannot be done unless we recollect ourselves interiorly in all things, raising our minds to those things in which there is nothing that can be perceived by any sense, as the Divinity of Christ, which is the same as that of the Father and the Holy Ghost, and seeking the Humanity of Christ in heaven rather than on earth; and so also the Blessed Virgin, and after the Blessed Virgin the angelic spirits and the rest of the souls of the just who are in heaven. But if we would remain on earth, being ignorant how to ascend to heavenly things, let us put before our eyes Jesus Christ fastened to the Cross, and His holy life, and in the same way the life of our Blessed Lady, and of infinite holy martyrs and confessors who despised the world.

[30] August 29.

On the same feast of St. Sabina, considering our Lord Jesus Christ under the species of bread and wine, there came to me in my mind a good sentiment, as to how His infinite goodness was willing to take upon Himself the office and form of material bread and wine for the nourishment of our souls and the reformation of our bodies to a better state, which material bread and wine are not able to bring about.

On the feast of St. Giles,[31] abbot, after I had delivered a short exhortation before some who were going to communicate, I felt a great desire to preach, a desire which I had often felt before, and I resolved to use all endeavours to preach and lecture in Germany, seeing that great evil came from the long silence of the pulpit; and I felt also that it was necessary for the future to correspond to that spirit which urged me on to fervour in the Word of God, both in public sermons and private exhortations, and not only in the church, but in the private houses and public places, even though there be few who listen, and also at the tables of princes and nobles.

On the first Sunday of September,[32] while applying my consideration on the mysteries of the life, and death, and resurrection of Christ, to the soul of a certain doctor, a theologian of Paris, I felt a great devotion to say Mass for him, remembering some matters in which he might have sinned, as concerning obedience, poverty, and chastity, for he had been a Franciscan friar, as also in defects in teaching, having been a professor and preacher, and as to overweening curiosity in learning, and also vainglory, which is wont to wait on such men. And at the memento for the dead, it occured to me with much devotion to beg the most Holy Trinity to deign to be glorified in that soul, and to receive him into the number of the holy doctors, according to the promise

[31] September 1.   [32] September 3.

of the Prophet Daniel—*Qui ad justitiam erudiunt multos fulgebunt quasi stellæ in perpetuas æternitates.*

On the feast of SS. Cosmas and Damian,[33] I felt certain great and interior yearnings for the veneration of the most Holy Sacrament and the saints in heaven and the images and relics of saints, and I could have wished to be able to be present before the most Holy Sacrament wherever it is kept in all Germany, and also before any picture whatever of Christ, or the Virgin Mother of God, or any saint, man or woman, whatever. And deeming this desire impossible to fulfil, I asked our Lord to supply, by our holy guardian angels, my defects with regard to this devotion and those of all others, so that what men fail to do may be done by their guardian angels.

While I was also considering, with a certain elevation of mind, Christ sitting at the right hand of the power of God the Father, and that He sees all things that take place under the sun, I felt a certain sense of wonder at His great patience and goodness, that being so powerful in heaven and on earth He yet tolerates so many iniquities. As I was reflecting on this, I seemed to myself to see another thing also, namely, that in old times men crucified the Lamb bodily while He was mortal, and now that He is immortal and is reigning in heaven, they nevertheless crucify Him spiritually. And in this I found more to wonder at in His patience, inasmuch as it is a greater evil to offend Him now that He is in glory than it was to offend Him when He was liable to suffering.

On the feast of St. Michael the Archangel,[34] I had many reflections and pious feelings with reference to him and all the angels. While saying office, I felt a desire that the angels should praise our Lord as often as such

---

[33] September 27. [34] September 29.

words are said, inasmuch as it is they who feel and understand them better. I desired also that the saints should do the same, not only those who are named in the prayers, but also all the others, and that my saying office, my words and thoughts, might always be to them an occasion for praising our Lord, of thanking Him in our behalf, or asking favours from Him for us; and that they may not on account of my want of attention omit taking note of the good words which are pronounced by my tongue, and in like manner of the actions and ceremonies performed for God, although they are often done only in the faith of the Church, or in my own habitual faith alone.

At the offertory of the Mass, I felt a certain desire that it might be applied to the glory of St. Michael and the army of the angels, just as if they had been in this world in mortal flesh and perfectly imitated Jesus Christ; as also for my own greater merit and that of others, just as though we, having the power and knowledge of the angels, praised Christ here below even as He is praised in His glory. And so I should rejoice much if God had given me grace to take the place of the angels in many labours, and if they, on the other hand, supplied for me all that I am bound to for the honour of His Divine Majesty, to Whom thousands of thousands minister, and ten times a hundred thousand stand before Him. But I know very well that it should be enough for me to serve, praise, and honour Christ, considering Him in that guise in which He lived in the world, and with which He chose to be satisfied, seeing that in this He has left here those who hold His place, of whom He says, *Qui vos audit, me audit*, and also the poor of whom He says, *Quod uni ex minimis meis fecistis, mihi fecistis.*

On the feast of St. Jerome,[35] I learnt with special certainty, that to obtain his favour, and that of any other

---

[35] September 30.

saint, it helps much to have a great devotion towards that angel who was his guardian in this world. And so we may ask of such angels to obtain us the help of those saints, or, again, a share of that spirit from God which they had in this life.

Whilst saying office I felt great devotion, considering how the angels and saints can take occasion from our words to praise God and to help us to obtain what we ask; and so I felt it to be a very useful thing to implore them devoutly to assist us in contemplating and praising God, inasmuch as they see Him as He is. It is also of advantage that a man should desire that they should make up in all things for his deficiencies, and excuse his faults by the words of their blessed mouths. I felt likewise a great desire and a great joy that the saints who are in heaven should now have the means, power, and knowledge, and will to do and make up for all that which they had not the will, or the knowledge, or the power to effect with regard to undertakings for God or their neighbour, both alive and dead. I also felt a longing to be able to express in deed or words, or any other way, to all the saints and angels, all those things which God has done in this world, and whatever gifts God has communicated to us, that each one of the saints might in this manner be able to know and see in them God the Glorifier, to His own greater accidental glory, which admits of increase, even by occasions which come from us.

Here I also remarked a certain feeling of devotion, which I found arise from looking on the crucifix[36] in the Church of Holy Cross at Mayence, which pierced my heart so thoroughly, that I have retained an almost

---

[36] This seems to have been a crucifix which was said to have shed blood on receiving an insulting blow from a ruffian, on whom the blood fell, and who was converted.

continual remembrance of it, and a great impression of that high degree of God's goodness shown therein, in so often shedding His Blood for the sinner who has offended Him. So, too, He gave it after His death to the blind Longinus, who received his sight thereby. And so it appears to me that when I commit so many faults and show so much ingratitude to my Lord, He does nothing in return for so many wounds but to give me new grace in order that I may receive benefit from that very Blood so shed. And so it is, that whereas so many wickednesses and blasphemies in dishonour of God and of His saints are current in the world, the Divine Goodness still does not cease from shedding marks of the Blood of His love upon those who behave so, allowing Himself sometimes to be cruelly wounded, in order that after all they may enter into themselves, repent of their cruelty, and turn to that purest Blood, in order to heal their souls.

As I was making these reflections on the Blood of Jesus Christ, the Immaculate Lamb, I perceived the great force of that meekness which Christ taught us by words and work; for there is nothing more efficacious against cruelty and anger, and whatever is contrary to charity, than to be so meek as to make no resistance to the persecutor, so as at last to appease and soften him by patience and gentleness. But woe is me! I am too hard and savage, and too slow in believing and listening to Christ, Who has so many times shed tears and blood for me in vain! O wretched and cruel soul of mine! Why have not those tears softened thee which He shed for thee as soon as He had, for love of thee, left His heavenly Home and entered on the path of His mortal life? Why hast thou held out till He shed blood? See, even as a Child eight days old He shed tears and blood in the Circumcision, and yet thou hast not been moved. What dost thou wait for? See, unhappy soul, see that that shedding of tears which came upon Hin over Jerusalem, weeping over the ingratitude and ultimate ruin of that nation—that shedding of tears was made for thee and over thee. See also those tears which, as He gives up on the Cross His Soul into the hands of His Father, He sheds so plentifully for thy salvation! Ah! if these tears and this blood be not enough for thee, and if thou wouldst see a still greater outpouring, see Him in the Garden all sweating in His Agony, and how tears and blood are mingled there. See, moreover, the blood which issues from every part of His Body, bound, smitten, torn, and crowned with thorns; and, to end all, consider how on the Cross all His veins were entirely emptied of that most precious Blood, and how after death He opened His most sacred side, sending forth thence water and blood to heal and enlighten thee as well as Longinus. Do not seek, then, for any greater sign of His divine goodness in the sufferings of His Sacred Humanity, for now He can suffer no more. *Christus enim resurgens ex mortuis jam non moritur, mors illi ultra non dominabitur.*

The day before the feast of St. Francis,[37] whilst I was reciting the office of a martyr, my advocate, towards whom I have had for a long time a great devotion, I applied the sacrifice of the Mass for my relations living and dead, and for all of our family who have departed this life, and then also for all the families of my brothers who are in the Society of Jesus Christ. Whilst I was doing this, there arose in me a strong and pious recollection of those towards whom we are under obligations by nature. And so it seemed to me that it would be a very excellent thing to invoke the guardian angels of such families, past, present, and future, and at the same time to invoke the saints, after

---

[37] October 3.

our Blessed Lady, who have had special care of them, or who have now, or who shall have in future. And so I resolved to do three things — (1) to intercede for the remission of their sins; (2) to give thanks for the benefits which they have hitherto received; (3) to pray also that new blessings may be granted to them. I desired also that by means of that sacrifice, I and all my brethren might be excused for all faults and negligences committed in prayer, in thanksgiving, and in making intercession for those to whom we are under obligations.

After communion, I had a great desire, which I also had felt after the same action on the day before, that Christ, whom I had received within myself, might inclose me altogether within Himself and with Him, so that He might dwell in me, and might work with me for my renovation. I desired also that He, under Whose power lie infinite modes of being, would vouchsafe, at least accidentally, to renew my being within me—my being, my life, my working, that after a new manner I might direct towards Him my whole self and all other things, and that He Who alone is immutable in His being, His life, and His actions, might change all my doings day after day from good to better.

On the day of St. Francis,[38] among other good desires which I felt in my meditation, there was the special wish, which I begged with much spiritual fervour from our Lord, that by virtue of the sacrifice of the Mass He might grant me that St. Francis, and each one of the other saints, might for the future always remember me and intercede for me, and this as earnestly as if at the moment of the death of each I had asked it of him with tribulation of heart in those words of the thief—*Memento mei cum veneris in regnum Christi.*

[38] October 4.

Whilst thinking on that same day on certain points concerning the method of praying well, and of performing my actions well, and in a proper manner, also how good desires conceived in prayer are certain paths which lead to good works, and how on the other hand good works are like paths which lead to good prayers and good desires, I felt that one who seeks the Spirit of God in good works, will find it better afterwards in prayer. Whoever then seeks and finds the Spirit of Christ in good works, makes much more solid progress than the one who seeks it in prayer alone; for one who has Christ both in work and in prayer, is like one who has Him in affection and effect both. You must then mortify yourself and dispose yourself to gain all good by means of good works. For by this means you will perceive that this is a most excellent preparation for mental prayer. Let then your life be conducted in this manner, both with Martha and Magdalene, that is, made up of action and contemplation, pursuing the one for the other, and not one only for itself.

So you should practise prayer as a means for good actions, and so on the other hand, add good works as the best means for praying more fervently. It must also be observed that before going to good works, prayer, either mental or oral, should be well made, because it is in prayer that the good spirit is gained; and what I say of good works, I intend to be understood also of exhortations, sermons, and discourses, public or private. This is very necessary when things have to be done which are contrary to natural inclination, or to our own will, in order that thus we may better understand and more readily will the good that is to be found in such actions. And since for doing such things in which we feel difficulty or repugnance, we require greater grace, so also in doing them we acquire greater spiritual grace. One who is devoted to the mixed life must be adorned with many more virtues than one who leads a contemplative life, because he has many things above him, under him, within him, around him, which require various degrees of patience, humility, and charity, in due order; some to the sick, or sinners, or persecutors, others towards his inferiors or his superiors.

With regard to this subject of good works, we must know that there are three kinds of them, in which we must practise ourselves. Some have reference to ourselves, some to our neighbours, and some to God. To ourselves pertain works of penance, which consist in mortification and abnegation of our own will and judgment, and in the abandonment of riches and temporal comforts. To our neighbours we owe all those works which assist him either spiritually or temporally, such as consolation, help, alms. To God peculiarly belong all those things which relate to His honour and that of the saints, such as the administration of the sacraments, sermons, divine office, and the decoration of churches. In the first of these three ways, a man makes himself in a certain manner an enemy to himself; in the second, a friend to his neighbour; in the third, pleasing to God.

One day I was about to say a Mass for the dead in the Church of Holy Cross at Spires, for the benefactors, founders, and all the city, and it came to my mind to say the Mass of the Holy Cross, because there was there a cross which had wrought such great miracles. At that moment our Lord gave me a very great spirit of devotion to that cross and to any other, understanding with great clearness of faith the marvellous power of the cross against the devil. For this reason I desired always to have a cross actually on my heart, and to have by me always the pictures of the Crucifix, our Lady, and the saints, and their relics, and in like manner to have holy water always at hand, and to use it for everything.

Moreover, I desired that all that holy temple with its sacred things therein, and also all the most holy Body of Christ, the true temple of divine goodness, might ever be in me and I in it in spirit. O my soul, if thou couldst relish and understand well the sweet name of Jesus, in which is fulness of salvation, or at least the name of the the Cross, or of the Blessed Mary our Lord's Mother, and of the saints, how lasting would be thy joy and how much strength from God wouldst thou receive! Thou wouldst appear far different from what thou now art, both to angels and to devils. Advance therefore, my soul, in thy devotion to all sacred things, sign thee with the sign of the Cross, and consider all these things day after day, until thou comest to the fountain-head from whence they are all derived.

On another day I was thinking of that saying of our Lord—*Auferetur ab eis sponsus* and *numquid possunt filii sponsi lugere quamdiu cum illis est sponsus*, and a great feeling of marvel came over me, and in much piety of spirit towards our Lord, I exclaimed, 'O Lord, what is this? Thou speakest of Thyself to Thy disciples, and callest Thyself a Bridegroom, and nevertheless Thou showest Thyself not at all as a dainty Bridegroom, but rather as an abject servant and slave of all. Thou dost labour and sweat, Thou art despised and reviled even unto the Passion and death on the Cross. Thou dost toil, that Thine may rest, Thou dost afflict Thyself that they may rejoice, and to crown all Thou dost choose to die, in order to give them life.'

Truly this is something like that saying of the poet's—

> Sic vos non vobis vellera fertis, oves,
> Sic vos non vobis mellificatis, apes.

May Thy holy Name be blessed and praised and exalted for ever, O good Jesus, and for ever and for ever. Amen.

On a Sunday morning, as I was reciting the divine office, I found myself distracted, and implored the aid of God and of the Blessed Virgin. Then I received many good helps to devotion, which incited me to continue the actual attention of my spirit and my self-recollection, a thing God is wont to grant to those who use all diligence that they may understand the words that they recite well, and receive that grace which is in them as in a seed. And as I was drawing near to the end of the office, I considered that the nearer Christ drew to the end of His life, so much greater were the torments which He suffered, and so I ought to go on always increasing in my devotion to His Passion, so that when I came to the hour of none I might be able to feel the efficacy of His death and of the breathing out of His Soul, which took place at that hour.

On the day on which I recited the office of St. Mark,[38] pope and confessor, I had many good sentiments. Among other things it came into my heart to wish that all the good desires which that blessed Pope, when on earth, had for the salvation of the Germans and other infidels, might be fulfilled in our time, and also the desires of all the saints, in order that that saying might be more universally fulfilled, *Desiderium animæ ejus tribuisti ei*, in that each saint beholds fulfilled, not only the desires which he has in his life in glory, but also every other desire for the honour of God and the salvation of souls which he had in this life.

On the same day, as I was about to say Mass, I had another desire, that God might vouchsafe to accept that sacrifice for so high a degree of spiritual fruit for the benefit of this city of Spires, as I and all my companions might gain if we were to stay here until our death. After Mass, as I was examining myself how I had borne myself

[39] October 7.

therein, I begged earnestly by the merits of the Passion of Christ, which is our principal subject of remembrance, that I might have memory given me to call to mind all my past spiritual exercises, attention of mind for those which I am now occupied on, and a good desire as to those which I shall perform in future.

On the following day, as I was saying the office of St. Stephen,[40] pope and martyr, whose head is preserved and venerated in the chief church at Spires, I felt some strong desires, together with a firm faith, that they would be accomplished. They were that St. Stephen might be the first to open to me a door for the exercise of my spiritual ministry in the vineyard of Christ, and I prayed him to promote and arrange by means of God's grace the work in which I was to occupy myself, as it seemed to me not enough that I myself alone should be moved to it and disposed for such an undertaking.

When I made my communion in the Mass, I begged with great feeling that that most Sacred Sacrament might deign to make me an obedient instrument of His Divine Majesty, His Mother, the angels and saints, and all the souls in purgatory and all the living, an instrument which each might use to work with according to the will of God. May it please God to give me grace to accomplish what I have promised, and to be the property of all, to live for all, and to work for all, to the praise of God and to the salvation of the living and of the dead.

On the day of St. Denis,[41] the Areopagite, and his companions, I was visited by much devotion, praying them to vouchsafe to obtain for me some lasting grace from the Heavenly Father, another from the Son, and another from the Holy Ghost, and also some grace

---

[40] St. Stephen's day is the 2nd of August, perhaps the feast at Spires was that of his translation.

[41] October 9.

from the Blessed Virgin and the other saints whom I named.

Besides this, I asked them to obtain for me some principle of good sentiments in my heart, so as to break forth into words of love, of the fear of God, or of any virtue that I might be most in need of, and in the same way, some blessing for all the needs of my body. I felt also a new desire, that the Blessed Sacrament, when It entered my stomach, might deign to feed my soul, as the natural food of bread and wine feeds and nourishes the flesh and body which belong to my soul.

On the day of St. Cerbonius,[42] bishop and confessor, as I was reflecting on the life and death of Christ, there came to my mind certain colloquies with much tenderness of spirit, and I said, 'O my Lord Jesus Christ, let Thy death be my life, make me learn how to find life in Thy death, let Thy travail be my repose, Thy human weakness my strength, Thy confusion my glory, Thy sadness my joy, and in Thy humiliation let me be exalted. In brief, let all my good lie in the ills which Thou hast suffered, since Thou, O Lord, hast repaired my life, which was on the road to death without any hope of remedy.'

On the day of the Seven Friar Martyrs,[43] who were companions of St. Francis, I was celebrating Mass, and felt a sort of fear that I was not large enough in charity towards certain persons, whose defects came before me. On this I heard the answer—If you shut your heart against your neighbours, God will shut His Heart against you, and if you open your heart wide to your neighbours, God will open His Heart wide to you. Seek first the love of God, and then you will easily find the love that you ought to have to enemy as well as to friend. And whenever there may be need of some actual reconciliation with your neighbour either in word or deed, let it

---

[42] October 12.   [43] October 13.

be done as soon as possible as a means of making your peace with God. But when certain feelings come to you from nothing but what passes in your mind alone, then interior reconciliation of spirit is all that is needed. Such, for instance, are certain bitternesses and estrangements, which must be chased away at once from the heart, that it may take to itself feelings of kindness and patience towards your neighbour. In that way you will relieve your understanding from the error that was in it by means of false representations which beset it from mere human reason or from the evil spirit, and you will at the same time relieve your will from the error that was upon it in consequence of false impressions. Then you must be on your guard in such aversions of the mind not to let yourself attempt to conquer by flying, that is, by avoiding the person or the things from which you may feel averse. We ought rather to seek their presence, imitating Christ our Lord, Who was always, as it were, so given to drawing near to His persecutors, that even after His death, when Longinus came with hatred to pierce His Heart with his lance and so offend Him, not only did He not evade the blow, but with great love exposed His own Body and also shed His Blood in order to heal him.

On a Sunday, which fell on the 22nd October, 1542, I determined to consent to the wish of the Archbishop of Mayence, who desired that I should go with him to the Council of Trent, which was to begin on the 1st of November. Before I made up my mind, however, I had various feelings in my mind and some sadness, from which I was delivered by our Lord by virtue of holy and blind obedience, which knows how not to look at its own insufficiency, nor at the difficulty of the things which are commanded it.

As I was saying that morning the canonical hours, I felt myself distracted concerning the affair just mentioned, and as to a certain answer which I had to give to Mgr. the Bishop Suffragan, and then I had some clear lights which admonished me, that while one is saying the divine office, one must not admit any thoughts or applications which are not according to the words and their sense, in order that we may be entirely occupied in mind on that matter with which what we say is concerned. And when ever at such times we feel ourselves drawn off to any other subject, however good it be, as a sermon or an exhortation, we should remember at once that all that is outside the disposition of mind which is required for the divine office and the things which relate to God. May it please our Lord to grant us the grace not to bring ourselves into confusion as to the arrangement of our actions, our words, and our desires, but to do everything in its proper order and time!

One day in the same month I chanced to be lodged in a small castle of a certain count at Spires, and when I rose at midnight to pray, I entered on certain colloquies with God, praying for all the people there with much devotion and many tears, saying—'O Lord God, who is there among all these who acknowledge Thy great goodness, with which Thou hast brought it about that there should be so many temporal good things in these parts, and that for so long a time they have had the most holy Sacrament of the Eucharist, and the other sacraments, the ceremonies of Holy Church, and the true Christian teaching? Pardon, O Lord, this poor people which thinks not at all of these things, knows them not, nor asks for them. Pardon them also, because they are not mindful at all of the souls in purgatory. Vouchsafe, O Lord, to give and preserve to them all these blessings, and consider not their ignorances, or their ingratitude, but look rather on Christ our Redeemer, on the angels and the saints, who most perfectly acknowledge not only the greatness of Thy benefits, but also the grievousness of the sins which would have been committed in this place if Thou hadst altogether withdrawn the hand of Thy mercy from them.' And so I went on discoursing in my prayer, and I asked from our Lord for the inhabitants of this place abundance of the fruits of the earth, peace and good government on the part of their temporal lords, and also the Catholic faith, churches, holy pictures, Masses, holy water, relics of the bodies of the saints, and obedience to the bishops and elders of Holy Church, with many other good things, desiring that they should acknowledge them as received from God and Jesus Christ, and the Blessed Virgin.

On the day of SS. Crysanthus and Daria,[44] martyrs, before I began the office, I found great devotion, and in it I offered myself, with all the good works which I might in future do down to the time of my death, for my benefactors, of whatever state and condition, and for those of my companions, to the glory of God, and for the salvation of my soul and of my neighbours. This made me feel the abundance of the charity of Christ, and I invoked His grace, by which for all men, present and future, He merited superabundantly everything necessary both for their salvation in the state of grace and for their glorification in the heavenly country, although it is true that with an absolute will, according to the order of what theologians call the *voluntas signi*, He has not willed that all this merit shall be applied to everything. So I prayed our Lord that He would vouchsafe to receive me and each one of my companions as regenerated in Christ, and receive also all our works and labours as actually directed and ordered in Him, and as united to the life and Passion of Christ.

[44] October 25.

I also felt a very lively pain that I had not, from the beginning of my life, asked nor endeavoured to gain, or at least in some degree desired, that spiritual grace which has since been granted to me, and I thanked the Son of God, that in His everlasting charity He had determined to grant me those gifts which now I enjoy, and that He willed that all the labours and sorrows which He suffered in His Humanity for me, should be really applied to me, and be treasures of my own. May He be praised for ever.

And here I remembered a certain desire which I had before felt, after this manner—Oh, that God had granted me to be, for love of Jesus Christ, servant to Adam, to Abraham, to David, and lastly to the Blessed Virgin Mary, who conceived Him, bare Him, and nursed Him: and so again to the Apostles, to each Pope, successors of St. Peter, down to Paul III., under whom we now are, and of all the Popes who are to be hereafter. I desired, in the first place, considering the Sacred Humanity of Christ, to serve with bodily service all the ancient fathers, from whom He was descended according to the flesh, and then, dwelling on the thought of His Divinity, to serve with spiritual exercises the fathers of the New Testament, who have to serve Christ, and at the same time as in spiritual offices.

On the day of St. Evaristus,[45] pope and martyr, I rose three hours after midnight, and felt a great devotion and many pious desires to pray for the needs of my neighbours—Christians, Jews, Turks, heathen and heretics. And there came into my mind various kinds of maladies of men, that is, their various infirmities, sins, despair, lamentations, deaths, famine, pestilence, and other travails. And in relation to all of these I set before me our Lord God and Redeemer Christ, our Comforter and our

[45] October 26.

Deliverer, praying Him to vouchsafe to give to all succour, comfort, and aid. And here again I desired and prayed with an abundance of feeling, that I might be allowed to be servant and minister of Christ, so that by means of Him I might have power to succour, console, and liberate many from divers evil, spiritual as well as corporal, so as to practise in such a manner all the offices of charity to my neighbours, whether in relation to the soul or to the body. Remember this, my soul, and that at that and other times it was given thee to confide, not in thyself nor in thine own merits, but in Christ alone; and this as to things which cannot be done by natural power, such as healing the sick, giving sight to the blind, cleansing the lepers, driving out devils—so far did thy desire and thy spirit stretch, and that without vanity or foolishness, making thee desire all things possible unto charity, from which, even though it be no larger than a grain of mustard-seed, confidence is wont to spring without rashness or presumption. Otherwise, that faith which is not kindled by charity is of little help to him who worketh, as the Apostle says—*Si enim habuero tantam fidem ita ut montes transferam, charitatem autem non habuero, nihil mihi prodest*—although it may profit my neighbour. It is necessary, therefore, that the faith which is to work great things towards our neighbours, be the child of and awakened by this charity which we feel towards them, by means of which we come to understand what is useful and what is necessary for our neighbour, and this without being moved by any other feeling than pure charity— for this is often wont to be the case when we see others in extreme necessity, and less often in others, on account of our human imperfection, which makes it difficult to feel the smaller needs of our neighbours, as we do our own smaller needs. A man in love with the glory of God, who by the grace of the Holy Ghost knows how to weigh to the very life the things that are of God, will be able more easily than another to obtain this faith by the gift of the Holy Ghost, by means of which he will be able to work great and wonderful things to the glory of God at a fitting time. Again, in your own necessities, especially when they are very extreme and great, and tend to deep affliction of the heart, it is not difficult to find faith, by means of which, contrary to all human hope, you may be able to obtain some small grace for soul or body, such as a deliverance from some evil or the acquisition of some necessary good which otherwise could not be had. In such a case it is of the very first importance that a man should not love himself for himself, but should be directed in everything to the glory of God, the salvation of his own soul and of his neighbours. Keep, therefore, thine eye in everything on the most perfect of graces and gifts, that is, on charity, and practise thyself in this, making continual advances therein, and then it will be easy for thee to acquire other graces also relating to good for thyself and thy neighbour. Ask the grace of little things, and thou shalt find grace to aim at and hope for great things. Practise thyself in the least matters, and God will give you the greater; do all that thou canst do, and then God will give thee strength also to do what is above thee.

There are many who are often very anxious and eager to do good works that are great and universal in their range, and meanwhile they neglect lesser and more particular good works, for which they might well have found sufficient grace to help them. If you find you have one single talent, do not hide it, but make use of it, and you will gain thereunto another in addition to it. Never fail to execute the good works that are present to your hand, for the sake of the idle consideration of other future good works, which are far off from thee. Desires are good, when they are from God and conceived for Him and directed to Him. Hence, also, it sometimes happens that in our prayers we desire impossible things, and things which will never be granted to us: the desires are, nevertheless, not displeasing to God, to Whom they are directed.

It often happens that when you look on yourself, and on your own strength, you seem to yourself not to have the knowledge or the power to do anything at all for the service of your neighbour. But if the Spirit of our Lord guides you, He will make you see the most difficult things accomplished most easily by His grace, so to excite you to undertake great works, and that you may never be without hope in any matter. And even if the Spirit of the Lord, as is possible, were to make you feel a perfect certainty as to some misfortune, some utter condemnation of certain cities or persons, and you were to seem to know that such was the will of God, not for all that ought you to cease from supplicating His divine goodness for such cases, and asking for mercy on them, knowing by faith that that will of God is not absolute but conditional, since God declares many things to His servants as well as in the Scriptures in an absolute manner, while yet He does not decree them absolutely, on account of the many variable conditions of contingent things.

On the vigil of SS. Simon and Jude,[46] I happened to be making my prayers in the silence of the night, and I felt myself strongly inspired to use every effort in order that the poor sick people who are to be found up and down the streets of the city of Mayence, might be collected together and received into some hospital, where they might be well tended and governed.

[46] October 27.

And here I remembered many cases of negligence of my own and of want of care for certain poor persons with wounds and sores, whom I had seen and even visited more than once, but with tepidity. And although I had then no means of helping them, yet I might have gone from door to door begging for them, and I might have found others who might have helped them, prelates, lords, magistrates, or doctors of the places in which these poor creatures were.

I felt myself also moved to pray all those of the Blessed in heaven who had been weak and of bad health in this life, to deign to be the advocates of the poor sick people of this and other cities, and also to obtain for me fresh grace to help the poor in such a state.

On the day of the holy Apostles Simon and Jude,[47] I had much consolation after Mass in certain meditations and colloquies which I made either immediately with God, or with the Father, the Son, and the Holy Ghost, as also with the Sacred Humanity of Jesus Christ our Lord, and in them I felt greater consolation than I am wont to feel when I invoke the saints, or when I pray for the salvation of others, although in these two last ways I am more frequently visited by our Lord than in those reflections which I make immediately upon the knowledge and love of God. But it is abundantly enough for me that our great and mighty Lord should communicate Himself to me in His saints and through them, for my good and the benefit of my neighbours, towards whom I am warmest in feeling when I am coldest in work. Hence it is that I am often most anxious and full of various desires for their salvation and profit, at the time that I do not exert myself enough in doing for them what I can, and hence I often fail

[47] October 28.

in external execution of good at the time that I am overflowing with internal affections. May it please our Lord God to set in order, direct, and arrange all that I do according to the good pleasure of His will, so that I may not only be in search of what He is, but also of what He desires me to do. He in His own Essence is most high and infinitely great beyond all capacity and intelligence of all men, and yet in His will, which He lays on us by precept, He is so modest and limited that He never obliges man to anything which He cannot do, never commands anything that is beyond the force of any one, however weak, and more than this, He helps him with His grace which is always more ready at hand to help man than he is to himself. It is right therefore that God should be greatly praised for this, in that being Himself in all respects infinite and immense, He yet contents Himself with what our nature, so limited and measured, can do, and that the burning force of the grace that He gives us is so tempered that He does not require, as of necessity, that we should do the very extreme of what our power and knowledge and will can effect.

On the following Sunday,[48] after I had been delivered from a certain perplexity of mind and had regained all that serenity which is of the good spirit, I seemed to hear some words of consolation, to the effect that He Who knows how to take away from us the fear of an evil, knows also and is able to drive away as well that evil from which that fear and anxiety of mind proceeded, and He Who can give us good hope in adversity can also give us the thing itself which we hope for. May He then be blessed, Who is not less powerful in overcoming all the obstacles that meet us and contradict us, than in soothing all the disturbances of our spirit!

[48] October 29.

On the solemnity of All Saints,[49] I felt a great desire that there should be the same sort of solemn remembrance made of them in heaven as on earth to-day, as well as great mercy and pity for all that now dwell in the world, especially sinners, so that no one should be left out, and memorial of all be made in heaven. I desired the same thing for the souls in purgatory; for each of the saints can easily see in the mirror of the Divinity every one who is on earth or in purgatory, and so remember them before God.

On All Souls' day, I had from the beginning to the end of Mass, and even from the time that I began to prepare for it, great devotion in the thought of the dead, such as I never had before on this day, and it all came by the spirit moving me to compassion for the departed. There was given to me an abundant flow of tears; I thought of my father and mother and relations, of my deceased brothers of the Society, of our benefactors, of the relations of all my brothers; there were present to my thoughts those who in life were specially devoted to the Blessed Virgin Mary, and to certain particular saints, and to the angels, and also to those who had no one in this world, which is the place of meriting, to pray for them.

I had also a feeling of humility as to the continual hunger and thirst I have to be able to serve Christ in His work of saving souls. The words which seemed to come to me with this feeling were to this effect—' For as much as thou art not worthy to serve Christ Himself, the Lord of all lords, nor even to be employed in the harvest of souls, take comfort in this at least that thou mayest find something that thou canst do for Christ's sake, as the servant of some lord of lesser dignity, as some particular saint, or the souls of the departed who

---

[49] November 1.

are being punished in purgatory. And this last is indeed a great affair, and one to which in times past great many others have served Him.'

On that same All Souls' day, just as I had finished none after dinner, I felt great devotion accompanied with various illustrations of holy light as to certain classes of men, which may be put down as five. The first, in every way more perfect than the rest, of the souls already in heaven and blessed. The second, of souls in purgatory, who are afflicted with the deepest sorrows, and for a time are kept fast in the greatest torments. The third is of the souls of children in Limbus, who have died in original sin and who have missed all the good that Christians can gain through Christ, although they neither have nor ever will have any pain of sense internal or external. The fourth is of the souls of those who have been condemned to eternal punishment, and who are now and will be for all eternity tormented in every way. The fifth is of the souls of those who are in this world and who are journeying on still between the hope of life in heaven and the fear of the pains of hell. These have in their own hands power to save themselves or to be lost; the latter, springing from their own nature alone, the other springing from that divine grace which is always in our power and may be said to be more ours than our own free will.

I pondered then these five classes with varying affections, feeling chiefly moved in the thought of the souls in purgatory, and the souls of those still alive in this corrupt world. I felt desires that the saints, who, now that they are in their glory can do so much, should pray for us; and that the souls in purgatory should also pray for us in those groanings and contrition of theirs, which, for the rest, do not profit themselves, but which if they were the sorrows of heart still mortal, could not fail to merit in the shortest moment anything in heaven, and thus can avail much and far more than can be said for us who live in faith and have not yet come to know by sight the things of God. May Christ grant that these groanings may plead in His sight for us! I understood also that it might be most salutary that the souls in purgatory should be invoked to obtain for us a true knowledge and a true sense of our sins, diligence in good works, solicitude in bringing forth fruits of penance, and in general all those graces for want of which they themselves are now suffering so great a punishment.

On the day after All Souls' day, in the morning, I observed many things that occurred to me as to the nakedness of my soul and spirit, and for that reason I begged our Lord with some fervour of devotion, that through the intercession of all the saints He would deign to clothe me with a garment of purity, innocence, chastity, and cleanness, against all the stains and defilements of this deceitful life, and with the garment of a fervent love of Himself and of my neighbour against all the chills of the evils that threaten us from without, against the wickedness of men or any other adverse accidents.

I had also, it seemed to me, a clear understanding of the nakedness of the souls in purgatory, which taught me that I ought to account their sufferings as far heavier, inasmuch as they suffer in the soul deprived of the body. For just as a soul which does not yet possess a glorified body is better able to feel consolation when separate from its body than when united to it, so a soul which suffers away from its body because this has not yet been given up to punishment, suffers more in this naked state than if it were still clothed with its mortal body; and the reason is this, that pain which pierces through soul and spirit directly, is deeper and far more keen than pain that only reaches the soul through the body, because a mortal body, and even the senses of the body, would necessarily absorb or divert not only some of the corporal punishment that is inflicted, but also all that part of the spiritual punishment that is received either through the organs of the body, or through those faculties of the soul that are, as it were, buried therein.

On another day within the octave of All Saints, I began to feel a new and lively desire for greater perfection, so as to stretch myself out to those things that are before, forgetting the things that are behind. Hereupon I determined to direct my thoughts and desires and affections to the things that are better and higher, more perfect and more pleasing to God. This favour, too, was granted to me, at least in part, while saying office and Mass on that same day, namely, that I strove to attain to a more perfect attention and more perfect understanding of the words that I said, and that my soul, instead of being drawn away to other things, should attend more resolutely to its own greater and better profit.

I noted also here how very much every one must be on his guard not to let himself be pierced by those cold winds which arise from the attentive consideration of the defects of others, for from this it often comes about that we lose the hope which we had of our neighbour's salvation, our good opinion of him goes, and our confidence in him, our love and charity towards him. These evils must be overcome by the fervour of the spirit, not only when they exist only in our opinion, but when the defects are truly to be found in our neighbour; that so evil may be overcome in good, and we may not desist from intercourse with him and care concerning him on account of his miseries. On this account it is of the highest importance in such cases that things should not be considered in themselves but in God, and in what we know of His good pleasure. A man who does not raise his mind and his spiritual senses to the things which are of God, but rather dwells on things in themselves, full of defects and evil, as they are in themselves, such a man will be quickly disturbed and quickly grow cold, and despair of success in what he undertakes. He will be dejected and take to flight in sadness and indolence, will easily be deceived, and will judge of the issues of things all on the worst side and be filled with many suspicions.

And here I noted how sometimes it may help us very much not to have great sensible devotion, for it is very expedient that we should learn to work with but little grace to help us, or, to put it in better words, to co-operate to that lesser grace which our Lord gives us, straining ourselves to do what we can and what God requires of us, so that, with but a small aid of grace to help us, we may cherish some good desire or gain some sort of spiritual profit. Sometimes God pours into the soul His holy fear, and this fear is often more profitable than a great fervour of devotion. Hence we must esteem highly, not only devotion, but also the desire and the effort to have devotion, as also the sorrow because we have it not. These are seeds of great worth, which in due time bring their fruit to maturity.

Desires, therefore, are good things, and so are prayers and petitions, although they be accompanied by but little grace of devotion. For in this way we go on, although slowly, though with difficulty and tears, we go on and we arrive at God; whereas with an abundance of devotion and consolation we are in a certain way drawn to Himself by God, Who consoles us. When St. Paul says that we are not sufficient of ourselves even to think anything of ourselves, he does not infer that we can do absolutely nothing as of ourselves, but he says that we are not sufficient, that our own forces alone are not enough to do good. For it behoves us that grace should go before, and accompany, and follow that very little or nothing which comes from us, as of ourselves, and which is of itself insufficient. In order, therefore, that we may have sufficiency given to us, even in the least things, our own work is required, which is to cooperate with the grace of God, and receive therefrom its sufficiency even in the first apprehension of that good which it does. Let no one, then, say that he cannot do good always and everywhere. For although our sufficiency comes from God, Who works in us, yet nevertheless it is always within us, because grace is always standing at the door and knocking, it is always and everywhere anticipating and expecting us, but we may work together with it with that force which is our own.[50]

On the fifth day within the octave of the same feast of All Saints, in the morning, after I had made my daily prayer and contemplation of the life of Christ, I felt a great devotion to the holy angels, and the saints, and the souls in purgatory, and I besought the angels of all the saints, and of the souls in purgatory, that is, those angels who had at one time been their guardians, that they would be propitious to me through the merits of Jesus Christ, that so I might be able to overcome the malice of the evil spirits who by God's permission try even the saints in their cause of virtue.

I made my petition also with great devotion to Christ our Lord, pondering how He had subjected Himself externally to the power of the bad angels, as of Herod, of Archelaus, of Annas, of Caiaphas, of Pilate, and of the others who afflicted Him with bodily sufferings; and

---

[50] In these few sentences it may be said that the whole treatise of Divine Grace is summed up. We may learn from them what were the doctrines on that subject taught at the time in the University of Paris, where Father Favre learnt them.

even to Satan, the tempter, who with external violence tempted Him in the desert, as if wishing to allure Him to the things that belong to the flesh and to the pride of life and to the love of riches. I desired, therefore, that by the grace won by this so great humility, it might be ordained that the devils and bad angels should have no power over my interior, but rather, if it were not expedient that it should be otherwise, over my exterior only. Here I considered how the devils were able indeed to afflict Christ by the hands of men, by the scourges, the nails, and other external things, but could not do so by any evil thoughts or suggestions so as to provoke His flesh, or spirit, to evil. In the same way I thought how the Blessed Virgin Mary and many of the saints, suffered external afflictions, but not internal, although some holy men and holy women (but not the Blessed Virgin Mary) were sometimes, even repeatedly, attacked by interior trials connected with the vanities of the world and the pleasures of the flesh, caused by the ministry of evil spirits.

On the 13th of November, the day on which the Canon Bartholomew Monson was buried, I was in the town of Lower Ingelheim, two leagues from Mayence. I felt some sadness, thinking I had not taken all the care I might of him. I seemed to myself to have done nothing for him; but then I took comfort from a sort of answer that came to my mind that it was well that a person's will should go far beyond any good work that he does, and not that the will should be exhausted and borne down by its works. I received also instruction in thinking over the repugnances that are wont to be experienced by those who exercise themselves in such works of charity to the sick, and especially if they are poor, wounded, or if there is contagion. And the instruction came to this, that it behoves every one who attends to such good works, or to any others for Christ's sake, to be willing to give even his life in the performing of any such work of charity. Here also, whilst I was searching within myself for some reason for devotion and thanksgiving, and reflecting on the time of the death of the aforesaid Master Canon Bartholomew, which was after midnight on Sunday night, that is, about two o'clock on Monday morning, this reason for good hope occurred to me, that the deceased had been for many years most earnestly and constantly devout in honouring St. Michael the Archangel, to whom, together with all the other angels, Monday is consecrated in many churches by a special commemoration. I rejoiced that he had died on that day, and was thus myself consoled.

Another day when I was celebrating Mass for one of our religious brethren, who had died at Louvain the preceding day, as I, unworthy that I am, held in my hands the most Blessed Sacrament of the Eucharist, I saw and understood a great benefit done me by God that I had hitherto not thought of, this, namely, that He had left me my body as the instrument of my soul, to aid me in many ways in the service of both Christ Himself and His Father. I besought Christ, therefore, that He would vouchsafe to bestow this grace in answer to the prayers of all my friends and others, that I might not breathe forth my spirit from my body till such time as my soul should be rightly disposed to merit to be received into the hands of Almighty God.

On the feast of St. Catharine of Alexandria,[51] I received a singular light as to a practice which would help very much to the proper reciting of the divine office. It was this—'Persuade yourself that as long as you give the attention you ought to the divine words, so long will our Lord Himself be solicitous for your interests, both in

---

[51] November 25.

your affairs of business and your other works; and take care, therefore, not to allow yourself to be distracted by thoughts of good and pious works, be they of what sort or what importance they may, lest you should thereby prevent God Himself from being solicitous for them in your stead.' I saw also how fitting it would be when saying office to consider on the one hand God Himself present and His good angel, who notes and weighs most exactly all my exertions, on the other hand the enemy of men, that is, the malignant spirit, who notes down every fault I commit, that he may some day be able to charge it against me before God.

On the day [52] before the feast of St. Saturninus, as I was saying the translated office of St. Cæsarius, martyr, I experienced a great feeling of devotion towards this holy martyr, and this, although I knew nothing special about either his life or martyrdom. The favour was then, for the first time, granted to me to understand the benefits to be gained by making a contemplation regarding each saint as his feast occurs, the contemplation to have, after the ordinary preludes, five points, as follows. (1) Offer thanks to God the Father, Son, and Holy Ghost, Who from all eternity predestined this saint, Who chose, called, justified, sanctified, and finally placed him in glory. (2) Thank the Blessed Virgin, St. Michael, and the saint's good angel, and all the saints, men and women, who, by their prayers, or in any other way, helped this saint before God in the saving of his soul. (3) Pray to God and to the saint himself for the souls in purgatory, and all those still alive, who were or are devout to the saint. (4) Beseech God (pondering at the same time how much profit must ensue from your prayers being granted) that He would vouchsafe to preserve for us the writings and books from which we might be able to keep

---

[52] November 28.

in our minds, either some of the words of the saints, or at least some of the good deeds that the saints performed for our edification when on the earth. (5) Consider how good and profitable it is that the relics of the saint have been preserved to us, and are held in such great veneration, or how good and profitable it would be if they had been so preserved. If, however, any one should not find in these five points matter on which to exercise his understanding, let him exercise his will by desiring from his heart that all the things named should be done, and should be still better and better done.

On the feast of St. Saturninus,[53] which was also the vigil of St. Andrew the Apostle, when I was about to say Mass, the grace was given me to make the following petitions with my whole heart, namely, to God the Father for the grace and all other things needed by my memory, to God the Son for everything needed by my intellect, and to God the Holy Ghost for everything needed by my will. In this way I commended to the Supreme Trinity my three powers. Besides this I commended my soul to the Soul of Christ our Lord and Saviour, and lastly my whole self, all that makes what is called man, to Christ made man for us.

Here also with a singular feeling of misery and depression of spirit, I prayed for the grace of the elevation of my mind; both that it might not now remain, as it had hitherto been, inclining downwards to the things of earth, and that by the grace of Jesus Christ it might be always turned and soaring up to that which is above. While thinking of this prayer, this also occurred to me as it had indeed often occurred to me before, namely, to recommend myself to that holy woman who was delivered by Christ from the infirmity by which she had been made unable to look upwards

[53] November 29.

even with the eyes of her body, but who, after her deliverance, was at once able to do so. For it is of much avail to invoke those who have received certain graces with the view that they may obtain the same or similar favours for us. It is, therefore, consonant to piety and true doctrine to say that certain particular saints should be specially invoked for certain particular graces both of the spiritual and of the temporal order. For although God can do everything directly Himself, or by any one saint He chooses as well as by another, it is not His will to bring about everything by one and the same means.

On the feast of St. Eligius,[54] bishop and confessor, I asked with great devotion for two graces that are contained in the collect of the common of confessors, when we beg *ut augeat devotionem et salutem*, that is, that we may be increased in devotion and salvation. In the Mass, also, I besought God that He would take from me all that can offend His divine eyes, all that can separate me from Him, or make me dry and wandering and unworthy of giving Him honour.

From the feast of St. Andrew to that of St. Saba,[55] I was considering a thing which before I had not considered, namely, that before this I used to pass from distraction to devotion, moved and exerted by external things, as for instance, the troublesomeness of temptations, or the remorse of conscience, or fear, which drew me to seek devotion and a remedy against distraction. But now I asked the grace of God, and partly obtained it, to be moved by interior things instead, the fervour of spirit and the affection of the heart. I took courage to ask this grace by considering the life of Christ, which began with interior things and then went on to external. In the first thirty years of His life, before He began to

[54] December 1. [55] November 30—December 5.

teach by word, it was His will to teach by deeds, to be first disciple, then teacher, first subject, and then master and Lord.

On that day of St. Saba, abbot, I was desirous to celebrate Mass for my confessor, and I called to mind all the confessors I have had in past times, feeling by the favour of God a great and unusual gratitude towards them. And in this same way I felt to him who baptized me, who gave me confirmation, and those who conferred on me Sacred Orders or any other sacrament. I remembered also to pray in general for all my teachers, and in short for all those who have ministered unto me any grace of God, either by their words or in any other way. I did the same in the name of all my brethren, desiring in this matter in the faith of Jesus Christ to supply for them, as they supply for me, and are my excuse in many things before God, as one limb of a body is wont to help the rest. For just as God, in regard of my gratitude or thanksgiving, may communicate to me some grace which He has not communicated to others, so on the other hand there will be very many things that others will think of acknowledging which I have never thought of. I felt also a great desire for the salvation of all those who have administered to me the sacraments, as I have said, or any other gift or good thing from God. I desired also that our good God might vouchsafe to allow that those whom He has chosen to minister to me His grace and the good things which are received in turn, may also be His ministers to me as to the glory and the good things of heaven. I had also a good sentiment of humility, and with it a desire to pray that by the grace and mercy of Jesus Christ it might be given me that my benefactors who have so kindly helped me in this life might be glorious in heaven, and that I might find grace to be subject in a glorious kind of servitude here to all those whom I have in any way served in this life, which is led in the state of grace. So be it!

On the solemn feast of the Conception of the most Blessed Virgin Mary, I felt what seemed a new interior firmness and stability, by means of which it seemed that I should be stronger in future to overcome the floods of temptation. I did not find great devotion in the apprehensive part of my soul, moving me to great tenderness and feelings of lively devotion, but, on the other hand, neither was I so much disturbed by thoughts from the evil and unclean spirit, because I felt in myself, by the grace of God, a kind of new strength and vigour, much as if a man were to say that his house had been repaired and strengthened in the foundations, the walls, and the supports, although it had not received any increase of decoration. At other times I felt very frequent impulses of divine inspirations and movements, though I acknowledged at the same time that I was very weak and inconsistent. May our most gracious Jesus, the Saint of saints, grant me by the intercession of His Blessed Mother, and all the angels and saints of heaven, that I may be able to renew myself every day, advance in grace, and diminish my imperfections. Oh, that God would so have it! that He would renew my being and my life, my senses and my powers, my qualities and all that is necessary to me for the heavenly life, and all that may give pleasure to my God!

At the same time, that is, on the feast of the Conception, I observed something as to my temptations, that is, that I was no longer overshadowed by darkness, but that I had a greater interior clearness, my memory more capable and vigorous, and that I was no longer so much disturbed as used to be the case before. Oh, that these things might be the beginning of so great a good to me that I may at last, once for all, pass from my darkness to that inaccessible light, and from the depth of my confusion, weakness, and infirmity, to that most bright life, full of all strength and firmness! Our Lord knows who I am, and what I am worth, my own peculiar deformities, the stains of my soul, and all that I have of evil; but the Blessed Virgin Mary, our Mother and our advocate, altogether fair and entirely without stain of any kind, she, our gracious Lady, can obtain for me from the Father, the Son, and the Holy Ghost, that grace whereby I shall be entirely formed anew, adorned and sanctified. *Fiat, fiat!* Whatever thing may be granted me, it will proceed from the Power of the Father, it will be communicated to me by the Wisdom of the Son, and given to me by the Goodness of the Holy Ghost. *Fiat, fiat!*

On the most sacred night in which our Lord Jesus Christ was born, while I was at matins in the cathedral church in front of the relics, and was saying the nocturns, I felt great devotion and shed an abundance of tears from the first beginning on to the end. The words of the Prophet Jeremias that are read in the first nocturn, especially affected me. There were given to me also great desires, that so I might beg from my heart that I might be 'born of God,' and 'not of bloods, nor of the will of the flesh, nor of the will of men.'

I desired also, my soul thirsting and longing for the granting of the petition, that there might be born on that night some good and efficacious means to build up what is good and pull down what is evil in this our century. I felt, too, a great desire that I myself might now be born to the performing of every good work, both for pursuing the work of my own salvation, and for the glory of God and the good of my neighbour. I should be thus born again, I understood, if our Lord gave me such a spirit that in it and through it I should be able to devote and order my whole self to every good work, imitating Him Who with His whole self was for each one of us conceived, for each one of us was born and died. Hence we ought in spirit to wish to live all that yet remains of our lives so as to do everything for this end, the good of our neighbour and the praise of God. It is enough, and more than enough, that we have lived hitherto for ourselves and for our own temporal commodities, as if, indeed, we had been born for ourselves alone.

Here observe that three things concurred to produce our carnal birth. First, the flesh and blood of which we are made, as the material cause; secondly, the will of the parents that begat us; thirdly, that other intention and will of our parents to have sons that might be rich and prosperous in this world, which is so often the reason of the wish for children. He, therefore, who is to be born again of God Himself, of Him Whose nature is most perfect, and His every will most right and holy, must so be born and so live that he be no longer guided by the inclination of his own corrupt nature of flesh and blood, or be moved to act according to those movements of his will that belong to the men of this world. It is in fruits like these that can be seen the signs of a true birth, that is, of birth that is from God.

The first Mass which I said at midnight I applied, as far as depended on my intention, to our Society, for which I earnestly begged the birth to all good desires, to sanctity, and to justice before God; and I prayed that every member of it might be born to a new life, so as to help the whole world. I said this Mass in the Cathedral. I offered up the second in the monastery of the Carmelites, and I applied it for the prosperous issue of all good desires of the Bishop of Mayence, and for the spiritual birth of the whole district of the Rhine intrusted to my charge. I said the third Mass in the Church of our Lady, where I took an opportunity of contemplating her birthgiving. And I offered up this Mass to obtain the remedies which these sad times so much need—that is, peace amongst Christian princes, and the destruction of heresy.

In the first Mass, I felt no fervour before communion, and whilst I was grieving that the habitation of my soul was not better disposed, I felt an answer made within me which filled me with devotion and moved me to tears, that 'the present state of my soul harmonized well with the stable where Jesus chose to be born, because it was so poor a place. If my soul were filled with fervour, it would not represent well that lowly stable, nor should I see our Lord's Humanity come to me.' I was consoled then in our Lord, Who deigned to come to so unworthy a dwelling-place. I had wished my house to be well furnished, that I might draw comfort from that; but I was consoled instead in seeing my Lord come to me because of my very deformity. May it be granted to me henceforward, whenever I shall be unable to discover in myself the form, character, and disposition with which I would wish to present myself adorned in the sight of our Lord Jesus, of His holy Mother, and His saints, whenever, I say, this same shall be denied me for some just reason, may this be granted to me, to know how they, on the other hand, are disposed towards me.

Hitherto I have always sought to clothe myself in some feelings of devotion, or other splendid robes, with which I might invite God and His saints to come to me, and which would render me worthy of their love and acceptance. On the other hand, I did not employ a far easier method of approaching to them, which consists in contemplating the gifts they themselves possess, which render them so amiable and attractive. May the Almighty Father, and the Son, and the Holy Ghost, grant me the grace to know at the right time both of these truths, and may I have the power and the will to seek and to ask; to ask that I may be loved by God and His saints, to seek that I may love God and His saints. Henceforth I must be more solicitous to follow the better and the more generous course, and that which I have least pursued hitherto, that is, to wish to love rather than to be loved. I must therefore seek with greater diligence the marks which will prove that I love. These will be labours for Christ and my neighbour, according to the words of our Lord to St. Peter—'Lovest thou Me more than these? Feed My sheep.' Strive then to be first Peter, that afterwards you may be John, who was the more beloved by Christ, and in whom greater grace dwelt. Hitherto you have wished to be first John and then Peter. I wrote this on the eve of St. Stephen, after reciting the vespers of St. John the Evangelist.

On the feast of St. John the Evangelist, I said Mass for some spiritual needs of mine, and to obtain assistance against the chilling influences of certain evil spirits, which oftentimes so dispose me to some of my neighbours, and them towards me, that we are unable to endure or correct one another. I found in this Mass great devotion, and great confidence against the annoyance of the demons; against those annoyances, that is, which cause men to shut their hearts against each other, and which are wont to render them unable to endure one another, or, when their defects ought not to be endured, make men unable or unwilling to correct each other, but rather anxious to be entirely separated, on account of the disquiet caused by that spirit of division.

Here I earnestly begged the guardian angels of men, and all other angels, that they would deign to be born to us with Christ, and I prayed in like manner with regard to the holy saints reigning in heaven. I also desired the same for all those in this life, that every one of them should be born unto his own salvation, and the salvation of all his neighbours; that is, that each would now begin seriously to adapt and direct his whole being, first to the spiritual profit of his neighbours, and then to their temporal profit.

During the Mass, whilst I was reading the words which tell of the love of Jesus for St. John, I felt a great desire to love and honour this saint, for it was given to me to understand that our Lord is much pleased when this is done, for whosoever wishes to love Christ must love all that He loves, but above all he must love the salvation, the spiritual life, the consolation, and the refection of souls, which are the sheep and lambs of Christ, according to the charge which He gave to St. Peter after He had asked him three times over, 'Lovest thou Me?'

On these Christmas feasts, it seems to me that I have gained for my spiritual birth this special grace, that I desire, with an anxiety hitherto unknown to me, to seek the marks of love for God and His Divine Son, and what concerns them, and this grace will urge me henceforward to think more, to desire more, to say and do more willingly, the things which are of God. My chief anxiety hitherto was about such feelings as might prove to me what it is to be loved by God and His saints; for I wished especially to understand what were their dispositions with regard to me. And this is not a bad thing, on the contrary, it is the first thing that happens to such as are going to God, or, to speak more exactly, to such as are appeasing God in their own regard. For we must not suppose or assume with unwavering faith, as some wrongly do, that in the very beginning of our conversion, and much less before the beginning, God Himself and His Divine Son, and all the heavenly court, laid aside the great anger they felt, and became most favourable to us. Neither must we conceive that when He is appeased, so far as the threats of eternal punishment are concerned, that therefore He does not threaten us with labours and penances, since He said of St. Paul, whom He had chosen for a vessel of election, 'I will show him what great things he must suffer for My name.' We are wont then, and it is the right way to proceed in our first attempt to lead a good life, to be most anxious to please God by preparing in ourselves a dwelling-place corporal and spiritual in body and soul. But there is a certain period (which the unction of the Holy Ghost alone teaches every one who advances correctly), when the grace is granted to us, and demanded from us, to direct our attention principally to love God, instead of seeking to know what He likes or dislikes in us His creatures. In that former stage we endeavour to draw God to us, in the latter we go towards Him. In the first we seek that He may remember us, and be careful of us, in the second that we may remember Him, and be careful to do all that pleases Him; the first is the way of fear and filial reverence, the second of perfection and charity. May our Lord then grant to me and to every one these two feet, true fear and true love, for with them we must mount the ladder of the way of God. Hitherto, in my case, fear, I think, has been the right foot, love the left; now I desire that love may be the right foot, and the one I depend upon most; fear the left, and the one I depend upon least. And oh, may God will that I may be born now in this new grace, to grow therein unto the perfect man !

1543.

During first vespers on the feast of the Circumcision of our Lord Jesus Christ, I was at the Cathedral of Aschaffemburg, and I experienced great devotion in listening to the vespers and in looking at the decorations of the church. And I had many desires both for myself in particular, and for all nations, that they might be renewed in peace, love for the Catholic faith, and for the splendour of the worship of God.

During Mass this morning a good spirit strongly moved me, and made me feel how good and happy a thing it is to be manifest to God alone, and to be seen by Him alone in our work, without caring for anything else.

This too I observed, that Christ was unwilling to take His name Jesus publicly in the Jewish Church before He shed His Blood. And from this I concluded that we ought to pray Him most earnestly to grant us the grace that whatever abides in us that does not work to perfect fruit may be circumcised so completely that we may deserve to bear some name in Jesus Christ. And let us seek no name for ourselves in this life which is not included under the name of Jesus—that is, Saviour. For he who seeks the name of father, or teacher, without doing what belongs to the name, would work in a different way from Christ, Who took the name of Jesus when He was fulfilling the work of Saviour, and also all the other parts of Father, Teacher, Leader, and the like, all which titles are included in this most holy name.

On this feast I desired with a holy desire that the four seasons might run their course spiritually in my soul during this year. I desired a spiritual winter, that the divine seeds committed to the soil of my soul might be fostered and be able to take root; a spiritual spring, that the soil of my soul may have power to put forth with vigour its fruit; a spiritual summer, that the fruit may have the opportunity of ripening into a rich harvest; and lastly, a spiritual autumn, that the ripe fruits may be collected and stored in the granaries of heaven, and may be preserved and never perish.

I desired also that through the grace of our Lord Jesus Christ, Who was circumcised in the flesh, and finally suffered death in the same as a proof of His obedience to His Heavenly Father, that there might be granted to me some real circumcision of the spirit which might be a mark and a warrant of my love towards Christ and of His love towards me.

During vespers, whilst I contemplated the modesty expressed in a picture of the Blessed Virgin Mary, I felt in some degree how powerful is that grace of God which makes a person throw his whole being into serving God Himself, and retaining His grace in his soul, like one who does not know how to induce any creature to love him or think of him. In this way, then, all the beauty of Mary was within, and was hidden within her for God.

On the octave of the feast of St. Stephen, I celebrated Mass in a chapel of his lordship the Bishop of Mayence. The chapel was solemnly adorned on my account with all its relics and treasures. On the following day, the octave of St. John the Evangelist, I celebrated Mass in another chapel in the Cathedral, which was also solemnly decorated. Yet in both these places, though they were decorated in this manner, when I approached the altar, I felt very little devotion, nay, more than this, I entered the sanctuary, remained there, and came forth from it, full of dryness. Hence it came to pass, through the grace of Christ crucified, that I became much colder in the desire of seeking for myself so many and so great external helps to increase my devotion and to find more easily Christ crucified. For it often happens, as it did to me on these occasions, that whilst one finds great favour amongst men, he is more abandoned interiorly by Christ and His Spirit. Hence I felt in my soul an aversion to the favour of men and to influence with the great ones of the earth, seeing how much more efficacious a means to obtain the grace of God it is to be abandoned of men, and to become most like Christ crucified. All human favour, then, if any must be sought and must be accepted when offered, is to be referred and directed to our neighbour's edification and not to our own profit, since we can more easily find the Saviour of our souls without such human favour. We must, therefore, direct our course, and incline in spirit towards that road which leads to the Cross. For Christ crucified is the true way that leads to the glory of our soul and body, and not the way only, but the truth and the life as well. When, therefore, you shall desire for yourself your own edification, or shall seek true consolation, or your own advancement, see that you always despise favour or influence with men, and seek instead the lowlier things which are the companions of the Cross.

There are some who up to a certain point will advance better in thanksgiving, and will with greater ease be strongly moved to glorify God, Who is Almighty, and in every manner infinite, by the sight of His Eternal Beauty, Power, and Goodness as they are presented to them. Nevertheless it is necessary (if it should not have been done from the beginning) that we should finally come to the Cross upon which hung our Salvation. For in Christ crucified is our salvation, our life, and our resurrection, and these three things precede the glory which awaits us in heaven, and which, like the rest, is through, from, and in the same Christ crucified.

We must seek, then, first the virtue of Christ crucified, and then of Christ in His glory, and not the opposite, that is, we must seek the virtue of Christ crucified, by which our death was destroyed. He dissolved, destroyed, and reduced to nought death, He Who alone of His own free choice took flesh and offered Himself for our sakes to undergo sufferings and death. So we ought to arm ourselves with the same thought, and resolve to offer ourselves voluntarily for His sake to sufferings and death to the laying aside the body of sin, that we may at length find the body of the grace and the glory of God in Christ our Lord, in which our souls must find their existence and life and motion.

On the Epiphany, which is the feast of the holy Wise Kings, I felt great spiritual consolation, and especially in the litanies which I am wont to recite, whilst I prayed that all the saints would deign to adore in my name Almighty God and His Divine Son, Jesus Christ our Lord. Here in great earnestness I desired for myself and all others that all the external movements of my body and of others who desire to serve God, might be always acceptable to Him, even though the heart and soul, though free from the flesh, should at times know not how to rise to God.

On this day, also, I felt compassion for the insults which our Lord Jesus Christ suffered during His lifetime up to the moment of His death, and which were so unlike the honours He received from the three Magi. I had also a desire that the grace might be granted to me never to rejoice except in God or my neighbour, and never to be sad on account of any temporal discomforts of my own, but for such only as affect my neighbour or for offences against God Himself. I also felt the highest esteem and value for the good works of the different persons who are engaged in any way in labouring for me or for others, or who in any other way occupy themselves for the love of God.

Whilst I was present at the Mass which was sung at the altar of the three Kings, I felt a great desire that the grace might be granted to me to leave behind me various outward objects which would serve to remind people of God and His saints, and I desired also that if their memory should perish in these parts, all memory might be lost of me in the world. These desires were suggested to me by pictures of the saints, and different representations of the mysteries of Christ, by means of which many recollections and perceptions of holy things were given to me at that time, just as at other times they are always granted to me. For the same reason my love and veneration increased for his lordship Albert, Archbishop and Prince of Mayence, who has had during all his lifetime and still has so great an anxiety about the relics of the saints, and so great a desire to preserve their memory and to hand it down to posterity. Moreover, these outward memorials are so much the more necessary in proportion as men esteem them of little value, and are themselves cold and indifferent. For unless they were so much honoured, it might easily come to pass that men would despise everything of this kind. For how could they help despising all sacred things, if they were treated without fitting respect, since they seem utterly to contemn them when they are held in so much honour?

During Mass I felt a great desire that Alvaro Alfonso, who is at Cologne where the bodies of the three Kings are preserved, might remember in particular to supply my place at their tomb, and not my place only, but that of all my companions. I also desired that the same might be done by all others who are in any place where such saints as are held in peculiar veneration amongst us are worshipped.

On the Sunday within the octave of the Epiphany, I applied the Mass amongst other intentions as a sacrifice and oblation of thanksgiving, which I owe and have never sufficiently and can never sufficiently render for the gifts of faith and humility in spirit infused into me in common with other Catholics, in answer not only to our own prayers, but also to the prayers of the Church, and by force of its faith.

On another day I perceived and noted how those who withdraw from the Church begin first to grow tepid in works and holy exercises, and consequently make little account of and place no value upon whatever they do not know to have discovered themselves and approved by their own judgment. So it comes to pass that they begin to seek reasons for their faith and hope, making everything doubtful, and in this manner they lose the infused gifts of the Holy Ghost, and the true faith which depended upon the Catholic faith and the communion of saints. And when they have lost this they make another for themselves, according to their own judgment. For they seek reasons and examine them for themselves, and they search for the interpretations of the Scriptures, and judge of its meaning according to their own caprice, and so form a faith of their own, or rather, erroneous opinions. And when they wish to draw any one into their errors they ask this first from him as a foundation and first principle, that he must lay aside all passion, for so they style the tenacity with which it becomes a Christian and a Catholic to cling to the opinions and teaching of the doctors, and the authoritative decisions of the Church. What else is it for a man to lay aside this passion, as they call it, except to abandon and lose of his own free choice the Catholic faith, and the simplicity and humility of an understanding submissive to the obedience of faith? And when they have emancipated a person from this holy and necessary submission, then they ask him to seek another faith altogether after their fashion, and if any one doing this finds that he has either already lost, or is gradually losing the faith he had, then they say that faith and the power to form by oneself a good judgment upon the Scriptures and other matters, must be prayed of and sought from God, for that faith is of God, and that not every one has it, and other such assertions, which are indeed most true, but which are not made by them with good intention, and do not help to the edification of others. Oh, how much better would they have done if they had understood that these gifts can be lost by any one!

Whoever, then, of his own accord has thus lost the faith which he possessed as long as he belonged to the Church and had not yet abandoned her, ought not to wonder if he perceives that when he seeks faith by other ways which he has chosen himself, he does not find it. Much less ought he to blame God as if he were unwilling to give it to him, for God wishes to give faith to everyone, but He will not give it to one who desires not to live in the Church, for out of her there is neither salvation, nor life, nor true resurrection. Every faithful Christian, then, in the Catholic Church, has knowledge of religious things and many graces bestowed upon him, but if he were to seek by himself the reasons for each of them, he would suffer harm in many ways. Eve had received a great gift of grace to believe the word of God's command made known to her by the mouth of Adam, but as soon as she listened with attention to the question of the serpent, and began to seek for reasons with which to answer him, she lost the gift of faith. And when this was lost it was easy for the serpent to deceive her and persuade her to do what she afterwards did. And so she who had received, not by reason, but by infused grace, at the word of Adam, the faith that in whatsoever hour she should eat the forbidden fruit she should die, by reasoning about the commandment and judging for herself, ran into the false opinion that by eating the apple she would attain to the condition of God, the knowledge of good and evil. We must, then, acknowledge with much thanksgiving the gifts we possess, and which we have received from God, apart from any judgment of our own, and though we did not pray for them nor understand what was given to us, as happened in baptism, in which, in the faith of the Church and of our parents, the seeds of the Catholic and orthodox faith, hope, and charity were infused into our souls. So, too, is it in the other sacraments, for in all of them graces are bestowed, not in accordance with the measure of our intelligence, nor in proportion to our knowledge and appreciation of the form and matter of the sacraments, but graces which far exceed what we pray for, or what we could ever conceive or desire. If a person puts questions to you, and is neither able or prepared to edify, and cannot or will not be edified by you, do not join in conversation with him, but avoid and shun him as you would a serpent or a scorpion. Do not reply to his questions, for if you answer well he will not be edified, and if, on the contrary, you answer ill, he will not show you your mistake.

On the same day, during Mass, whilst I held the most precious Body of our Lord in my hands, I saw in a very clear manner how great a grace it is to assist at the sacrament of truth, and at this sacred pledge which contains within itself all truth and goodness, and to which we must not approach except after much purification and examination of our transgressions. For he who approaches this sacrament without first reconciling himself with God, in receiving it shall receive his own condemnation. Take the case of one who has received a command in the name of his earthly prince to leave the country on account of some crime by which he has incurred the anger of the prince. Now, if he were to despise that command and would not attend to it and fly from the country, and if, moreover, before being reconciled, he were to presume to go into the presence of his prince, it is evident that he would receive a severe condemnation from him. For inasmuch as the crime was evil, and on many accounts unendurable, the prince was unwilling that the culprit should appear before him, and ordered him to be exiled from his State; but the culprit in his pride takes the pains to approach still more nearly and to present his fault before the eyes of his prince. So is it with the man who, loaded with the burthen of his sins, on account of which he had been dismissed from the number of God's children, presents himself unreconciled before the face of Jesus Christ, Whom he receives in Holy Communion. It is just as if these words were spoken to the sinner—'Take away this disgusting thing out of My sight, that I may not look upon it,' and he, instead of removing it, draws near to the Prince in order that he may not only look upon it but even touch it and embrace it with a kiss. So the sinner answers in effect —' I know that You cannot endure to look upon me, but I would have You kiss me: I know, my Lord, that You cannot bear the sight of me, but I will introduce You into my inmost soul, which is full of all foulness and uncleanness.'

On the third day of the octave of the Epiphany of our Lord, there came to my mind a train of thought I had formerly conceived as to the graces which I had understood were to be sought and asked for according to the order of the litanies which I am wont to say. And this instruction was given to me by means of a comparison to be taken from one who was to serve some great king. Some of the good qualities of such a man may be put down in this order: First, and above all other qualities, he should know and have the power and knowledge and desire to serve his Lord. So we must beg from the three Divine Persons of the Trinity the triple grace that we may have the power and knowledge and the will to serve Jesus Christ our Lord. Secondly, he who would thus serve must be in the good graces of the prince; and as I have need of grace and our Blessed Lady was full thereof, I will beg her to obtain it for me of our Lord, that my service may be wholly pleasing to God and His saints. Thirdly, it is necessary that such a servant be diligent and fit to fulfil his duties, and for this I will beg the ministering spirits who serve God to obtain for me this aptitude and assiduity in serving. Fourthly, it is necessary that this servant should be a lover of all that is seemly and decorous, lest anything should present itself to his lord which might offend his gaze; he will, therefore, be always anxious and desirous that everything may be becoming and well prepared. I will, therefore, seek the intercession of the patriarchs and prophets, that I may be able to prepare all the ways of the Lord like a faithful forerunner of Christ. Fifthly, this servant must be quick and diligent in following the Court whithersoever it shall go, and for this I may invoke the apostles to obtain for me the grace to follow our Lord, as His holy will shall think good. The sixth quality of a servant at Court is that he should be most attentive to every word of his lord, and for this I will ask the intercession of the disciples, that I may be in truth a disciple of Christ, and an attentive listener to His words and those of all the saints. The seventh quality required in such a servant, is that he must be always on his guard never to offend any of those who live at Court, but must strive on the contrary to be useful to all in every way, and hurtful to none, so that no one may be able to lodge a complaint against him with his lord. In accordance with this, I will beg the grace from the Holy Innocents never to injure, or scandalize, or disedify any one. Eighthly, this servant must be ready to suffer even unto death, for the honour and interests, or in the just defence and preservation of his master. And for this I will invoke the martyrs to obtain for me such virtue as to be ready to undergo any tribulations for our Lord Jesus Christ, for His honour and for the fulfilment of His will. Ninthly, this servant ought to speak in all places and at all times in praise of his lord, from a desire to extend his renown and fame. So I will invoke the confessors of Christ, that through their prayers I may be able at all times and in all places to praise and magnify in every way our Lord Jesus Christ. Tenthly, a servant such as we have been describing should dilgently fly from and avoid all pleasures, amusements, places, conversations, and all other things which could prevent him from duly fulfilling the wishes of his lord. For this I may invoke the intercession of the monks and hermits who abandoned all worldly things that they might be able to fulfil the will of their Lord as it was revealed to them. Eleventhly, this servant should strive to be spotless in person and dress, that so he may be beloved by his master; and for this I may call upon the holy virgins, who strove in every way to be pleasing to Christ, their Spouse, alone. Twelfthly, after one has won the affection of his master, and has been admitted to his familiar confidence, he should strive to be faithful, not abusing the love of his lord, but corresponding to it; for this I will invoke the holy women who have kept their faithfulness in matrimony. The last quality may consist in this, that if such a servant be deprived of the presence of his loving master, nay, even if he be for a time quite separated from him, his affection for him is never lessened, and he never turns aside to seek the favours of others, by which he might easily be prevented afterwards from reunion with his lord. This suggests to me the form of my last petition, and in it I ask the aid of the widows and such as lived in chastity, that they would obtain for me the grace never to seek any consolation except from God, nay, when it shall be denied me to enjoy our Lord, to prefer rather to mourn and sorrow for His absence than turn to seek any pleasure whatever which has its source in anything else but Him, and is not supplied to me by Him. So be it!

Another day, during the same octave of the Epiphany of our Lord, I considered what a great favour of God it was that I now beheld, for the thirty-seventh time in my life, this feast of the Epiphany, and so I went through the other feast-days which have passed during the recurrence of so many years. I however have gained but little fruit from them, and was never grateful enough even to acknowledge that so great kindness of God, Who has on these occasions offered me so many means of procuring my salvation, and of repairing the losses of past neglect. I gave thanks therefore, and I acknowledged my ingratitude, carelessness, negligence, and thoughtlessness, beseeching Him to grant that henceforward I may increase daily and in many ways in the holy knowledge of Him. For this divine goodness and mercy, which has given to me and to others to understand our own negligence, I offered the divine sacrifice of praise and propitiation as a holocaust and victim for our sins, and may God the Father deign to accept it as pleasing in His sight. After matins, when I went to say Mass, I received a very clear light about the Child Jesus, lately born and given to us. I understood that by the power of His Divinity He had drawn the shepherds to Him, though they were far removed from the power of recognizing His Divinity, hidden in the Humanity; so too in the case of the Magi, for though they were by no means poor in mind and intellect, yet were they, on account of their worldly greatness, far removed from the knowledge of the Divinity of Christ, made a little Babe for us. I reflected too, on the Innocents who were called to martyrdom, without any cooperation of their own. I prayed to Jesus, Who in these different ways had manifested Himself to those who were far distant, that He would deign to receive whatever supplications and prayers are offered for those who either know not how to seek their salvation, which is in Him, or will not seek it, as sinners or little children who are still in their mother's womb.

After Mass there occurred to me the various salutary uses for which Christ gave Himself to us, and was given to us by the Father. For He was given us as medicine, as food, as drink, as victim, as physician, as salvation of body and soul, as strength in death, as pledge of resurrection, and lastly, what is most striking of all, He gave Himself to be ill-used in all ways and killed by us. Here then I grieved from my heart that I had not as yet, in any way, given myself wholly to Him, to do with me whatever He wishes, or shall wish in life or death. I asked Him therefore now, to employ me and all my labour in every way just as it may seem good to Him, for His own glory, the good of my neighbour, and the salvation of my soul, and that He may grant me to will, and feel, and think, and do in all things according to the order of His holy will and wisdom.

After the feast of the Epiphany, on the 15th of January, I celebrated the feast of the most Holy Name of Jesus, and I found very great devotion and many different affections towards this sweet name. I said Mass on that day for the whole of our Society, because it is called the Society of Jesus Christ our Lord. During these days, I found out a great means of help to concentrating my mind in prayer. This help was to represent to myself the presence of Christ hanging on the Cross, and uttering the words, *Mulier, ecce Filius tuus! Parce illis! Deus, Deus meus, ut quid dereliquisti me? Hodie mecum eris in Paradiso! Pater, in manus tuas commendo spiritum meum! Sitio! etc.* And whilst I reflected upon these words, and considered Christ in this way hanging on the Cross, I felt that my heart was sensibly drawn and calmed, and attained a more perfect peace, nay, was lifted up with greater attention.

About this time there came from the Sovereign Pontiff the Bull of the Jubilee, and in accordance with the contents of it, I prepared myself to receive the grace which that Bull spoke of, and for that end God infused into my soul a great increase of faith and hope with regard to such spiritual goods. I besought our Lord to bestow on me the grace to regain back whatever riches of the soul I ever alienated or lost, considering the example of the Jubilee among the Jews, in which each used to return to the possession of his property, which he had before lost. I had also many affections with regard to reconciliation with God. I desired that all the faults I had contracted by ignorance, or culpable weakness, malice, ingratitude, or which in any other way had stained my soul or body, might be so blotted out that nothing might remain in me which would offend God, His Mother, or the saints. And with regard to the temporal punishment I had incurred, I desired most earnestly that I might be perfectly reconciled with God and His saints, and that no more public evils might come about in the world on account of my sins. For it almost always happens that calamities, such as plagues, wars, famine, and the like, befall men on account of the accumulated sins of multitudes of men, so that every one is partly the cause for this kind of affliction.

On the Saturday[56] immediately preceding Septuagesima Sunday, while I was praying during the night that all my sins might be pardoned, and while I prayed especially that I might not fall back into them on account of past demerits, I experienced intense consolation, considering the joy which one would feel if he knew and felt that God, His Mother, and the saints were reconciled to him. I seemed to hear within me the words that Christ, the Blessed Virgin, and some saints, my special patrons, might say to me; but this thought was one connected rather with their possible than their real presence. As if one addressed me in this manner—'Oh! if you were to hear the voice of such a saint, who is your friend!'

On St. Agnes'[57] day, the glorious virgin and martyr, whilst I was pondering and reflecting upon different necessities of those in this life, in which men can have no relief except by means of Christ and His saints, I felt a great desire that the saints in heaven would deign to pray for us and excuse us, each pleading in particular for those who labour in his own country, and for the souls in his own lands. While I was offering Mass for this end, I prayed the Father of Heaven that as often as I should pronounce the name of His Son, that is, Jesus, He would condescend to look favourably upon all those in any quarter that need help for their salvation, whether in this world or in purgatory, and also that He would remember all the merits of Jesus Christ, and all the desires that He had for the salvation of men as long as He lived on this earth.

To-day, when the thought once presented itself to my mind that a time might come when we might lack even necessary food, I felt a great and strong desire to possess nothing; and so from the bottom of my heart I prayed Christ, Who lay on the altar before my eyes, that

[56] January 20, 1543.   [57] January 21.

if it were His will and pleasure, I might never as long as I am in this life pass a year in which I might not find myself once at least in extreme indigence, without having anything to support me. And if this grace, and I looked upon it as a great grace, should not be brought about by human changes and chances, I prayed that light be given me to know whether it were God's will I should deprive myself once in the year of all earthly necessaries, and in this way reduce myself to true and actual poverty. The desire of effecting this has through the grace of God often been in my soul. But God then granted me grace to know what His will is in this respect, and what I say of myself I say also of my brethren who live with me. As for myself, God has long since given me grace to wish and desire everywhere to beg my living from door to door. I pray God that this desire, as well all other desires which tend to my own abnegation and abjection, and to any virtue or grace, may always increase in my soul with increase of virtue and grace. For many persons not being accustomed to the exercises of actual poverty, and other holy acts of the Cross of Christ, easily lose the affection they ought to have to these acts. But we must beseech Jesus Christ crucified, that it may not happen to us to be diverted or even retarded in the race which we ought to be ever running towards the Cross and the death of our Lord Jesus Christ. For whosoever runs in this direction, runs safely to salvation, true life, and true resurrection. But, on the other hand, the lovers of this temporal life pursue difficult and dangerous ways.

On the festival of the virgin St. Emerantiana,[58] I understood that I ought to bless our Lord Jesus Christ, who, on this day, drew to Himself this virgin and martyr, whilst but a catechumen. And I think it was the effect of her prayers that I felt great devotion both during my

---
[58] January 23.

office and at Mass, for whilst saying the latter I received abundant consolation, and I shed many tears. And I desired especially that our Lord, looking on the sacrifice I was offering, and the sacrifice which was offered to Him on this day in the person of St. Emerantiana, would forget the sins of the men who had stoned this saint. And so I felt that it was a good thing in God's sight, that day by day as we celebrate the memory of the martyrs, we present to Christ the good works and merits of these saints, so that by the sight of them God may be appeased towards us who of ourselves perform no such deeds, and at the same time may not remember the evil and malice which were displayed against these saints.

On this day, finding myself in great consolation and spiritual joy, the desire came to me that this consolation might be communicated to a certain person and to others, but it was quickly answered by a response which seemed to say—'Would that you yourself could taste and partake of the consolation which Jesus would communicate to you, which the Blessed Virgin and the martyr St. Emerantiana would gladly make you share.' At the same time I had a strong feeling which I had never felt before, and which I may thus express—'Would, my Jesus, that I might clearly know Thy will in all my actions, for this would be to me the sweetest life in the world!'

On the day of the Purification of our Blessed Lady,[59] I received many lights concerning the Gospel, and felt great devotion during the blessing of the candles. I earnestly desired that I might not depart out of this world ere I had attained an intimate knowledge of Jesus Christ and beheld Him abiding, as it were, in my soul, keeping it in peace despite all the assaults of the enemy, delivering it from peril, enlightening it as to whatever regards His service, and strengthening it against sadness,

[59] February 2.

trouble and perplexities. On the same day I was in many ways made sensible of the misery of my imperfections and shortcomings, chiefly in my outward work. Yet was I encouraged in spirit, seeing that God was ever favourable to me, and that if I but cleave to Him, I can make myself all that I ought to be. I also felt, on this very day, a certain joy in beholding how needy and destitute I am in spirit, since this affords the Blessed Virgin Mary an opportunity of compassionating me on account of my shortcomings. I proposed, moreover, frequently to recite the following prayer—' O Lord God Almighty, grant me this grace, that till my death I may enjoy the peace which consists in beholding Thy salvation, in the light given to all nations, and the glory of Thy Christian people.' For by obtaining this, I should come to the perfect knowledge of Christ our Saviour, Enlightener, and Glorifier.

Soon after the feast of the Purification, I had a lively apprehension of the promise made by Christ to them that forsake father and mother, &c., saying that they shall inherit life everlasting. On that same day, while questioning myself interiorly about the account we shall have to give of time, I understood how it is that He Who alone can give us time, is to call us to account as to our use of it. Another may inquire into what I have done with the things he has intrusted me withal, but God will ask an account of time itself, no less than of all His other gifts, as He alone can give and prolong time.

In the Carnival time, I felt overwhelmed with sadness at the sight of my natural imperfections, arising from the corruption of human nature. This sadness of mind came not so much from the imperfections themselves, as from the consideration of them, suggested not, as is usual, by the Divine Spirit, but either by my own, or by the angel of Satan sent to buffet and to exercise me. I was at that time very slack in well doing, distracted and withdrawn from the intimate knowledge and feeling of the things that are above. Mine only consolation was in the thought that this was to be my cross, as I had heretofore so often experienced: a cross made up of these three parts—of the inconstancy of my carnal mind in regard to spiritual things, of the effect of the imperfection which compasses me round about both on the right hand and on the left when I consider my shortcomings in respect of charity to my neighbour, and thirdly, of what arises from my want of devotion and inattention to what directly concerns God and His saints. This consideration of my three chief defects forms, so to speak, the three arms of the cross that has so long pressed heavily on my shoulders, of which I oft-times feel the burthen, that I may learn to bear that other cross far more pleasing to God, which is to undergo grievous and continual labours in order to kindle within me the love of God, for the sake of mine own sanctification and my neighbour's salvation, ever rising higher and higher to God, ever descending in myself into lower depths of humility, and as regards my neighbour, never failing to stretch out on both sides helpful hands. But because I fail diligently to bear this cross, my spirit groans within me under the weight of the other.

On the feast of St. Dorothy,[60] virgin and martyr, I yearned longingly for the salvation of my neighbours who are in affliction or any strait, I therefore earnestly intreated God that He would move them that were in misfortune to implore His mercy on their sufferings; and I was deeply grieved at thinking of the numerous sufferers who, knowing not how to lay open their misery before God and His saints, have constant recourse to human and temporal means of relief wherein there is no

[60] February 6.

help. Let us then ever pour forth our afflicted hearts in His presence Who beholdeth sorrow and trouble, and knows full well what each one is able to bear.

On St. Apollonia's day[61] I found great devotion in applying the Mass to the person who was most desirous of the suffrages of the Church. I further begged the release from purgatory for the soul that had best reason to complain of me and the greatest claim to my prayers. I also called to mind how, when a child, I was wont to recite a prayer to St. Apollonia, in thanksgiving for her having cured me of toothache, which I have never since felt. I therefore rendered fresh thanks to this virgin, who was able to obtain for me at so light a cost to be preserved from this ailment, and I asked that henceforth through her merits and intercession with Christ, that not only I, but every one of my brethren, might be kept from this and all other diseases. I, moreover, besought this saint to intercede in our behalf with the other saints, according to the ministry allotted to them by Christ in the care of the faithful, that they would obtain for us not only increase in virtue and the salvation of our souls, but vigour of body, deliverance and preservation from bodily ailments. For myself I desired that some one of them would obtain for me humility, and have especial care of me in this respect; that another would get me patience, another bodily health, and so forth. And I put up the same petition on behalf of all who belong to the Society, descending to the most minute particulars in the spirit of holy piety, and with faith unfeigned and steadfast hope.

May God, Who has created us and all things, enable us by His Spirit to discern all that we receive from Him, and to render Him due thanks. Oh, that we could know all that God works in us, both in our bodies and in

---

[61] February 9.

our souls, whether of Himself or through His several ministers! Oh, that we could at length behold Him, Who is and Who works all things in us, by Whom all things are, and are moved, and in Whom are all things! But we must ascend to this first and supreme principle and cause of all by the second causes, even as we reach the first Mediator by intermediate steps; and the final end, the term and perfection of all that is, by other intermediate ends and forms. The Father is the first principle, from Whom are all things; the Son the first by Whom, the Holy Spirit the first in Whom, are all things. The Father from Whom all created being derives its origin, the Son by Whom all things are made, the Holy Ghost in Whom all is brought to perfection. This, of course, is to be taken in an attributive sense, the Father, Son, and Holy Ghost, being the sole principle of whatever is created, formed, and perfected; from which sole principle all things do proceed, by Whom all are directed, in Whom all subsist. Blessed be God for evermore. Amen.

On the festival of St. Scholastica,[62] virgin, I celebrated Mass in her honour for my own intention. I observed and understood on this occasion that it was most necessary and suitable on these festivals of holy virgins, to ask for those graces which help one to advance in perfection. All these holy virgins, who spared no pains to build up in themselves the temple of God in the Spirit, and sought to become vessels of holiness to please Jesus Christ, the Bridegroom to Whom they had vowed themselves, such souls as these, I say, cannot but desire most earnestly to see us decked with spiritual graces, so that cleansed from all blemish offensive to the eyes of God, we may be pleasing to Him in all holiness and justice. Hence, these virgins are anxious to obtain for us the graces we

---

[62] February 10.

demand through their intercession. The other saints may be fitly invoked according to the rank they hold, and the peculiar merits and graces wherewith it pleased God to distinguish them here below, and whereby they have attained glory everlasting in Christ Jesus, their Lord and ours. For God, in His dealings with His saints, keeps to this order, in virtue of which, each one desires that God should be imparted to others, even as He has graciously communicated Himself to them. For each one was led by a different path in his lifetime, nor were all endowed with the same gifts, nor was it God's purpose that they should be exercised in the same good works and spiritual practices. Wherefore, then, should it be otherwise than pleasing to the saints that we should be led to the knowledge and worship of God by the same path as they followed, that the good works wherein they found God should be practised by us, by such of us, at least, as call upon them here below?

On the first Sunday in Lent,[63] while praying and beseeching God to drive from me all mine enemies, I received this answer—'Do thou strive that the Lord may raise thee far above the dwelling-place of thine enemies, for not here below is thy dwelling, yet is it the abode of thine enemies.'

This same day, while reciting office, I wound up the clock without any necessity, and it was suggested to me to beseech God that by His grace He would fit and dispose me for praying well, for it were far easier for Him so to dispose me, than it could be for me to arrange and set in order with mine own hands any mechanism whatsoever. I further took occasion herefrom to rebuke myself for having heretofore too frequently allowed myself to be distracted by handling, looking, or putting things in order without necessity, when I ought rather to have kept

[63] February 11.

myself attentive and disposed for my prayers or godly meditations, inasmuch as my sole care at such times should be to set myself to perform aright, both in speech and thought, the duty I had in hand. For we can acquit ourselves perfectly of these holy exercises, only when they are performed by the whole man, and with the concurrence of all his requisite powers. When this is the case his good angel will not fail him, and the Holy Ghost, Who is God, will not be absent, and will surely perfect his action.

On the day that I kept the transferred feast of St. Martina, virgin and martyr, the lessons of the nocturns inspired me with a lively faith in her credit with the holy angels, and her power over the spirits of evil, whose temples and idols fell in her presence. I therefore, while celebrating Mass, made a firm resolution of invoking her protection against them, and I further determined to put this resolution into practice every Monday, a day whereon it is my wont to commemorate the good angels. For as it is profitable to invoke the good angels and to be devout to them, it is of no less advantage to choose a day whereon to beg the grace of God and these blessed spirits, and their protection against the fiends who in so many ways molest, delude, and ruin us. God send that I may ever enjoy the favour of this holy virgin whose feast I kept on the Monday after the first Sunday in Lent,[64] that I may never fail to recall to mind every Monday, not only of the good angels (which has long been my wont), but also of the evil spirits, in order to baffle them. I had never until then felt the importance of this latter. Blessed be He from, by, and in Whom such sentiments and lights as these have been vouchsafed to me.

[64] February 12.

On the 14th of February, St. Valentine's day, Stephen took leave of us and set out for Rome. I felt urged to invoke, with great devotion, his good angel, as well as the angels of others, on his behalf, that he might be encouraged with a lively hope in face of the perils of his journey. I moreover felt a great desire that many good and patient travellers might confront these dangers, and so by their patience and prayers obtain God's grace for those who shall hereafter make the same journey.

On the occasion of his departure I felt moved by the good spirit, at considering how long his good angel had tarried in our household, yet that I had never noticed him, and that he was now locally parted from us. And I grieved that I had not invoked him concerning the care of the youth of whom he was in charge, for all that this angel had kept him humble and submissive to me, nor had allowed his bad spirit to be as troublesome to me as I deserved. Thus, while considering the ministries of angels on behalf of men, I fully realized how necessary it is that the Divine Spirit, Who upholdeth all things most perfectly, should quicken our souls, and guide them by the outpouring of His gifts. We must, therefore, beseech Christ that He would keep His Spirit within us, failing Whose influence, the good angels themselves would be powerless to direct our souls. For without this Spirit, their inward suggestions would be void of efficacy, and could not penetrate into our innermost soul. It is the Word of God that is quick and powerful, and sharper than any two-edged sword,[65] piercing even to the dividing asunder of soul and spirit, of the joints and marrow, of the thoughts and interests of the heart. Such is the virtue of the Divine Word when taught and recalled to us by the Holy Ghost.

[65] Heb. iv. 12.

On the same day, while considering the divers spirits that frequently disturbed me, and made me in turns hopeful or despondent about the possibility of doing good in Germany, I observed that we ought not to rely on the words of that spirit whose wont it is to exaggerate the impossibilities and difficulties of every undertaking, but rather to give ear to him who shows how possible things are, and who gives encouragement. Yet must we take heed lest we run too far to the right hand, and forsake the middle path which prudence marks out for us, so as neither to be unduly elated by groundless hopes, nor to be weighed down by despondency. If this may not be done, and we must needs go either to the right or to the left, it would be safer and less perilous to yield ourselves up to the hope that cheers us, than to the opposite extreme, where there are countless errors and delusions, countless roots of bitterness, involving us in a trackless labyrinth. He who can discern the spirit of hope and his words, and likewise the spirit of temptation and trouble, is enabled to gather useful lessons from both. We should then strive to lay hold of and to keep the spirit of hopefulness, and when we have lost it, to seek it anew, to preserve the joy, the consolation, the peace, and other dispositions that arise from good inspirations; to these must we ever come back in order that they may strike deeper root within us. We must not, however, receive all the thoughts that may occur to us, as if they could not possibly have some ingredient of truth, for even the wicked spirit can disguise himself as an angel of light. In regard of the adversary and his suggestions, we must deal with them by way of contradiction; the spirit himself, and the sentiments he inspires, is to be driven forth and to be shunned. Not so, however, as to all his suggestions, for you may draw from them many warnings, and learn thereby prudence in secular business, for many of them may be true and useful, if they be quickened hereafter by another spirit.

On the transferred feast of St. Hyginus,[66] pope and martyr, when about to celebrate for the intention of the Sovereign Pontiff, Paul III., I considered the goodness and liberality of Jesus Christ, Who deigns to impart Himself not only to the just, but to sinners likewise, as He did to the traitor Judas at the Last Supper. And here I was reminded that as Jesus Christ imparts Himself to me daily in the holy sacrifice, and is ever ready to communicate Himself in manifold ways, whether in prayer or in other pious works, I ought in like manner to dedicate, and wholly yield up myself to Him, and for His sake, to the welfare of my neighbour in preaching, instructing, consoling him, and by spending myself for him with all that I have.

On the feast of St. Brigid,[67] virgin, I had various thoughts concerning the salvation of souls; and I grieved at the remembrance that in this province there are so many parishes without a pastor, even wholly destitute of any priest. Yet had I then great consolation in considering how earnestly St. Brigid yearned for the salvation of souls, as appears from her writings and prayers which are still extant. I therefore gave thanks to God for all the benefits conferred on Holy Church by means of this sainted woman.

On the transferred feast of St. Gilbert,[68] confessor, I was affected during Mass with a great devotion and compassion for the departed souls, and my tears ceased not to fall during the Mass. I felt a desire of giving

---

[66] Transferred from January 11.

[67] Transferred from February 1. This seems to have been the Irish St. Brigid, as the feast of St. Bridget, widow, occurs either in July or October in various calendars.

[68] Transferred from February 4.

myself up to Christ, and I saw that there was no better way of so doing than to take part in His sufferings, not bodily only, but those He underwent in His Soul, which grieved over the everlasting torments to which so many souls are doomed, and over their temporal sufferings, especially those of the souls in purgatory.

On the feast of St. Peter's Chair,[69] while saying Mass, I felt the wonted anguish my imperfections cause me, and there occurred to me this good thought, to wit, that I should not make so much account of these imperfections, nor spend so much time in considering them, since by making little of them they quickly vanish, and the mere contemplation of them adds to my imperfection.

On the day on which I celebrated the feast of St. Genevieve,[70] virgin and patroness of Paris, while my mind was filled with the thoughts of the innumerable difficulties in the way of the conversion of souls, difficulties which in nowise depended on me, I felt overwhelmed with disgust and grief, which undermined the confidence I had hitherto felt. In order to dissipate this melancholy, it was given to me to consider that the following things are necessary—(1) that I am not to undertake what does not concern me, or other work than what I have presently in hand; (2) that I ought not to extend my care to so many things at once; (3) that I ought to use all diligence in regard of what I have actually to do; (4) that I should proceed in these works of charity, as one who by their means paves the way to higher and more important deeds.

On the day on which I celebrated the feast of our holy Angel Guardians, which was on the 1st of March, I felt great devotion, especially during the Mass, which I

---

[69] *i.e.* at Antioch. February 22.
[70] Transferred from January 2.

celebrated for our Society, and I besought the Lord that it would please Him to compass it round about and to protect it, as with a hedge, through the guardianship and patronage of the holy angels.

While celebrating the office and Mass of St. Bruno,[71] the founder and patriarch of the Carthusian Order, I felt an earnest desire that this holy order, together with the other orders of monks and hermits, might flourish anew. I then said Mass for the Society, praying that it might, according to God's will, contribute by its labours and toils to the reformation of every religious community which the Roman Church has approved and instituted.

I felt at the same time an ardent wish that there might be many, who, for the love of Christ, would humble themselves even to the lowest works, and many so well trained in spiritual exercises as to be ready to undertake any duty, and to deem themselves as slaves who are prepared for all. I likewise prayed that there might be many who would account it gain and glory to serve at Mass and to assist the ministers of God. *Fiat! Fiat!*

The same day I called to mind how advantageous it was for a man to be held in the remembrance of the just, wherefore I conceived a heartfelt desire that the saints, who are for ever enjoying the visible presence of God, might be mindful of me.

I desired also to find place in the remembrance of Christ, for whatever belongs to His Manhood is most perfect and well pleasing to God, so that if He but vouchsafe to bear me in mind, I shall in a certain way exist in Him, and hence come to be most pleasing to God in that respect, for He takes delight in whatever

---

[71] St. Bruno's feast falls in October. This and the preceding paragraphs may perhaps show us the special devotion of Father Favre, as he may have said votive masses of the saints commemorated.

He finds in Him. I further craved that the fruit thereof might be a love wherewith I might love God and His Son, Jesus Christ.

As regards the Society, for which by God's help I have ever been most solicitous, I felt an ardent desire that it might increase in numbers and virtue, in the quantity and spiritual quality of its members, so as to compensate for the falling off of other religious bodies. I further prayed that there might be found a great multitude of laics and clerics, who, forsaking all worldly things, would offer themselves to obey in all things which with the approval and according to the order of the Church are practised in religious orders, and that of these some might select one order, and some another. God grant that this may come to pass, and provide fit persons to try the spirits whether they be of God, and to determine what calling is most suited to each one. May Jesus send a good number of persons so well grounded in faith, charity, and other virtues, so as to fill the religious houses, so that, what is beyond all else to be desired, they may all be sanctified and perfected in Christ.

Another day, while reciting the office of St. Roch, confessor, I had good thoughts concerning the advantages, truth, and necessity of the outward worship of Christ and His saints. I felt, thereupon, deeply grieved that the heretics make no account of the ceremonies and rites of the Church, which are so necessary to maintain men in humility, concord, and religion.

For if under the Old Testament there was so great a variety of ceremonies and sacrifices of irrational beasts, prefiguring what was to have its fulfilment in Christ, how can it be against God's will that we should have a form of outward worship under the New Testament, and make use of certain ceremonies with regard to the Body of Christ? The ceremonies of the Old Testament foreshadowed those of the New, and these last are entirely spiritual. The former rites foreshadowed not only the Spirit of Christ, but His most holy Body also. Thus in the outward ritual of the New Testament we practise that which was before represented in figure, and we worship the holiness of Christ's Body, and make Him our model, not only in the spirit, but in the flesh likewise, since our bodies are temples of the Holy Ghost. Under the former covenant, the flesh of beasts was offered, but under ours the Body of Christ; they washed their own bodies in material water, that we might understand to wash the old man in spiritual water. We have, therefore, an external worship consisting of actions cognizable by the outward senses, as a fulfilment of the Old Law and of its figures, and not that we prefigure or represent what is to come. We have also a service of worship for the Word of God, of His Christ, and of His Church, and also for the Holy Ghost. To hold this outward worship in no account is, therefore, to ignore the Manhood of Christ, and to show little care for the holiness of one's body and flesh. Certain ceremonies of the New Law are, however, figures of the heavenly and glorified worship paid on high to our Lord.

On the feast of St. Gregory,[72] pope and confessor, I was penetrated with intense gratitude to so illustrious a pontiff and doctor, for that, more than all others, he had left behind him the necessary teaching concerning the souls of the departed. For had he not spoken so plainly of purgatory, and of what may give relief to the souls therein detained, there might have been nowadays a greater number of those that withhold belief from this dogma. Blessed be God

---

[72] March 12.

for having divinely instructed so great a doctor concerning the compassion we ought to feel for these poor souls, and for having given them His Son, Jesus Christ, for their Advocate! I here made the resolution for the future to keep a remembrance of this sainted Pope when I call to mind the souls in purgatory, and to endeavour to inspire devotion to these holy souls to such as are devout to this saint; and on the other hand, to persuade those who pray for the souls of the departed, not to forget to implore on their behalf the aid of this holy Pontiff.

On the day of our Lord's Passion,[73] I was made aware of and noted down what follows. The first thought that occurred to me was, that though I had been much troubled and agitated throughout Lent, and though these trials had seemed to renew the wounds of my miseries and failings, yet I could not feel sorrow for the imperfection of my doings, whether they regarded Christ, my neighbour, or myself. My mind was distracted from all wherein it was wont to find peace. My flesh was wholly taken up with those things in which from childhood it had found disquiet and death. It seemed to me that torpor and ignorance had regained their hold on mine actions, and that all the sentiments I had fondly thought to have died out, were quickened anew. It was therefore not without cause that I grieved, and was saddened at these disturbances, which so much afflicted both my soul and body.

When the day on which is made the commemoration of our Lord's Passion had dawned, and I began to revolve these things in my mind, it came to pass that, feeling inwardly strengthened, I perceived that all this had been to my profit and advantage. For is not this the season, are not these the days, whereon we renew the memory of Christ's Passion, of His

[73] March 23.

stripes, His wounds, the reproaches and other sufferings of our Saviour? And surely it is expedient to me that my spiritual wounds and all the vestiges of my ailments, as yet so imperfectly cured, should be, as it were, renewed. I was thus moved by the grace of God to entreat Him, for the sake of Jesus crucified and dying for me, to grant me that I might be healed of these infirmities; and I moreover prayed that through the merits of Christ's Blood, all my carnal affections might be mortified, deliverance from which I craved in these words: 'Deliver me, Thou God of my salvation, from all these evils.' I also prayed that the virtue of Christ's most Sacred Body, entombed in the sepulchre, might heal the infirmities of my flesh; and lastly, I besought the blessed Soul of Jesus Christ, that had descended into hell on parting from His Body, to hallow my spirit and soul, by ridding it of all root of imperfection, &c. I resolved, moreover, this same day, to offer the divine sacrifice I was to celebrate on the morrow—namely, on Holy Saturday—to obtain of God the grace of hearty contrition and renewal, and this through the death of Jesus, whereby that most holy temple was destroyed and His Soul was parted from His Body. I purposed also to recite oftener and more frequently the prayer, *Anima Christi sanctifica me.* And I was at the same time specially touched by a light concerning the bliss and power of the Soul of Christ, when parted from His Body, yet united to His Godhead, as it appeared in Limbus to the holy fathers, and to the souls in purgatory at its descent into hell. While contemplating the soulless corpse of Christ in the sepulchre, still united to the Godhead, I felt powerfully moved to ask for a real separation from sin and all vanity, and the grace of being quickened by God through the merits of His risen Christ.

On Easter eve, there occurred to me some precious lights on the two articles of the Creed—'He suffered under Pontius Pilate, was crucified, dead and buried: He descended into hell, the third day He rose again from the dead.' To this God added the favour of an earnest wish for suffering somewhat for Christ, daily to bear my cross, to die to sin, to be buried to the world, by being deprived of all relish for this temporal life, and to rise again renewed both in soul and body, in order that I may be fashioned after the pattern of our Lord Jesus Christ, Who died for our sins and rose again for our justification, that we, being dead to sin, might live unto justice, so as not to relapse into sin, or fall any more under the yoke of death, the death of sin, conformably with Christ, Who having arisen, now dies no more, nor hath death any dominion over Him.

On the day of our Lord's Resurrection I experienced an unwonted consolation during Mass, yet without that sensible devotion I but too frequently desire for mine own gratification and the edification of others. There was in that desire something of mine own, and I was conscious of an inordinate impulse, inordinate, at least, so far forth as regards the vehemence of my craving.

While contemplating the glory of Christ's Manhood united to the Godhead, a clear knowledge thereof was vouchsafed to me, and I was penetrated with amazement and admiration. For it is surely a matter for wonderment that a human body united to the Godhead should serve as its instrument for corporeal operations, and more wondrous still that the principle of life within the body, in other words, the reasonable soul, should be immediately united to the divine nature, for the action in this case is just as much in kind and degree the action of a physical and organic body united to the Godhead, as it is the action of a sensible and rational principle of life.

The human spirit, that is, the rational soul, considered as exalted above the flesh and intent on things spiritual and eternal, is infinitely more noble, when we consider it as united with God, and deriving from Him its every impulse and motion.

I then prayed most earnestly that God, through the merits of His risen Son, Jesus Christ, would graciously grant my body and soul to be one day glorified for the praise of His holy name, from Whom, in Whom, and by Whom is all grace and glory and whatever natural gift I possess.

I also desired that the bodies and souls of all men, being as they are most capacious vessels of grace, might be filled from the overflowing fulness of the Sacred Humanity, which contains within Itself all the fulness of the Godhead. May God grant that I too may be enriched with this plentiful grace.

I made use of the consideration of the four qualities of Christ's glorified Body, to ask certain analogous gifts for my soul, to wit, that through His grace I might be ready and swift in well doing, and in bearing evil, more intelligent and enlightened, and less sensitive to sufferings.

On Easter Monday, after the nocturnal office, I fell into mine accustomed distress, that is, I grew sad for these three motives—(1) I failed to mark within me, as I desired, sensible tokens of God's love for me ; (2) I discovered in me more than I expected of the traces of the old Adam ; (3) I was not able to reap among my neighbours the fruit I wished for. In these three things does my cross consist. In the course of the day, while revolving these thoughts, I heard, as it were, an inward answer to this effect— 'Thou oft-times desirest to be taken down from the cross ere thou art dead ; Christ died upon His, wherefore then shouldst thou not begin to be willing to die upon thine own cross? But thou art willing just to suffer somewhat in order to lead a life full of consolations, and to be kept from feeling the burthen of thy corrupt nature. Henceforth desire rather to die to this life of thine, which is too fluctuating, too unstable and changeable. Thou canst no way die so well to this life as by the death of the Cross, which goes counter to it and consists in these three things—(1) that thy soul be so far in repose as never to desire, or to seek to feel, for thine own sake, any accidental devotion; (2) not to be troubled even though thy old man rise again by putting forth his roots and inclinations to mortal or venial sin; (3) to maintain thyself in peace, when thine outward works appear void of all fruit whether to thyself, or to those who look into thy doings, be it to profit by thy good example, or to slander and to slight thee. When thou shalt have died on this cross, and shalt, so to speak, be buried, taking no heed of the esteem or contempt of men, then shalt thou taste of a new spiritual consolation and feel thyself quickened with a new life, the root and fruits whereof shall not be of the same kind as the former, but far more excellent and lasting. Hitherto thou hast delighted rather in the greatness of the tree which draws its increase from divine grace than in its roots, in which its virtue mainly resides; thou hast regarded the leaves and flowers which are but passing, and not the fruits which tend to perfection. This is why thou canst not enjoy stable consolation. Seek not then the root of this tree for the sake of its fruits, but rather its fruits to obtain the root, and, moreover, desire that the root rather than the fruits may abide in thee, for it is by the root thou shalt attain glory. Let then the root be the object of thy toil and cares, for this it is that shall one day appear in glory, even as the root of all good, which is Christ, has now first been glorified. In the world to come, the root will be, and be seen to be, the fruit; not so in this wretched life, where it is laid low and trampled under foot. Wherefore, if thou wilt go in search of the fruits, seek such as are such in the next life.'

Another day during the Easter week, as I was moving into a house I had hired, I felt divers pious motions and desires for a prosperous entrance into this new dwelling; so I recited the following prayer of the Church in every part of the building—'Visit, O Lord, this abode, and drive far from it the snares of the enemy, let Thy holy angels dwell herein to keep us in peace, and may Thy blessing be ever upon us, through the merits of our Lord Jesus Christ. Amen.' This I did with a sentiment of devotion, feeling it was proper to act in this wise whenever one goes into a new dwelling. I also called upon the good angels of the circumjacent places to guard both myself and my companions against the assaults of the evil spirits lurking in the neighbourhood, especially the spirit of fornication, which, I doubt not, dwells with fallen women and fornicators, and other vicious persons who, as I learned, lived hard by. I also invoked St. Otillia, St. Jodoc, and St. Lucy, the patrons of the chapel near the house I had taken. I was penetrated with deep sorrow on beholding that this chapel was defiled and profaned by the fornications of those who pass that way, and felt on that account an earnest wish to repair it, and to restore the veneration of the saints aforesaid, whose memory had wholly ceased to be honoured in this chapel, which had in former times been a place of great devotion to them and of confidence in their help. I celebrated holy Mass for this intention, that it might remedy the sins committed through the neglect of this devotion, and that I might be enabled to restore it to some extent. God grant, through the intercession of these saints, and of all the others, that I may be allowed to labour at this restoration.

In the evening of this same day, when about to retire to rest for the first time in this house, as I felt an indisposition, which occasioned a certain heaviness of spirit, I began to beseech our Lord to grant me to prosper in this dwelling, by rendering the air of the place wholesome, or to dispose things otherwise according to His good pleasure. I begged the like prosperity for my neighbours, that they might be shielded from all evil, and my coming among them might be favourable and propitious to them, and I ended by praying that, by the merits of St. Lucy, we might be guarded against every ill. Thinking of this excited within me hearty gratitude to God, seeing that as I had been so often compelled in the course of my life to change my abode, though I never did so with a view to greater convenience, yet it had never befallen me to contract any illness through such change, though I had frequently gone to dwell in dangerous and unwholesome places. Thus, for instance, I have often had to lodge in filthy hospitals, more often still in wretched apartments, which sometimes were very cold; and now and then in miserable huts, where, saving a little straw, all was wanting—not to speak of those nights when I had to lie down under the canopy of heaven. Blessed be He Who in these straits, and many others of like nature, has preserved and helped me. On this account did I give thanks, which were well due, trusting that He Who never failed to protect me in other places of abode would surely not forget to come to mine aid in my present dwelling. I also prayed for all to whom it has happened, or ever may in future happen, to go to, or to dwell, in the places I have passed through, or where I had lived or prayed. May it please my God, Who has inspired me with these sentiments, to fulfil them according to His will, rather than according to what I may wish for or demand.

The same day, as I was writing to the Countess de Montfort, and the Vicar General of the Most Reverend Bishop of Spires, there occurred to me certain thoughts concerning the Resurrection which I never had before. They consisted in certain practical lessons, resulting from the fact that our souls will be glorified ere they are reunited to the body, even as Christ was glorified in the spirit before glorifying His flesh. Now, the consideration that our souls can, and, in very deed, will be, in bliss apart from the body, should teach us to despise it, and to realize more deeply those words of the Apostle, 'We are debtors not to the flesh, that we should live according to its lusts.' As also that we are not called upon to give full satisfaction to our bodily wants, seeing that the body is not so necessary to us as might appear from the care we take of it, as if without it we could not be happy; for, on the contrary, the soul will be in bliss before the body, and they who suffer in hell are tormented in the soul long before the body is put to torture. May Jesus, Who for our sake laid down His life, and ere He rose again shed happiness on the holy fathers, grant us to learn to lead a spiritual life, instead of this wretched life, which is wholly taken up with evil thoughts and guilty memories and yearnings, and to live a life which is the very opposite of this.

On the feast of St. George the martyr,[74] while saying Mass in St. Christopher's Church, I made a memento of a person lately departed, the day of whose burial or deposition was then being kept: I felt a great consolation at the lively apprehension of the glory Christ bestows upon souls. I was principally touched by the great generosity He gives proof of in rewarding what is done for His sake, in recompensing each work with the guerdon that is its due. And of a truth, the reward of any work

[74] April 23.

whatsoever done in and by His grace must needs be very great (those which are performed without grace can, of course, claim no reward), since to God it belongs to appraise them according to His charity and liberty, and to reward them in the measure of the Almighty power of His Godhead. And as the lowlimindedness of Christ knows no bounds, He disdains not to reward, and to make account of the slightest things which are done for His sake; and as His riches are infinite, immense too is the recompense He awards them. I next began to be intensely grieved, that nowadays so little thought is taken of the rewards awaiting our good deeds, whence comes heedlessness and want of fear of the chastisements in store for our bad deeds. In this way do we lose the hope of reaping what was sown in tears, and the dread of sin; since we are blind to the punishment that corresponds to it. In a word, while no heed is taken of good or evil doings, we lose, moreover, true knowledge of the deified Humanity, made manifest to us in the Incarnation of the Word, in order that our salvation might be wrought out by Christ, Who is both God and Man, Who is to come again to judge all the living and the dead and to take account of each one's doings in his lifetime, and to come in that same Manhood which was seen ascending into heaven, according to those words which were spoken to His disciples—'He shall so come, in like manner, as ye have seen Him go up into heaven.' The liberality, and gratitude men give proof of to their servants must exist in a far greater measure in Christ. It is unquestionable that any mortal prince can confer the greatest happiness on the meanest of his servants by merely taking notice of his work, and make him as it were beside himself for joy and wonderment at the condescension of his prince, who deigns to appreciate what the servant himself made little or no account of. They therefore are in the wrong, who preach and speak of Christ's Godhead, omitting all mention of His Manhood, thus doing away with all comparisons and resemblances between God and man, though not stripping Him of the flesh He took to Himself. He was pleased to take upon Himself a body and to become a slave, that we, despite the meanness of our origin, might more easily be brought to the belief that we are able to attain the likeness unto God promised to us, in that we hold for God and Man Him Whom we are to worship and serve, not only in spirit, but bodily too, since it pleased Him to take that nature of ours wherein He suffered, and wherewith He is now gloriously reigning at the right hand of God the Father. This human nature, so highly exalted by God, claims to be venerated by us in holiness and justice, seeing that it is a most perfect instrument of our redemption, justification, sanctification, and consummation in glory, and the temple of the whole Godhead.

Lucifer refused to submit to this nature, and by submission to the Humanity of the Word to become subject to the Most High; he chose rather to enter into the joy and glory of his Lord by his own strength and virtue. He had set before him the mystery predestined in the eternal counsels, the mystery of the humiliation of the Son of God, whereby it had been foreordained and decreed from eternity that He should become Man, and by this means to be subject to Him Who before all ages had begotten Him coequal to Himself. Lucifer refused to humble himself to the God made Man Who had thus from the greatest become the least. And since he would not consent to humble himself, by means of the faith and grace wherein he was created, to Him Who was to take our human nature, he lost the gift of faith, and fell back upon himself, saying, 'I will ascend above the height of the clouds, I will be like unto the Most High;' an ascent which was his ruin and degradation.

Before celebrating Mass on St. Mark's day,[75] I became conscious of a downward motion to evil, and was overwhelmed with such grief and sadness that I was moved even to tears that I should still be liable to such disturbances. I therefore besought the Lord in the spirit of compunction, which, as my past experience taught me, was the true remedy for these temptations, to enable me by His grace to employ myself wholly in discovering and acquiring the good that is still wanting to me, so that if I have occasion to grieve, I may grieve rather at beholding myself so devoid of virtue, than for the evil motions I may chance to feel, and may be so taken up with desiring and seeking after my perfection, that no room may be left for thinking of what may draw me down or backwards.

I perceived most distinctly on this occasion, as was most frequently the case before, how necessary it is to distinguish the several degrees of perfection, so that when once we know them we may strive to attain them; not that we are to take our rest at any determinate stage, but rather should make good our footing in order to an advance. Now this advance can be made in three ways, according to the three-fold relation of our virtues—(1) with regard to what appertains to the knowledge and love of God; (2) with regard to what concerns our neighbour, for it is certain that we daily stand in need of fresh knowledge, and renewed affections, concerning the interests and the spiritual and bodily needs of our neighbour. From these two things results a third, to wit, our own progress in good, which is to be directed toward God, and through God to our neighbour. But as our progress in perfection necessarily supposes that we

---

[75] April 25.

strip ourselves of the old man, and put on the new, we must needs, whether we like it or not, suffer temptations and prickings both in the spirit and the flesh, for this it is which helps us in our path, and by temptations and prickings are meant not only such as disturb our peace, but those that goad us on to sin, otherwise we should have no knowledge of our own soil, on which we might be building before having laid the foundation-stone, which is Christ, a stone which cannot be laid ere our old man is destroyed. We have then need of patience, and as we have heretofore observed, we should strive might and main to acquire what we still lack, and to endure the stings of sin until it shall please God to send us relief. It is to be borne in mind that these distinctions drawn out above need no new terms, or names which are not in use with doctors of positive or scholastic theology.

The reason whereof is, that we should be most careful not to depart from the common mode of speaking of Catholic doctors, nor should we multiply the books to be read, especially those of the Divine Scriptures, according to the diversity of spirits, since the same passage may suit different dispositions. Besides, if every man writes and composes books in terms of his own devising, we shall see, what has partly come to pass already, countless sects, and diversities of doctrine and of views concerning sacred things. We are not therefore to think that we should adapt what has already been written and approved to our new-fangled terminology, but rather our terminology should be made conformable to what is written. Wherefore, every spiritual light and sentiment not in conformity with the teaching of the Catholic Church and its approved doctors is to be rejected.

On the feast of the holy martyrs Cletus and Marcellinus,[76] Popes, after saying matins, I felt intense devotion

---

[76] April 26.

in considering how the mercy of Christ brought to a better mind the holy Pope Marcellinus, whom fear of death had led into idolatry, so that he attained the martyr's crown.

It was given to me by the grace of the good spirit to mourn on this occasion over my backsliding in the way of virtue, for which I had never yet wept enough. I also admired the mercy or justice of God in my regard, which consists herein, that I have never or but seldom felt within me the threatenings or rebukes of His Holy Spirit on account of my sins and shortcomings, since the reproaches inwardly addressed to me came either from my conscience, or from the spirit given me to buffet me and to exercise my virtue. I then received grace to beg earnestly of the Most High, that He would enable me for the future to hear the warnings and rebukes of the Holy Ghost. For the which end I said the following prayer—'My Lord and my God, methinks that Thou hast hitherto kept silent at the sight of my past sins and my present imperfections; that no word of Thine has yet been spoken to my heart and soul concerning my sins, while Thou hast in manifold ways taught me to follow Thy counsels and to do good. Begin therefore in a new way, that is with no intermediary, but by Thine own Spirit to suggest to me the words and sentiments of true contrition; stir up my soul by Thy Spirit to mourn for my sins, even as Thou hast hitherto done so by means of other spirits.' I conceived this desire, not because I was depressed by any sin, or that I felt the prickings of conscience, but because I was conscious of that higher spirit, the Spirit of God within me, and therefore I desired that the sense of my sins, and the knowledge of what it is to offend God, should be renewed in my soul.

Another day, while visiting Master Peter of Gueldres (Canisius), who was going through the Spiritual Exercises, most cogent arguments came into my mind, which gave me to understand far more clearly than ever before, that it is of great advantage for the discernment of spirits if we attend not to the thoughts and inward suggestions, but rather to the spirit itself, which is wont to manifest itself by means of desires and affections, the strength or weakness of the soul, tranquillity or disquiet, sadness or joy, or other spiritual affections of the like kind. By means of such marks one may more easily know and judge of the soul, and of the spirits which move it, than by means of thoughts. There are some, who, by means of many and various exercises of prayer and contemplation, are scarcely able to distinguish the diversity of spirits, but seem always agitated, now more now less, by one and the same spirit. The most effectual means, however, for distinguishing this diversity, is to propose the choice of the state of life to be embraced. But generally speaking, the more any one applies himself, with all his affections, to do, or hope for, or believe, or love, a higher and more perfect thing, the better he will be able to know the diversity of the good and the evil spirit. In some the evil spirit is not recognized, chiefly in those who are given up to piety and devotion, because they have no thoughts which are outside the limits of goodness and truth, nor any evidently inordinate affections. But if these persons can be induced, however perfect they may be, to examine themselves, and see to what higher degree of perfection they might aspire, and whether the sort of life already embraced by them is immutable, and what more perfect sort to embrace, they will then easily distinguish both these spirits, that which strengthens and that which debilitates; that which enlightens, and that which produces darkness; that which justifies, and that which defiles—that is to say, the good and the bad spirit.

On the fifth Sunday after Easter, I noted certain things, the order and manner of which had been already clearly enough shown to me the preceding Friday, and they had reference to what may be and usually is asked in the colloquies of the four weeks of the Exercises. In the first, these three graces are rightly asked for, namely, a true knowledge of and contrition for the sins committed in our past life, knowledge and resolution of a real amendment, and a true regulation of our life for the future. In the second week, in accordance with the end of the contemplations of the life of Christ, which end is to know Him in order to imitate Him, these three graces are, with good reason, put into the colloquies (I am speaking of the principal colloquies to the Blessed Virgin, to Christ, and to the Eternal Father). The first is the abnegation of self, the second the perfect contempt of the world, the third the perfect love of the service of Christ our Lord. There are many persons who think that they have a great esteem for the Person of Christ, and that they love Him, when, notwithstanding, they do not like the things in which the service of Christ consists. Such persons, to say the truth, think frequently, and not without consolation, of Christ, and of His virtues and perfections, but very seldom of the works which He requires from His servants, and in which He desires His followers to be exercised, in order that, being where He was, they may hereafter be where He now is. In the third week, during which we meditate on the Passion of Christ, those three graces seem to me very suitable, namely, compassion for Christ's bodily sufferings, compassion for His poverty and His privation of all things, compassion for the insults and reproaches He suffered, for there are many sufferings in these things the diversity of which we cannot feel without the help of God. In the fourth week, which has for its subject-matter the contemplation of Christ, risen in glory, are placed these three graces—the first the love of God and of Jesus Christ, the second perfect joy in Christ alone, and the third true peace, which is only to be found in Him.

On the vigil of the Ascension,[77] when I was troubled and afflicted in considering that which is a hindrance in me to the service of Christ, I found myself, all on a sudden, strengthened, and full of consolation and resolution. Then it was given to me to see that such consolations are no less to be shunned than desolations, in so far as both are hindrances to the solid profit which sometimes is delayed by both, that is, by vain sadness and vain joy, and sometimes more by the latter than the former, although it is true that the joy with which there is united a little spiritual vanity, is more helpful in doing good than the sadness with which some disturbance is mingled. This disturbance proceeds from the evil spirit, although afterwards it ends in the good spirit, just as, on the contrary, the joy usually proceeds from the good spirit and ends in the evil spirit. For just as the good spirit is wont to take occasion from sadness to draw us to what is good and solid, to give us true and not vain consolation, so our enemy is wont to take occasion from joy to lead us to a vain gladness, the end of which is real sadness. Let us then consider attentively, and observe these things both in the beginning and the end, in order to know from which spirit the interior movements of the soul proceed.

On the feast of the Ascension, it was given me to understand what is meant by seeking God and Jesus Christ above every creature, and by desiring to know them perfectly. I was also able to understand the difference that there is between knowing the creature in God, or God in the creature, or God without the creature. And this is the

[77] May 2.

true ascent of mind and spirit, to ascend, by means of creatures, to the knowledge and love of their Creator, and not to rest in considering them only. In the second place, we ought to rise to the Creator by considering Him as He lives and works in creatures. But neither ought we to rest there, but to seek God in Himself above every other creature, without, for that reason, excluding Him from the creature. After that, let all creatures be known in Him more perfectly than as they are in themselves. Oh, quickly may that time come in which I shall neither see, nor love, nor fear, any creature apart from God, and from this may I rise as by a ladder, to know Him in Himself, and lastly, all in Christ that He may always be to me all in all. By means of these steps I will strive that Christ, Who is the way, the truth, and the life, may be in the centre of my heart and my interior, that is, within myself; and then above me by the mind, and outside of me by the senses. And thus we ought to pray that the Father, Who is said to be above, may communicate power to us; that the Son, Who in His Humanity is said to be *ab extra*, may give us wisdom; and that the Holy Spirit, Who, in a certain way, is beneath, that is, within us, may give us goodness. For in no other way could our interior open itself and see God there, nor could our superior part rise to invisible things, nor feel within our body Him Who is outside of and above all things.

The day after the feast of the Ascension,[78] on which was kept that of the most Holy Cross, I celebrated Mass in the church called the Church of the Cross, which is outside the city of Mayence, and in which is preserved the memory of those wonderful miracles which once

---

[78] The feast of the Ascension in 1543 fell on the feast of the Invention of the Cross, May 3, the latter feast being therefore transferred to the following day.

happened, one of which was with regard to the crucifix that is kept there, which was found floating on the Rhine, going against the current of the river. The other miracle happened to another crucifix, also venerated there, which being struck by a gambler, there gushed forth blood from the wounded head, and to this day it may be seen to have oozed from the picture. While celebrating the holy Mass, then, in that church, I experienced very great devotion, and felt great sorrow at seeing how forgetful men are in these days of such illustrious miracles. After which, I prayed to my Lord to give me grace that I might be able to know all miracles and favours of this kind, and that He would receive these particular feelings of mine as though they were those of all the members of the Society, and of all the pious persons I have known, and as though this sacrifice were offered by all those to His praise and in thanksgiving for similar benefits.

Then I promised to return once more to this church, before I left Germany, in order to celebrate Mass at the altar of the other crucifix which floated on the water.

On the feast of the Apparition of St. Michael the Archangel,[79] I had a special inspiration to thank God for the gifts bestowed upon the holy angels. And it seemed to me that one of these benefits was their exemption from the infirmities belonging to our souls, which are shut up in the prisons of our bodies, thereby causing in us so great a difference and contrariety of feelings, and so many inclinations to do evil, which those angelic natures cannot have. It is also a great advantage to the angels, that they have not, like us, a superior and inferior part, and those interior conflicts which we have, but which they did not have even before they were confirmed in good, although the evil angels then made

[79] May 8.

war upon them. But in us there is so great a variety, that even if some part seems to be good, we have many others which lead to evil. For the entire will does not at once go with the understanding, nor the understanding with the will; and, again, sense often inclines to go begond what reason proposes. It thus comes to pass that man is not altogether good and upright all at once, because there is in him a part which is not so. I was enabled, however, to know this is a great benefit, for although some part in a man may be bad, it does not therefore follow that he must be wholly lost; and, in like manner, though he may be lost for a short time, yet his very changeableness and inconstancy make it possible that he shall not be eternally lost. Often the sensitive part in man seems corrupt, although the rational part is not so; and this is a misery which could not exist in the angels, even when they were not confirmed in grace. Yet from this very thing sprang a great danger, that, namely, of their being lost like the other angels who were apostates; for immediately on their contracting evil, it would have happened, through the simplicity of their nature, that that nature would have been infected therewith, and there might have been in them no possibility of one part consenting, and the other resisting, but, of necessity, their nature must either have instantly remained good, or been wholly infected by evil. I, then, seeing myself so prone to evil, and surrounded by so many seductions of the flesh, the world, and the devil, rejoice that I do not possess this simple nature: for if it were so it would speedily happen that my soul would be imbued with some evil spirit and be wholly defiled. In my actual state, although some evil spirit may imbue, for example, my flesh, my understanding, or appetite, my nature does not therefore become bad at once, because I am able not to consent to such things, but to resist them with the full force of my will. I desired, therefore, to be so imbued by the good spirit, that in this respect my nature may be entirely simple and constant; but when bad spirits assail me, then I would rather it was not so, that is, I would rather have a nature that was inconstant, and not simple, otherwise I should run a grievous risk of being instantly defiled, and of my fall being irreparable.

Blessed, then, be our Lord Jesus Christ, Who for us became Incarnate, and died; because, having given us so variable a nature for our help in the various accidents we may meet with, He nevertheless permits us, by His grace, to attain to that perfect simplicity and immutability in good in the kingdom of heaven, although the state of the damned is that of immutability in torment and in evil. And thus the saints will be one day wholly penetrated by that chief Good to Whom they will be eternally united, and the wicked, on the contrary, by every kind of misery by which they will be always overwhelmed.

On the holy festival of Pentecost I had a keen desire to receive from the Holy Spirit an understanding and a will that were wholly spiritual, and therefore I asked also that my existence, and life, and thoughts, and words might be spiritual, for which word I had a particular affection. I understood also the very great difference that there is in divine movements, which may take place in the vital, animal, and rational spirit of man; and I also considered how great a difference there is between feeling a thing in the flesh and feeling it in spirit—between existing and living in the flesh, and existing and living in the spirit.

Then, with many prayers I besought that Holy Spirit, that for the time to come my being, life, and thoughts might be spiritual, and that I might thus perform the work of my salvation, and be delivered from those carnal motions and thoughts by which I am now distressed.

For then are things truly appreciated when they are apprehended by the spirit, especially when the things are spiritual and suggested by the Holy Ghost. I also noted the manner in which I experienced carnal movements in my flesh, since it happens that they sometimes come from the evil spirit in the flesh, and sometimes, also, by means of the same wicked spirit, in the vital, or animal, or also in the rational part of man. Again, it may sometimes happen, that spiritual things are learnt in a carnal manner, as it also happens with regard to corporal things that they are felt and understood spiritually. We ought therefore, above all things, to beg the Holy Spirit to vouchsafe to guide whatsoever spirit is in us, both that which is the cause of life and of sensation, and that which is the reason of thoughts and affections, and to continue to do so till there comes that time and blessedness when God will be to us all in all.

Another time, during the octave of Pentecost, I experienced great devotion in thinking of the gifts of the Holy Spirit, considering what it is that is meant by the gifts of understanding, of wisdom, of fear, of knowledge, of counsel, of piety, and of fortitude; and so, in order to obtain them, I prayed to the Holy Spirit by His Procession from the Father and the Son. In like manner I prayed to Him as He was the Guide and Sanctifier of the Soul of Christ, as He it was by Whose operation Christ was conceived, and He it is Who enriched with His gifts the Virgin Mary, the angels, prophets, apostles, martyrs, confessors, monks, virgins, widows, and the rest. Furthermore, I prayed to Him as He is the Destroyer of the suggestions of the devil, and, in short, as He it is Who fills all things and in Whom everything has movement. Then I understood how excellent and great a grace it is to enjoy the protection of Him Who abides in all things, as their beginning, middle, and end.

On that occasion I prayed the Holy Spirit to be for ever my Guardian and Protector, that, indeed, I might be, and live, and feel in Him, and that I might be able to drive away the wicked suggestions of the evil spirit, which are those bad thoughts and affections, and the incitements to do wrong which come to us from our malicious enemy. For bad spirits have great power in our bodies, but the Holy Spirit strengthens us against them either by Himself, or by means of the angelic spirits.

On the feast of the most Holy Trinity, I desired greatly that it might be celebrated with much solemnity, as it is the festival of those Three Persons, than Whom it is impossible to believe or imagine anything more excellent and worthy.

I also prayed that all my powers and strength might be employed by the means of the Divine and Eternal Father in His service, that they might be guided by the Son, and lastly, that all my appetites, inclinations, and affections might be purified by the Holy Spirit.

I experienced great devotion whilst I was occupied in considering and understanding, as clearly as I could, the manner in which God the Father, the Son, and the Holy Ghost are in every place, and outside of all things, and within all things, and everywhere, and in us all; and I asked God that He would be pleased to grant me grace that I might be able to seek Him in every way, and to find Him according to my desires. I understood, also, in some degree, how God is said to be omnipotent, that is to say, that He is so great as to be able to cause, in every possible way, everything which, of itself, could not exist either corporally or spiritually, or, to speak more generally, either in a substantial or accidental, a simple or complex manner. And here I began to reason on the order and gradation which there is from less perfect to more perfect things; and this was the order in which they came before me. In the first place, I considered all the accidents, the perfection of which may be classed and arranged from the subjects to which they are united; next, the matter of corporal things; thirdly, the substantial forms of inanimate and corruptible things; fourthly, the form of the heavens; fifthly, the corruptible forms of animate things, such as plants and brutes; in the sixth place I considered inanimate and also corruptible vegetable substances; seventhly, heavenly substances and the corporeal heavens; then brute animals, rational souls, and, lastly, the angels. After that I considered the Father, the Son, and the Holy Ghost, God, Three in Persons and One in most perfect Substance.

On the Tuesday after the feast of the most Holy Trinity, while saying Matins, I felt within myself a certain grace which I had never before had, though I had greatly desired to have it, namely, an elevation and fixedness of my mind in God, Who is in heaven. At other times I had often had greater devotion concerning the understanding of the words that I recited, and concerning the spirit of them by which I was moved to compunction; but what I now felt was a sublime elevation of mind, by means of which it was given to me to know the power of God, Who dwells in heaven as in His temple; and thus I was moved to desire and ask for an increase in myself of this grace, in order to be able to attend better to vocal and mental prayer. This concentration of the mind on God appeared to me a difficult thing to attain; but I hoped to be assisted and strengthened by grace in this matter.

It seemed to me, also, easier to fix the mind during prayer on Jesus crucified, or on His Virgin Mother, or some saint, as though they were present, or on God, as He truly is in heaven. And here I took note that it was very necessary for every one who desires to pray, either mentally or vocally, to have present to him these three things, namely, the thought of the person to whom the prayers are addressed, the meaning of the words which are said, or which are in the mind during prayer, and lastly, the spirit of devotion and affection with which these things are to be done.

It will also be a help to the perfection of prayer for the memory to be raised to the throne of the Divine Majesty, for the understanding to be enlightened by the wisdom of the Son, and the will inflamed by the love of the Holy Ghost, without which there is no sweetness in the interior of the soul. May Jesus Christ give us grace that we may be able to attain to this, and to increase in it every day! These feelings which I had concerning the devotion of the mind to God, as soon as I paused to consider the miseries of my flesh and spirit, I recognized to be a fruit, so to speak, of the festival of the most Holy Trinity. Wherefore I resolved to recollect myself every year, in readiness for this feast, and to see whether I had made progress in preparing my soul to be a habitation of the most Holy Trinity, in which mystery meet together all the mysteries of the life of Christ, and all the feasts and solemnities of the Church.

On the feast of the most Blessed Sacrament of the Body of Christ, I had many lights with regard to the manner of celebrating that festival and of adoring Jesus Christ. During the procession I was moved to devotion by the sight of its pomp, and of the multitude of people, and by the way in which every one endeavoured to increase the devotion of the function by his reverence, his actions, and the affections of his soul; and I rejoiced to think how the senses and members of the body and the mechanical works of artificers may be made useful for this purpose, in the same way as the voice in singing, instruments of music, plants, flowers, garlands, and other things which are additions to the ceremony. Thus all men may serve God with their bodies, and offer their members as a homage to Him from Whom they have received them.

On the same day I felt great devotion in offering my whole being for the worship of Christ. I offered my understanding, my memory, and my will, my five exterior senses, and all that is in me, both to glorify and honour Him, and to serve and obey Him with regard to my own sanctification, as also to labour for the good of my neighbour, having for my object the love of God. I also desired to imitate Jesus Christ with my whole soul and body in these two things, namely, to be altogether used and consumed for Him in good works, and to accustom myself to endure sufferings in soul and body, as He suffered for me and for all men, in all His members, even to the death upon the Cross.

On the Octave of the same feast, whilst anxiously considering my defects, it was given to me to ask grace that the punishments of those sins which proceed from bad habits and inclinations, from temptations, and from the concupiscence of my nature, might be remitted to me. I also felt, in a certain way, how it is the will of Christ, by means of this admirable Sacrament of His Body and Blood, to exercise the faith of His spouse, the Church. For in believing that under those sensible species there is the Body and the Blood of Christ, we are exercised in the faith of those things which are not seen, and we believe the Real Presence of the Body under the species of bread, and of the Blood under the species of wine, and, by concomitance, the presence of the Soul and the Divinity. Furthermore, we are exercised in adoring the Divine Sacrament in various ways and by various acts, not only in spirit and by interior acts of faith and devotion, but exteriorily also, by the worship of *latria*, as though Christ were visibly present. Lastly, we are exercised in promoting our salvation when we make use of this heavenly food for the nourishment, strengthening, enlightenment, and consolation of our soul, and for receiving within ourselves all heavenly treasures. Those, therefore, are very wretched and unhappy, who do not pay to this Sacrament the same veneration and worship which they would pay to the visible Person of Christ. No less a thing is given to us than that which was given to the Apostles at the Last Supper; that Body, not dead, but living, was given to them, which was, shortly after, to be betrayed and crucified.

On the fourth Sunday after Pentecost, as I was about to say Mass, I asked the grace that my soul might be defended from the evil spirits of devils and men. I took notice that I had often been troubled and distressed by the idea that some wicked men were plotting against my soul and spirit. It seemed to me that I was weak in opposing these imaginary plots, and I thought it would be a lesser evil if all men in the world were to set themselves to persecute me in the body, than if a single man were to set to work to attack the weakness of my soul. And then I invoked the protection of God that I might bear those persecutions of spirit which we suffer by means of the demons and of men.

And here began again that torturing affliction which I have experienced ever since I came to Germany, on witnessing the defection of this nation. God grant that the event may not verify what was presented to my imagination by the operation, not of the good spirit, but rather by the spirit of diffidence, which has tormented me in various ways, suggesting to me to hope for no fruit from my labours, to flee away and quit these parts committed to my charge. I pray God that the tepidity, malice, and defection of these wicked men, whether real or imaginary, may cease to assail my soul and spirit, which is already in itself so tepid, cold, and imperfect; that there may be an end of this changeableness of mine, which makes things appear to me at one time prosperous and favourable, at another adverse and desperate. This would not happen if I did not know the causes and the occasions from which such great evils proceed and grow. I have spent too much time in considering and weighing them, and inquiring into the ways which lead to error and sin. My experience also of the infirmities and imperfections of others has increased my alarm. Hence it has happened that I have not given heed to the virtues and good qualities which God has sown in men; the consideration of which good qualities with a single eye, contrasting them with the bad, would bring greater peace, and greater fruit would be gained by endeavouring to cherish those good qualities.

On the 10th of June, which at Mayence is a solemn feast of St. Albanus the martyr, I celebrated Mass at the high altar of the Church of St. Albanus, where, besides other relics, the body of that most blessed martyr was exposed. I had great devotion in reflecting on the many journeys of this martyr, and that he came here, in the time of the Arians, to give his life for the salvation of the people of Mayence. Hence I took courage and confidence of gaining some fruit out of these Lutheran heresies, which desolate almost all Germany. The consequence of these heresies is that many persons, falling away from the Catholic Church, and rejecting her discipline, believe and say whatever they please, so that the heretics of these days may well be called teachers of rebellion and defection. God send us men of opposite sentiments, who may, by word and deed, promote unity and obedience to the Church, and progress in every Christian virtue.

On St. John the Baptist's day, before Mass,[80] I was moved to devotion, and to ask the grace rightly to regulate myself and all my spiritual exercises. In the first place, I desired to be pleasing and acceptable to God, through the merits of Jesus Christ; in the second place, to perform worthily all offices of the priesthood, such as preaching, offering the holy sacrifice, meditating, and the like. Thirdly, to be enabled to exercise my ministrations to the profit of my neighbour, according to the dispositions of the divine will, both in respect to my friends and to all others. Fourthly, to have a particular grace for well directing those whom I am to instruct.

While considering St. John the Baptist as a model of penance, I received some lights illustrating the teaching of the Exercises with regard to sins. It seemed to me that the first thing of all is to inquire what is penitence, and not to desire all at once a compunction full of tears and tenderness, although this is the end towards which we tend, but to discover the various ways of performing exterior penance. Many persons complain that they have not compunction of heart, when they have not the patience to seek that in which this compunction consists. They would like to feel inward sorrow of soul, but they are not willing to afflict their flesh in anything. God often delays communicating to us His more perfect gifts, and leading us to the attainment of the end, in order that we may learn to make use of His lesser gifts, and of the means which lead to the end. Some persons desire to have spiritual feelings, and to experience in their flesh compunction of heart, whilst, on the other hand, they lack patience and other virtues,

[80] June 24.

the want of which they neither feel nor know. But it is the will of God that we should possess our soul, and we can only possess it by patience, according to the words—*In patientiâ vestrâ possidebitis animas vestras.* And how can he who does not possess his soul by patience expect to possess God by sensible consolation?

On the day of SS. John and Paul, on rising from bed in the morning, I had a very remarkable grace of preparing my heart to say office without admitting affections of sadness and of joy. Nevertheless, while dressing and arranging other things, I was very careful to desire to pray with all devotion and attention, and my only fear was of not continuing in these dispositions, which, however, lasted till the end of Mass; and I desired that it might be so always. And here I noted that it was a good thing that our heart should always be in a state either of a certain sadness at the privation of the divine assistance and illumination, which is wont to come from actual devotion, or of a certain consolation in consequence of possessing them. And this seemed to me a good exercise for knowing thoroughly what it is to be deprived of the vision and fruition of God, which is the portion of the damned, or what it is to possess it, which is the portion of the blessed.

That day I said Mass for the soul of that most pious and learned man, Lansperg, the Carthusian, whose good state I desired. While making the memento of the dead, I came to know that the deliverance of a soul from purgatory must bring great glory to God and the saints, as well as great assistance to those who live upon this earth. For in purgatory the soul is, as it were, bound, and can do nothing for our salvation and for the glory of God, whilst the blessed, who are in heaven, cause the Divine Father and His Son, Jesus Christ, to be evermore glorified, and the glory of God and Christ for the salvation of the souls of the living to appear upon earth, according to the angelic hymn—*Gloria in excelsis Deo, et in terrâ pax hominibus bonæ voluntatis.*

Another day in the octave of St. John, whilst hearing a person's general confession, I received great knowledge concerning works of mercy towards the living and dead, and I wept abundantly, without, at the same time, being distracted from listening to my penitent. I learnt that to show mercy to others is a very effectual means of finding mercy ourselves with God; and how easy a thing it is freely to receive from God His spiritual gifts, if we will freely practise towards others the corporal works of mercy. Thus it happens, that some persons much given to prayer do not find sometimes that which they desire for their spiritual consolation, because they do not show spiritual mercy towards their neighbour. There are others who, being entirely occupied with the salvation of their neighbour, though they may be able to spend but little time in prayer, find God propitious, not only as regards the remission of their sins, but also as regards the gaining of various heavenly gifts. Henceforth I resolved to exhort all persons to pay greater attention to works of mercy.

On the day of the holy Apostles SS. Peter and Paul,[81] while saying Mass for a friend, it was granted me to hope that he might be able to obtain some necessary graces from the mercy of God, by the intercession of the Blessed Virgin and of the holy Apostles. While meditating on the mysteries of the life of Christ, and considering the shedding of His Blood, and the other sufferings of His Passion, I recited this prayer—'O Lord God Almighty, I pray that by the merit of Thy Blood shed upon the earth, Thou wouldst grant me the grace which I ask for this person, that thus there may not be

[81] June 29.

lost so great an abundance of Blood, which has not, so to speak, been yet applied.' For I represented to myself that some drops of blood, some particular sufferings of the members of Christ, some of His words or actions, had never been applied by any one to his healing and salvation; therefore I prayed that they might be applied for that grace which I was asking.

After the feast of the Visitation, I had a great desire to know, in my works, what was the good, pleasing, and perfect will of God. I had also great consolation in perceiving the manner in which I ought to manage a certain affair.

On the feast of the dedication of the Cathedral of Mayence, I found great devotion in offering my prayers and actions in the name and in the person of those of whom I bear especial remembrance. I adored Christ in my person as though I were representing my brothers and relations. In like manner I venerated the relics exposed on the altar in the name of others, and particularly of those who are wont to delight in honouring them. I desired also that the saints who are in heaven might adore, honour, and glorify God, giving thanks to Him for me and for the rest of us who are in the world.

On the day before the octave of the holy Apostles, I had many good desires for myself, and for my brothers and relations, and generally for many others who came into my mind; and I asked the Lord to be pleased to accept these desires as though they had been offered by the persons themselves for whom I prayed, desiring in this matter to be, as it were, the vicar of Christ, and especially in the Mass I was about to celebrate.

On the Octave, I had great devotion in taking holy water on entering the church, and I besought the Divine

Father that all the power of sanctification and benediction possessed by that water might be applied to the cleansing of my soul, and to its defence against invisible enemies. Then, on turning towards the crucifix, I had a lively understanding of the usefulness of images or pictures which represent persons to us to the life, as though they were present. Moreover, I besought the Divine Father that I might enjoy in my mind the presence of Christ as I enjoyed that of the figure; and the same thing I desired with regard to the Blessed Virgin, namely, that she might be always present to my mind, and also that I might receive greater fervour of devotion in church, that my prayers there might be better heard, according to the divine promise. In short, I understood the virtue of these holy things to be very great, not only in consequence of the piety and faith of Christians, but by divine ordinance and the commandment of our holy mother the Church. Then, kneeling before the Blessed Sacrament, I experienced great devotion, thinking that there in reality was the Body of Christ, and consequently the assistance of the most Holy Trinity in an ineffable manner, such as does not exist in other things and in other places. Other sacred things, as pictures, holy water, churches, represent to us Christ and the saints spiritually present, but in this Sacrament we have Christ really present under the sacramental species, and for this, blessed be His name!

On the same day of the Octave, while calling to mind the graces and benefits of God, I felt in my soul a kind of lamentation, such as I had never felt before. It seemed to me that, by the grace of God, I enjoyed interiorly an abundance of consolation and peace, but that I corresponded very ill with the grace of God in the exterior works of charity. First, I did not feel my defects whether interior or exterior, as also I did not, either interiorly or exteriorly, reflect on grace. Afterwards, it happened that I sought grace and peace purposely, and then I complained of my exterior, which seemed to me without feeling, though both mind and body were working much. Lastly, by the superabundance of divine mercy, it was in addition given me to know that I was too inactive in the love of God and my neighbour, and that I failed in exercising and making the most of my talents. May the good Jesus grant that I may not find so much peace in myself till I am, in every way, exercised in the victory over myself, and in fighting with the devil and my evil inclinations.

On another day within the same octave, as I was considering the various necessities, tribulations, adversities, and oppressions of men, I conceived a great desire of having them always present to me, so as to be able always to pray to God, and, like Moses, to hold up my arms, while those I pray for are fighting, and suffering, and waiting for help from others; and for the obtaining of this grace I offered the divine sacrifice. In the Mass, at the words, *Orate, fratres*, I eagerly desired that all present might pray for me, and as I saw that many were not doing so, I asked the guardian angels of those present to make up what was wanting in men. The same day I felt and knew clearly, that whoever desires to be united with God, and to grow in His love, must be humble in spirit, and mortified in his flesh and his passions. For by mortification of the flesh and abnegation of spirit one comes to possess God. We must enter by the narrow gate, and this gate is that which leads to the heart where dwell truth and life. The heart of man is that part which is the first to receive life and the last to lose it. To the heart, then, we must go, so that being there recollected and united, we may have that spiritual life which is hidden with Christ in God.

On the octave of the Visitation of the Blessed Virgin,[82] I remembered the grace that I received on that day to make my profession according to the rule of the Society of Jesus, and I prayed to be enabled to grow in perfection, so that by the vow of chastity I might be pure and clean in mind and body; that by means of the vow of poverty I might be free from every worldly affection, and from the desire of possessing anything; and that by means of obedience I might be a fitting instrument for diligently performing all good works.

On the day of St. Anacletus, pope and martyr,[83] having to celebrate Mass in the convent of the monks of St. Augustine, for the intention of their prior, it came into my mind, and I desired to do everything that I could for every superior whatever of a community, as though I did it for a disciple of the first founder of that order, as for instance of St. Augustine, of St. Francis, St. Dominic, St. Benedict, St. Bernard; and so also with regard to the nuns. And if I did it for any particular religious, I desired to do so as for a disciple of the disciple, or for a brother of the disciple of that saint. I resolved to demean myself towards the generals of orders, as towards the vicars and immediate representatives of those saints. So, with regard to the Roman Pontiff, as to the vicar of the Person of Christ, and His successor and lieutenant; and to bishops, as vicars of the other Apostles; and to priests, as vicars of the disciples of Christ; and to deacons, as successors and vicars of the disciples of the Apostles. But the Sovereign Pontiff should be honoured by me and by all Christians as though he were the very Person of Christ, inasmuch as Christ is the Head of the Church, the Priest and Prince of pastors, the Dispenser of graces, gifts, virtues, and all good things, of Whose fulness all we have received.

[82] July 9.   [83] July 13.

While saying the office of SS. Processus and Martinianus,[84] as I fastened my eyes upon the crucifix, there came into my mind these considerations concerning the Five Wounds. The Wounds of the Hands and the Feet admonished me to be diligent and to increase in good desires and in good works, and with that object to undertake with good courage long journeys and wanderings, so that we may show in our hands and feet the marks of our labours, as St. Paul says of the whole body—*Ego stigmata Domini Jesu in corpore meo porto.* I took notice that the Wound of the Side was opened after the death of Christ, when our redemption was already accomplished; and the water which issued from it was a superabundance of the merits of Jesus Christ. And from this we may learn that we shall not be able till after death to taste those interior gifts which constitute the perfect and complete salvation and glory of the soul.

1544.

On the feast of our Lord's Circumcision, which was the first day of the year 1544, as I was considering how Jesus Christ was pleased for us to receive the sign of circumcision, and to be accounted as a man of the Jewish nation, and how He was pleased to take a name among men, I asked of God these two graces: first, that by God's grace a sign of true circumcision might be seen on my soul; and secondly, that henceforth my name might be written in the book of life.

After the feast of the Epiphany I was called from the journey which I had already begun in the direction of Portugal, and returned to Cologne. I sent to Portugal Francis Strada, Andrew Oviedo, John Aragonio, and nine others whom I had won at Louvain. These were Master Peter Favre de Hallis, Master Hermes, Master

---

[84] Transferred from July 2.

John, Master Maximilian, Don Leonardo, Master James, Master Daniel, Thomas, and the young Cornelius. On returning to Cologne I took with me Master Lambert and Master Emilian; and I hired a house in which I lived till the month of July, preaching in the Latin language every Sunday and feast day in the College of Arts, besides other occasional sermons. I left at Cologne Don Alvaro with nine other scholastics; and God grant that they may be, as it were, the foundation of the Society in that place. Having received fresh orders to go to Portugal, where the King wanted me, I set out on the 12th of July, taking with me seven heads of the companions of St. Ursula, with many other holy relics. One of these heads was given to me by the nuns of St. Maximin, another by the Convent of White Ladies, another by the parish of St. Columba, and one came from Don Alvaro Alfonso through Doña Leonora Mascareñas, who received it from a good lady of Cologne.

On the day of St. Bartholomew the Apostle I landed at Lisbon.

1545.

On the feast of the Three Kings in the year 1545, these reflections suggested themselves to me for my sermons: that Jesus Christ, among other reasons, was pleased to hide Himself in His humility, in order that men might learn to show themselves such as they really are in regard to Him. He chose to hide beneath His humility all the treasures of divine wisdom and knowledge, to give us the opportunity of better understanding the treasures that we have received from the Divine Majesty. And thus He ordered it, that the Magi, seeing His poverty, should open their treasures. And so, again, He hides His power, and so He causes the angels to manifest it; He hides His purity, choosing to be baptized by St. John the Baptist, and so He moves the Father to reveal Him in these words—*This is My beloved Son:* He hides His charity at the marriage of Cana, and so He moves His Mother to speak, and to manifest His glory before the time. These are the three manifestations which the Church celebrates this day.

The Magi offer to the Infant Jesus gold, as though they wished to assist Him in His poverty, and at the same time to acknowledge that they received every good thing from Him. They offer incense for the odour of sweetness, as though they wished to comfort His mind and spirit, and notwithstanding, they believe and declare that it is from Him alone that they can have good desires and a good understanding. They offer myrrh with the desire that that holy Body of the Infant may not be subject to corruption, while, on the other hand, it is from His Passion that the glory and incorruption of our bodies is to come.

And here I experienced in myself a certain dryness and desolation which debarred me from the devotion and joy which I desired to have on so great a feast. Only, I heard within myself a reply like this—'This is the day of the Three Kings, and of the adoration of the true King. Bear, therefore, with patience this dryness and desolation; for by this means thou shalt be the better able to know whether or not thou art master of thyself. It is not difficult to govern and to conquer oneselves, when we are near to Christ by devotion. The real victory and dominion is shown when our King and Lord is far from us, Who fights for us till such time as we are made masters of ourselves.'

When is it said—*Omnes de Saba venient et omnes reges adorabunt eum, omnesque gentes servient ei*, we may understand that God desires all men to be saved, and that Christ, as Mediator, gives to all means sufficient for their being saved; and it may further be understood, that as such great kings submitted to Christ, it is to be hoped that others of greater, equal, and, still more, of less authority, will do the same.

On the Saturday before the octave of Epiphany, while I was hearing confessions, I considered how a confessor ought to endeavour, not only to instruct, correct, and perfect his penitents, but also to move them to help the souls of the departed, and to relieve the corporal and spiritual necessities of their neighbours by their prayers and works of charity and almsdeeds.

On the Sunday within the octave of the Epiphany, in considering Christ's going up to and remaining in the Temple, I noted seven things which He teaches us in this action—(1) That He chooses to absent Himself from His natural parents to do the will of His Heavenly Father; (2) that it is His will to be sought for by His parents; (3) that it is His will to be found in the Temple in the midst of the doctors; (4) that it is His will to place Himself again in subjection; (5) that it is His will to condescend to His parents; (6) that it is His will to dwell at Nazareth, and (7) to be subject to His parents.

His parents, having fulfilled their ceremonial observance, went back from Jerusalem according to their custom; but Jesus Christ has greater things to do in the temple, which cannot be accomplished in the usual time. And so we ought not to regard ordinary custom, when it involves the discontinuance of practices of devotion. It may well be that we have satisfied ourselves, but not God; and therefore, if we know that God requires from us greater and longer service, let us abide with Him. I certainly would rather be forsaken by relations and friends, than forsake God. Let all, then, who boast of being learned and prudent, learn of Jesus, Who, at the age of twelve years, sits in the midst of the doctors, to hear and ask them questions; let them learn, I say, not to desire to know more than ought to be known. Let heretics also learn a lesson from the humility of Christ; let them listen to, and inquire of the doctors of the Church, who are seated in the midst of them.

In the octave of the Epiphany, having taken for the text of a sermon those words—*Vidit Joannes Jesum venientem*, and, as I was about to say Mass, I conceived a great desire, as it were, to see and to feel Jesus coming into my heart. And afterwards, when I received the Blessed Sacrament, I knew that Christ had entered into me without my having seen Him enter. Hereupon, I prayed to God, the Blessed Virgin, and the saints, that I and my brethren and all who communicate might, with the eyes of our mind, see Jesus coming to us, and so might be able to reverence Him, and dispose ourselves to receive Him by a worthy preparation. Whilst putting on the sacred vestments, I stirred myself up to have that modesty of demeanour which a person would have who saw with his own eyes Jesus coming towards him.

By withdrawing in time from His subjection to His parents, in order to go to receive baptism from John, Jesus teaches us that those who think of changing their state of life, ought not to seek the liberty of the flesh, as he does who passes from a strict rule to an easier one, but rather to attach themselves to that which is more perfect. In leaving the obedience of His parents, Christ submits in a certain way to John's discipline. Hence, He does not seek for some one of greater consideration than His parents, nor to shake off all obedience, since He is desirous to make Himself the servant of all. He comes into the world to accomplish the salvation of all. It is fitting, therefore, that every one should go forth to meet Him, to receive the grace of this Immaculate Lamb, Who. Himself bears and takes away the sins of the world.

The day after the octave of the Epiphany, while considering the coming of Christ as Judge, I called to mind those tremendous signs which will precede the judgment: the wars, seditions, earthquakes, pestilences and famines, as also the disturbance of the heavens and the sea, the darkening of the sun, and all the other appearances which will cause men to tremble; and considering all these things, I prayed the Lord, with tears, to give grace to me and to all men, present and future, that we may watch over ourselves and fear His Judgment. War, famine, earthquake, and pestilence, are things which fill men with exceeding fear: much more, then, will those awful signs in heaven terrify those whose hearts cling to earthly things, and are weighed down with gluttony and drunkenness. It is right, therefore, for men to be very vigilant and careful with regard to the Day of Judgment, which is to be preceded by so great tribulations. And here there came into my mind those words in the twenty-first chapter of St. Luke—*Vigilate itaque, omni tempore orantes, ut digni habeamini fugere ista omnia quæ futura sunt, et stare ante Filium hominis.*

The following prayer, therefore, seemed to me a good one, which I should like to be recited in public and private by all Christians—

'O Lord Jesus Christ, Son of the living God, Who hast commanded us always to watch and pray, that we may be able to escape all the evil signs of Thy tremendous Judgment, and to be worthy to stand before the Son of Man; graciously hear us, we beseech Thee, asking this thing with fear and confidence, and let not that day overwhelm any of us unprepared. Who livest and reignest,' &c.

Once, when I was saying Mass for my spiritual brethren and children, there came into my mind the words of the

Apostle—*Patres debent thesaurizare filiis;* and I desired greatly that I, too, might be able to heap up spiritual treasures, which should be for the advantage and consolation of others, in imitation of Him Who has in Himself all the treasures of the wisdom and knowledge of God. I also took consolation in considering that the holy fathers, whose true sons we are and ought to be, have amassed for us many treasures, not only of glory in heaven, but of grace on earth. And in this all also who lead a religious life, subject to obedience, ought to find consolation, because, although they may not have much opportunity of laying up spiritual treasures, they nevertheless know that their fathers and ancestors have gained them for them. Superiors, also, who govern, ought to be careful to amass these spiritual treasures for those under them, first making themselves capable of such gifts. And, generally, it is fitting that he who has temporal goods from others should return spiritual goods for them. And I would say the same of those who serve Christ in offices which are meaner and of less account, with regard to those who serve Him in higher and more dignified positions. For, as they share in the labours and sufferings, so, also, ought they to share in the rest and consolation. And to this those words refer which Christ will say to all His saints—*Intra in gaudium Domini tui;* that is, thou who hast entered into a share of My labours and consolations.

On the day of the five holy martyrs of the Order of Friars Minor, Bernard, Peter, Accursius, Adjutus, and Otho,[85] while present at the divine office in the Church of Santa Croce, at Coimbra, where their bodies rest, I was filled with a great feeling of compassion towards all those in general who are in evident danger of damnation. There came into my mind Luther, the King of England,

---

[85] January 16. This was the day of their martyrdom.

the Turk, and many others. I then considered the great mercy of God, Who had waited so long a time for their conversion. And reflecting upon myself, I noted how it can be that God not only gives to men like these time for repentance, and waits for their conversion, but that He also waits for some one who may be willing to pray for them, and to labour to convert them. Wherefore we, to whom is given the power of preaching and instructing, ought to fear greatly lest many should be lost through our fault and neglect. Many are stretching their arms towards us; let us, then, hasten to help them. The blood of the martyrs calls to us to win the salvation of those amongst whom and for whose salvation they were slain. And thus may God grant that one day some of the Society may have the opportunity and means of cultivating that country of the Mahometans where these five martyrs shed their blood.

On the day of the holy martyrs Fabian and Sebastian,[86] there was at Coimbra a great flood which did much damage, not only to the country, but to the houses also. I offered the Mass in suffrage for a deceased monk whom Father Martin Santa Croce recommended to me as a holy man, and thus I experienced a great desire to deliver the souls in purgatory. I had also a new spiritual feeling with regard to souls who are detained in purgatory for very small faults, imagining them to myself as arriving by successive degrees at the possession of eternal happiness; and here I am speaking of accidental beatitude, because that which is essential is, as theologians say, *Tota simul et perfecta possessio vitæ interminabilis, statusque bonorum omnium aggregatione perfectus.* I conceived great hope of the fair weather which was desired, praying God to take pity on the poor people whose property was suffering by the flood; and l imagined that property as belonging

---

[86] January 20.

to pious and holy persons, such as the monk in question, and others already blessed in heaven. I also desired that the will of God might be always done in us, and the will of the saints which is inspired to them by God, especially in that which concerns the honour of God, the salvation of souls, and our perfection. Then I took courage to ask of God the fulfilment of certain desires of mine, which came to me from Him, with regard to the bringing back of Germany and of the heathen to the true faith and the profession of Christians.

On the day of the glorious virgin martyr, Agnes,[87] when I said Mass, I prayed God to grant the grace to our Society by a special privilege, that the sins of those who enter, or shall enter it, may not be imputed to that Society. And I say this both in reference to sins committed before entering it, and to all others which may be committed afterwards. And this I asked of the Lord, because I had felt a certain pious fear lest the Society should be less flourishing and less esteemed by our neighbours in consequence of the sins of its present and future members. Ascribe not, then, O good Jesus, the particular sins of each one of us to this holy Society, and suffer not anything we attempt to succeed which is opposed to Thy honour and to the salvation of souls; but let those things only have a favourable issue which are good and edifying. O Lord God, I pray Thee to forget our old offences; and even if it is Thy pleasure that we should suffer for them chastisement, reproaches, bodily sufferings, and poverty, at least permit us not to be punished with those scourges which are inflicted on wretched sinners as the punishment of their sins. May these punishments for sin, I pray Thee, O Lord, be far from this young and tender family of Thine.

[87] January 21.

On the feast of the Purification,[88] I conceived a great and lively desire not to pass out of this life till I should have settled all the affairs of my soul, according to the will of God; to see my mind at peace before the dissolution of my body; to taste true life in Jesus Christ before my death; and lastly, to witness the glory of the Church and of our Society. I desired also to have the grace to let no day pass without gaining some fruit, since God gives me health that I may work, and prolongs the days of my life that I may do good. Do Thou, O my God, continue in me these good desires, so that I may do not only what at the end of my life I should desire to have done, but that also which Thou wouldst have me do daily. Oh, how happy would that man be who should be able to know what God requires of him every day!

On the feast of St. Blaise,[89] I gave Father M. Simon Rodriguez one of the heads of the holy virgins, which was taken to the College of Coimbra in the confidence that it would there be honoured and venerated till the day of the general resurrection of the body.

On the Friday[90] after Ash Wednesday, as I was thinking that our fathers, who follow the Roman Breviary, recite a shorter office than others, I desired that they might make up for this by exercising themselves in mental prayer, and in the ministrations of preaching and hearing confessions, and in everything profitable to the living and dead.

On the Saturday[91] after Ash Wednesday there came into my mind the affliction of a person who had opened his whole heart to me; and thinking over the various tribulations and adversities which many people suffer in temporal things, my eyes filled with tears of interior compunction, because, while all others who are in the world have some

---

[88] February 2. [89] February 3. [90] February 20.
[91] February 21.

trouble, I had not any. It is true, indeed, that one who aspires solely after eternal and invisible things, is free from the tribulations which spring from temporal and visible things; but I lamented that in order to attain these eternal goods, I did not suffer what worldly persons do in order to gain temporal goods.

On the same day, as I was leaving the King's palace towards evening, I fell in with a party and cavalcade of gentlemen who were preparing to receive a duke, and many people were crowding to see the sight. To avoid the meeting and the noise, I turned into a church close at hand, and feeling a certain curiosity arise in my heart to see the very thing that I had been avoiding, I fixed my eyes on the crucifix, and I understood that to be the one sight truly worthy of contemplation—how God was pleased to take human flesh, and to die between two thieves. Let those who are possessed with a curiosity after external things gaze on Him, and then there will be an end of all insatiable appetites of the eyes, ears, and other senses. And if, as yet, thou dost not take pleasure in this sight, at least desire to do so: so shalt thou take from thyself the curiosity of worldly and earthly spectacles. If, as yet, thou canst not enter into the sepulchre, at least stand outside with Magdalene and weep before the sepulchre.

On the day of the Apostle St. Matthias, I gave the King and Queen of Portugal two heads of the holy virgins which I had from the Carthusian Convent and the Monastery of St. Maximin, and two of the four bones of the companions of St. Gereon, which I had from the canons; and to the Prince of Portugal I gave a bone of the eleven thousand virgins. I said that I did not know where to place them better than in their Highnesses' hands, and they ordered me to place them in a casket in the Queen's oratory.

On the Wednesday after 'Invocabit' Sunday,[92] while reciting the litanies according to custom, I prayed the Lord to grant to me and my brethren the grace to perform well all those actions of which we ought to render a special account, namely, observing the order and discipline of the house, examining our conscience, reciting the canonical hours, making a good confession with sentiments of sorrow, celebrating Mass, communicating, administering the sacraments, handling the Word of God well in public and private, and giving good edification to those with whom we have intercourse.

On the 4th of March, having obtained permission from the King of Portugal, I started with Father Antonio Araoz from Evora; we reached Salamanca on St. Gregory's day, and on that of St. Gabriel, the 18th, Valladolid; and thus I have, by the divine favour, accomplished the obedience which commanded me to go from Cologne to Portugal, and thence, with the King's leave, to proceed to Valladolid. And blessed be the Lord, Who was always and everywhere propitious to me in this long journey.

On the eve[93] of St. Benedict I commended myself with many tears to God, to the Blessed Virgin, and to all the saints who, in this life, endured labours and sufferings. I also begged that all sinners might have sorrow and contrition, having in my mind those words—*Lavabo per singulas noctes lectum meum, lacrymis stratum meum rigavi.* Afterwards, having heard some persons in the adjoining rooms talking improperly, I was much grieved at their preparing themselves for sleep in such a manner, and I recited this prayer—'Visita, quæsumus, Domini, habitationes istas, et reliquas omnes in quibus homines degunt,

---

[92] *i.e.* the first Sunday in Lent. Ash Wednesday was February 25, the day after St. Matthias.

[93] March 20.

et omnes insidias inimicorum invisibilium ab eis longé repelle; angeli tui sancti habitent cum ipsis, qui nos et reliquos omnes in pace custodiant. Per Christum;' etc.

On St. Benedict's [94] feast, I offered the Mass for our Society, begging that holy patriarch, that as he had great power with God, he would protect it from all evil spirits, and defend it from all error, culpable ignorance, and from all sin.

Thou oughtest to pay honour, reverence, and submission to those over thee, and especially to thy superiors, and to all who are thy betters in authority, learning, virtue, and age. There are many persons who bear affection for parents and superiors, and who obey them, and help them in their necessities; but there are few who really honour and reverence them from their hearts. Do thou love all thy neighbours, and do them all the good in thy power. Have, to thy superiors, affections of honour, reverence, and modesty; to thy equals, affections of brotherly love, endeavouring always to yield to them; and to thy inferiors be amiable, kind, and courteous, nay, be friendly and gracious even to the lowest and meanest; and so shalt thou imitate Christ, Who stooped to the very lowest.

One day, when I had gone to the palace to hear the sermon in the Prince's chapel, the porter, not knowing me, did not admit me, and so, remaining outside the door, I called to mind the many times that I had given free entrance into my soul to so many vain thoughts and bad spirits, and had refused it to Jesus, Who was knocking at the door. I also thought how Jesus Christ was everywhere ill-received by the world. I prayed for myself and for the porter, that the Lord might not make us wait very long in purgatory, before entering heaven. Many other good things came into my mind on that

---

[94] March 21.

occasion, and therefore I felt great affection for that porter, who had been to me a cause of so much devotion. I also desired that none of the Society might suffer any hurt to their souls through similar or greater repulses, as often happens to the proud and impatient.

On the feast of the Annunciation [95] of the Blessed Mother of God, I desired that I, too, might have announced to me the good news of my eternal salvation. I considered, on that day, how I might be certain of eternal life; and deemed him happy who knows that he has found grace with God, is united with God, and does work well pleasing to God. Oh, how unhappy are those who place all their anxiety in seeking the favour of men, in expecting a reward from them, and in rejoicing that their services are pleasing to them! Then, considering how on that day the Eternal Word became Incarnate, and, in fact, began the work of our salvation, I prayed the Lord to give me grace to begin with works and actions that which had hitherto stopped short at intentions and affections.[96]

On Maundy Thursday I greatly rejoiced that Jesus Christ has been pleased to leave to His Apostles and to us, not only the example of all the good works which He did in His Body, but also that very same Body. Woe to us Christians, if, having as our meat and drink the instrument made use of by the Divinity, we do not become active and unwearied labourers!

On Good Friday, while hearing the confessions of some children, who were the sons of a nobleman who

---

[95] March 25. Wednesday in Passion week.
[96] Here several manuscript copies of this 'Memorial' end; among them that which has been already lithographed at Vals. But I have in my possession a very old copy, which formerly belonged to Father Antonio Spinelli, and was, perhaps, copied by him; and this continues almost up to the October of this year, 1545, and concludes with a short appendix of 1546. [Italian translator.]

was a penitent of mine, there came into my mind some annoying thoughts, as though I was losing time with those little ones, when I might be labouring for older and more capable persons. On becoming conscious of this, I resolved to spend my whole life even, if such were the will of God, in those employments, which, in themselves, seem small and mean; and I found great comfort in the spirit of humility, and understood better the value of those works which are done, with a right intention, for the good of low and obscure persons. Wherefore, I desire for my part, and esteem it a very honourable thing, always to be able to teach children and uneducated people, the poor, and above all, the most abandoned. For, although it may seem to us that more fruit is to be gained by attending to the great ones of the world, yet God is wont to grant greater fruit to the labours which are spent on little ones, according to those words of His—*Quod uni ex minimis meis fecistis, mihi fecistis.* Certainly He values more highly what is done for the sake of one who is abandoned by all, than if thou wert to perform the same work for the good of the Emperor. As, then, the poor man is left to the care of God, so do thou think that he is left to thee, that thou mayest help him who has no one else to do so.'

Another time I was sad, considering that I was performing nothing great, and deeming myself, for that reason, the most unhappy of my companions. But presently I took notice that in this God is wonderful, that He adds something of His own even to the least of our works. And, therefore, that if we are united to Him, we shall receive from Him a more abundant blessing on our labours. Do not, therefore, consider what the work is in itself, but how, and with how much perfection thou hast done it. Endeavour to increase grace in thyself, and thou shalt be great in little works while, in the other way, thou shalt be little in great ones. Little works, accompanied by much grace, last longer and edify more than very great works with little grace.

Those words, *Popule meus, quid feci tibi?* which are said in the Adoration of the Cross, have touched and pierced my heart. More keenly than in past days, have I felt the words in which Jesus Christ complains that His vineyard made itself bitter to Him, that His people preferred Barabbas to Him, that they bound Him to the pillar Who had given them light in the wilderness by the pillar of fire, that they gave vinegar to Him Who made water gush forth from the rock for them. And I considered all these reproaches as addressed directly to myself.

On the feast of our Lord's Resurrection[97] I encouraged myself to raise my spirit to Christ, and to acknowledge the cause of my consolation to be from Him. Hitherto I have too much grieved and rejoiced at the good and evil I was conscious of in myself. God grant that henceforth I may love and value Jesus Christ rather for the price of my redemption which He has paid, than for my works and the changes in myself. God grant that I may fear, rather because I have been bought with the Precious Blood of Christ, than because of the danger that my soul may be punished with everlasting pains and banished from the society of God. God grant that, for the future, my life may consist in dying daily to the world, that so Christ may be my life and salvation, my peace and my joy.

Man hardly considers the dealings of God with him in all His works, in his creation, redemption, and glorification. And yet there is no one who, in human affairs, does not consider how men deal with Him in their

[97] April 5.

works. But do thou fix thy eyes on God, Who sees thee, and care nothing at all to be seen by men in thy actions. We see the charity of many persons suddenly fail, because there are few who freely practise the spiritual works of mercy, or who apply themselves to them in that spirit which the Apostle is speaking of when he says—*Caritas benigna est, patiens est*, &c. Even those who preside over works of charity are wanting in patience and kindness; they believe and hope little; they cannot bear any inconvenience, not feel a hearty compassion for the imperfections of others. It is thus that many persons inveigh against abuses rather from motives of impatience than of charitable zeal. Let charity, therefore, possess all the conditions enumerated by the Apostle, and then it will not fail.

One day I was expecting a young man, who had twice promised to come to confession, and had twice deceived me. I was feeling some sadness of soul, and it seemed to me that I had fruitlessly wasted six hours in waiting for him, when I received great consolation from God, for Whose honour I had so done; and there came to my mind this consideration—If, for the love of God, thou spendest many hours in waiting at the doors of nobles and princes without feeling weariness, knowing that thou will have a reward from Him, why art thou sad when one *ex minimis Christi* makes thee wait a little while? Dost thou suppose, because he is lower than those others, thou wilt not therefore have a reward from God? How many times dost thou keep Christ waiting at the door of thy heart, and then wilt not allow that He has any reason to complain of thee! Do then, as Jesus Christ would do, if He were here upon the earth in visible flesh. And at this point I conceived the wish and desire to labour and suffer in every way, not only generally, but particularly, even for one single soul, in imitation of Christ, Who gave His life, and suffered and died for each one in particular.

On the 16th of April I gave one of the heads of the eleven thousand virgins to Don Philip, Prince of Spain, son of the Emperor Charles V., and another to the Princess, his consort. I desired to see each of them placed in a befitting casket; and far more, that by the intercession of these holy virgins, those two royal personages might live in a perpetual bond of peace and charity.

On the last day of April, the feast of St. Catharine of Siena, I said Mass for the good success of the Council of Trent, beseeching the Lord to be pleased to help His Church by means of that Council. I had before my mind the necessities of sinners, who would be more easily converted after the reformation of the ministers of the Divine Word and of the sacraments, the necessities of poor troubled souls, who would find help when charity should receive fresh vigour; lastly, the necessities of the sick, and of the souls in purgatory, which would find relief when Church property and pious bequests should be distributed according to the intentions of the testators. These things I desired to be effected by the Council.

One day when I was greatly depressed and humbled, in consequence of certain vexations and heartburnings arising from a want of true brotherly charity and of humility towards those who had to give reproofs, I lifted up my mind to God, and the whole thing then seemed to me a mere nothing. And this I knew to be an excellent remedy in similar cases; because the more the soul is raised on high, the less can the arrows of human things reach it so as to hurt it. And this desire came to me while considering our Lord's Ascension into Heaven. If we would ascend with Him, we should rise above all earthly things, in spirit now, and in due time with our bodies also.

On the feast of the Apparition of St. Michael the Archangel,[98] I arrived from Valladolid, at Madrid, whither I came to visit several noblemen and friends in Christ. On the way, I had the opportunity of instructing a certain old man and some of the travelling party, and also of consoling a woman who was in great trouble, and who opened her whole heart to me in an inn. This made me think that it was a good thing to leave traces of good and holy conversation wherever one may be lodging, and to endeavour everywhere to sow and to reap fruits of salvation. For we are debtors to all men in every condition and in every place; as the Lord, with Whom we are fellow-workers, in every place assists and comforts us. And herein I acknowledged many negligences committed by me in various and long journeys, and chiefly with regard to the instruction, correction, and consolation which I ought to have imparted to the persons who conversed with me, or whom I had seen in the course of the journey. These opportunities ought never to be passed over; and our Lord Jesus Christ acted thus, seeking, by land and by sea, and in every place, to save souls.

I took note of a very effectual remedy against the carnal temptations which are wont to occur on going into inns where there is a crowd of men and women of all sorts. Not only ought we to say immediately, at our first entrance into these places, *Pax huic domui,* &c., but we should show plainly by our words and deeds that we profess piety and truth, and begin at once to speak of things leading to edification. By this means we shall bar the way against wicked suggestions. Some religious allow themselves to be overcome by this diabolical temptation,

---

[98] May 8.

namely, of concealing their religious character; and thus give an opening to others, and embolden them to display their impurity. By this method they think that they will be able to draw the others to themselves, and the end of it is that they are drawn by the others.

On the festival of our Lord's Ascension,[99] while turning over in my mind that saying of the Apostle—*Cum essem parvulus loquebar ab parvulus*, &c., I conceived a great desire that I too might be able to ascend and press forward, rising from the state of a child to that of a man, from these earthly and transitory things to heavenly and eternal things. And then I prayed that these things, which pass away, might not touch my soul, and that the esteem of eternal things might increase in me.

One day, as I was returning from Galapagar to Valladolid, there occurred to me the devotion of praying for each of the places through which I passed, by reciting a *Pater* and *Ave*, considering the various needs which might be there, and begging the necessary graces. I then extended this devotion to all the places where I or others of the Society are in the habit of staying, and for this intention I offered the Mass next day, in order that, by the merits of Christ's Passion, those whom we were not able to help, might find relief.

Once when I was saying office, and reciting that passage of the Psalmist where he says—*Ideo convertetur populus meus hic, et dies pacis invenientur in eis*, I experienced in myself a great sorrow because I had not truly turned to God, nor spent rightly every day and hour of my life. God grant that henceforth my days may be filled with good actions, not empty through idleness.

On the eve of the Visitation of the Blessed Virgin, at at a quarter past ten o'clock, the Princess Doña Maria, daughter of the King of Portugal, was delivered of a

[99] May 14.

son,[100] and the next day, in saying the Mass of the Visitation, I commemorated the Nativity of Christ, of the Virgin Mary, and of St. John the Baptist, which I had also done the day before, and I desired that the new-born babe might be blessed by these three heavenly persons. In doing this I felt great devotion. On the 12th of the same month of July, towards four o'clock in the afternoon, the Princess died. May her soul rest in holy peace!

On the feast of the Exaltation of the Holy Cross,[101] just as I was going to say Mass, a person stopped me, saying that he wished to confess and cleanse his soul from sins. And I answered, that I desired to be the Lord's broom, and to cleanse not only his conscience, but those of all others. And this saying of mine brought various considerations to my mind; and I compared myself to the broom which, while taking away dirt, remains sometimes dirty itself, and often, too, gets undone. Notwithstanding, I found great devotion in offering myself to Christ as a broom for His house, always ready to cleanse souls. I also desired that all our Society might be designed by God to cleanse the Church, that He might might make use of it as a preparatory and mean utensil; and for this intention I offered the Mass of the Holy Cross, beseeching God that after having on earth performed the part of a mean broom, of which lowly office even I am not worthy, He would one day admit me to the glory of heaven.

1546.

On the feast of SS. Fabian and Sebastian,[102] when I was with a person who needed comfort, the only thing which

---

[100] In the Life, p. 140, instead of the 1st of July, the 8th has been mentioned, by mistake.

[101] September 14.

[102] January 20.

occurred to me by way of spiritual consolation was this: that the spiritual tribulations which men suffer proceed from their too great fear of being brought into a state such as was endured by Christ, the Blessed Virgin, the good thief, and the holy Apostles. But in all tribulations, whether spiritual or temporal, there is this distinction to be made. Some are afraid of falling justly into condemnation, like the good thief; others, of being unjustly brought into the condition of Christ on the Cross; others are afraid, not for themselves, but for those they love, which was the case of the Blessed Virgin Mother of God; others, again, are afraid for those by whom they are loved, like the Beloved Disciple who stood with that Mother at the foot of the Cross of Christ, by Whom he was loved. Therefore, in our tribulations, let us put before us these four persons—Christ hanging on the Cross, the good thief, the Blessed Virgin, and St. John the Evangelist. While celebrating Mass, I begged the most holy martyrs to obtain for me light and knowledge concerning the troubles and adversities of our Society.

In the early days of this new year, while considering my faults, I sought for a new way of amending them; and I found that I need greater recollection, and that I ought to endeavour to be more united to God in my exterior actions, if I desire to find and to continue in the Spirit of God, Who sanctifies, corrects, and consoles. Above all, I was convinced that I require more solitude and silence. During these days, also, I knew, by the experience of temptations, that I require much grace, so as to arm myself against feelings contrary to poverty, and against vain fears of want and penury.

THE END.

QUARTERLY SERIES.

Conducted by the Managers of the "Month."

1872.

1. THE LIFE AND LETTERS OF ST. FRANCIS XAVIER. By the Rev. H. J. COLERIDGE. Vol. I. Price 7s. 6d.

2. THE LIFE OF ST. JANE FRANCES FREMYOT DE CHANTAL. By EMILY BOWLES. With Preface by the Rev. H. J. COLERIDGE. Price 5s. 6d.

3. THE HISTORY OF THE SACRED PASSION. By Father LUIS DE LA PALMA, of the Society of Jesus. Translated from the Spanish. With Preface by the Rev. H. J. COLERIDGE. Price 7s. 6d.

4. THE LIFE AND LETTERS OF ST. FRANCIS XAVIER. By the Rev. H. J. COLERIDGE. Vol. II. Price 10s. 6d.

1873.

5. IERNE OF ARMORICA: A Tale of the Time of Chlovis. By J. C. BATEMAN. Price 6s. 6d.

6. THE LIFE OF DONA LUISA DE CARVAJAL. By Lady GEORGIANA FULLERTON. Price 6s.

7. THE LIFE OF THE BLESSED JOHN BERCHMANS By the Rev. F. GOLDIE. Price 6s.

8. THE LIFE OF THE BLESSED PETER FAVRE, first companion of St. Ignatius. By Father BOERO.

LONDON: BURNS AND OATES,

PORTMAN STREET AND PATERNOSTER ROW.

QUARTERLY SERIES.

Conducted by the Managers of the "Month."

IN PREPARATION.

THE DIALOGUES OF ST. GREGORY. Old English version modernized. [In March, 1874.

THE LIFE OF SISTER ANNE CATHARINE EMMERICH, with a Prefatory Essay on her Contemplations on our Lord's Life and Passion.

THE DAUPHIN AND HIS COMPANIONS IN THE TEMPLE. By M. O'C. Morris.

THE LIFE OF LADY FALKLAND, mother of the great Lord Falkland. By Lady Georgiana Fullerton.

THE LIFE OF OUR LIFE. By the Rev. H. J. Coleridge. [The first volume will appear in the course of 1874.]

THE LIFE OF ST. STANISLAUS KOSTKA. By Father Boero.

THE LIFE AND LETTERS OF ST. TERESA.

THE LIFE OF PIUS THE SEVENTH.

ST. JEROME AND HIS CORRESPONDENTS.

THE CONFESSIONS OF ST. AUGUSTINE. Old translation modernized.

THE LIFE OF BLESSED MARY OF THE INCARNATION (Madame Acarie). By E. Bowles.

THE LIFE OF CARDINAL BELLARMINE. By Rev. Father Goldie.

LONDON: BURNS AND OATES,
PORTMAN STREET AND PATERNOSTER ROW.

www.ingramcontent.com/pod-product-compliance
Lightning Source LLC
Chambersburg PA
CBHW050847300426
44111CB00010B/1161